Mass Dictatorship in the Twentieth Century

The concept 'mass dictatorship' addresses the (self-)mobilisation of 'the masses' in and for twentieth century dictatorship. In contrast to tyrannies which imposed power from above, mass dictatorships have encouraged multiple forms of active participation of the people. In this highly modern process, distinctions between subjects and citizens are blurred. Through deliberate strategies of political, social, cultural and moral manipulation and persuasion, mass dictatorships tend to represent themselves as, ostensibly, 'dictatorships from below', and are indeed deeply entrenched at a grassroots level. Free of the Manichean dualism which had characterised both the totalitarian and Marxist models of the Cold War era, the series stresses the dialectical interplay between power and people.

Gender politics, modernity, everyday life, memory and the imagination are the themes explored in the individual volumes of the series. What they have in common, and what makes the series unique, is the global scale of the comparativist approach taken throughout. Readers are thus invited to explore and interrelate the pre-World War II dictatorships of Fascism, Nazism, Stalinism and Japanese colonialism with the postwar communist regimes and post-colonial developmental dictatorships in Asia, Africa and Europe.

Series Editor: **Jie-Hyun Lim**

Professor of Comparative History and Director of the Research Institute for Comparative History and Culture, Hanyang University, Seoul

Editorial Board:

Peter Lambert
Lecturer in Modern European History at Aberystwyth University

Alf Lüdtke
Honorary Professor of Historical Anthropology at the University of Erfurt, and Distinguished Visiting Professor at the Research Institute for Comparative History and Culture Hanyang University, Seoul

Karen Petrone
Professor and Chair, Department of History, University of Kentucky

Michael Schoenhals
Professor of Chinese Studies, Center for Languages and Literature, Lund University

Other titles in this series:

Jie-Hyun Lim and Karen Petrone (*editors*)
GENDER POLITICS AND MASS DICTATORSHIP: GLOBAL PERSPECTIVES

Michael Kim, Michael Schoenhals and Yong-Woo Kim (*editors*)
MASS DICTATORSHIP AND MODERNITY

Michael Schoenhals and Karin Sarsenov (*editors*)
IMAGINING MASS DICTATORSHIPS: THE INDIVIDUAL AND THE MASSES IN LITERATURE AND CINEMA

Jie-Hyun Lim, Barbara Walker and Peter Lambert (*editors*)
MASS DICTATORSHIP AND MEMORY AS EVER PRESENT PAST

Forthcoming titles:

Alf Lüdtke (*editor*)
EVERYDAY LIFE IN 20TH CENTURY MASS DICTATORSHIPS: COLLUSION AND EVASION

Paul Corner and Jie-Hyun Lim (*editors*)
THE PALGRAVE HANDBOOK OF MASS DICTATORSHIP

Mass Dictatorship in the 20th Century
Series Standing Order ISBN 978–0–230–30072–9 (Hardback)
978–0–230–30073–6 (Paperback)
(*outside North America only*)

You can receive future titles in this series as they are published by placing a standing order. Please contact your bookseller or, in case of difficulty, write to us at the address below with your name and address, the title of the series and the ISBN quoted above.

Customer Services Department, Macmillan Distribution Ltd, Houndmills, Basingstoke, Hampshire RG21 6XS, England

Mass Dictatorship and Memory as Ever Present Past

Edited by

Jie-Hyun Lim
Professor of History and Director, Research Institute of Comparative History and Culture, Hanyang University, Seoul

Barbara Walker
Associate Professor of History, University of Nevada, Reno

and

Peter Lambert
Lecturer in Modern European History, Aberystwyth University

palgrave
macmillan

First published 2013 by
PALGRAVE MACMILLAN

Palgrave Macmillan in the UK is an imprint of Macmillan Publishers Limited, registered in England, company number 785998, of Houndmills, Basingstoke, Hampshire RG21 6XS.

Palgrave Macmillan in the US is a division of St Martin's Press LLC, 175 Fifth Avenue, New York, NY10010.

Palgrave Macmillan is the global academic imprint of the above companies and has companies and representatives throughout the world.

Palgrave® and Macmillan® are registered trademarks in the United States, the United Kingdom, Europe and other countries.

ISBN 978–1–137–28982–7

This book is printed on paper suitable for recycling and made from fully managed and sustained forest sources. Logging, pulping and manufacturing processes are expected to conform to the environmental regulations of the country of origin.

A catalogue record for this book is available from the British Library.

A catalog record for this book is available from the Library of Congress.

Typeset by MPS Limited, Chennai, India.

Transferred to Digital Printing in 2015

Contents

List of Illustrations

Acknowledgements

This book, the third volume of the Mass Dictatorship series, owes its writing to the 'Mass Dictatorship as Ever Present Past' conference hosted by Jie-Hyun Lim at Hanyang University between 27 June 2008 and 29 June 2008. Focusing on the politics and remembrances of and under mass dictatorship, the conference was designed as the culmination of six consecutive 'Mass Dictatorship' conferences organised by the Research Institute of Comparative History (RICH) between 2003 and 2008. 'Global Perspectives on the Study of Dictatorship from Below' was the underlying theme of the Mass Dictatorship Project, and this volume is no exception. Most of the contributions to this volume were presented as papers at the conference and are the products of the lively discussions that took place there.

I am grateful to the National Research Foundation in Korea, which funded the Mass Dictatorship Project for six years. I would also like to thank my co-editors, Barbara Walker and Peter Lambert. Many of the contributions to this volume were penned by authors from the non-English speaking world, and I am very grateful to Barbara and Peter for their scholarly expertise and painstaking editorial work in producing this collected work. I am particularly indebted to this volume's copy-editor, Jenny Wang Medina, for finalising the manuscript with great professionalism and keen scholarly eyes. I would also like to express my very special thanks to Jenny McCall and Holly Tyler at Palgrave for their professional support and kind concern. Last but not least, I would like to thank all of the participants in the Mass Dictatorship Project from various corners of the world and the project researchers, fellows and staff at RICH. I have had the utmost privilege of spending six years on the Mass Dictatorship Project with all of them.

Finally, I must confess that the extraordinary experience of living through dictatorships of both rightist and leftist camps on the Korean peninsula and in the People's Poland was the inspiring and driving force of the Mass Dictatorship Project. I hope that the five volumes of the Mass Dictatorship series will provide scholarly empathy to all those people who suffered and are still suffering from the dictatorial past and present.

Jie-Hyun Lim, Seoul, 2013

Notes on Contributors

Sebastian Conrad holds the chair of Modern History at Freie Universität Berlin where he has taught since 2010. He is interested in issues of colonial and postcolonial history, transnationalism and global history, and directs the MA programme in Global History (a joint degree programme of Freie Universität and Humboldt Universität, Berlin). He has taught at the European University Institute in Florence and was a visiting professor at the École des Hautes Études en Sciences Sociales in Paris. Most recently he published 'Enlightenment in Global History: A Historiographical Critique', *American Historical Review* vol. 117 (2012), 999–1027. He is the author of *German Colonialism: A Short History* (Cambridge University Press, 2012); *Globalisation and the Nation in Imperial Germany* (Cambridge University Press, 2010) and *The Quest for the Lost Nation: Writing History in Germany and Japan in the American Century* (California University Press, 2010).

Jörg H. Gleiter (*1960, Prof. Dr.-Ing. habil., M. S.) is an architect and chair of architectural theory at the Berlin Institute of Technology (TU Berlin). He has studied architecture in Berlin (TU Berlin, Dipl.-Ing. 1989), IUAV (Istituto Universitario di architettura di Venezia) and Columbia University in New York (M.S. in Advanced Architectural Design, 1992). He holds a Ph.D. in architectural theory (2002) and a habilitation in philosophy of architecture (2007), both from Bauhaus-Universität Weimar. In 2003 and 2008, he was a fellow in residence at Kolleg Friedrich Nietzsche in Weimar. He held positions as a professor of aesthetics at Free University of Bozen-Bolzano in Italy (2005–2012), as deputy professor of Design and architectural theory at Bauhaus-Universität Weimar (2005–2007), as visiting professor of philosophy of architecture at Waseda University in Tokyo (2003–2005), and as visiting professor at Venice International University in Venice (2003). In 2008, he founded the book series *ArchitekturDenken*. Among his books on architectural theory and aesthetics are *Ornament Today: Digital, Material, Structural* (ed., Bozen-Bolzano, 2012, in English); *Urgeschichte der Moderne* (*Prehistory of Modernity*) (Bielefeld, 2010); *Der philosophische Flaneur. Nietzsche und die Architektur (The Philosophical Flaneur – Nietzsche and Architecture)* (Würzburg, 2009); *Architekturtheorie heute (Architecture Theory Today)* (Bielefeld, 2008). www.architekturtheorie.tu-berlin.de.

Suk-Jung Han is Professor of Sociology and Vice President of Dong-A University in Pusan, South Korea. He received his Ph.D. from the University of Chicago and is the author and translator of numerous works in Korean and English, including *The Reinterpretation of the Making of Manchukuo* (Manjugukkŏnkukŭichaehaesŏk, 2007), *Manchuria, the Space of East Asian Fusion* (Manju, tong asiayŏnghapŭikong'gan, 2008), and 'The Problem of Sovereignty: Manchukuo, 1932–1937', *Positions: East Asia Cultures Critique* vol. 12, no. 1 (2004).

Volodymyr V. Kravchenko is Director of Canadian Institute of Ukrainian Studies and a professor at the Department of History and Classics, University of Alberta, Edmonton, AB (from September 2012). Before that he was Head of the Department of Ukrainian Studies and Professor at the Karazin National University, Kharkiv, Ukraine (1992–2012, with interruption). He is the author of about 150 special publications (including five monographs) in the history of historical writing, regional and border studies of modern and contemporary Ukraine.

Peter Lambert is a lecturer in Modern European History at Aberystwyth University. He has published widely on historiography and on twentieth-century German history. His publications include 'The Professionalisation and Institutionalisation of History' in S. Berger et al. (eds), *Writing History: Theory and Practice* (2003); ed. with S Berger and P Schumann, *Historikerdialoge* (2003); ed. with P. Schofield, *Historians and the Making of History* (2004).

Jie-Hyun Lim is Professor of Comparative History and founding director of the Research Institute of Comparative History and Culture at Hanyang University in Seoul. He is the series editor of the *Mass Dictatorship* series and co-editor of two other volumes in the series, the previously published *Gender Politics and Mass Dictatorship*, and this volume, *Mass Dictatorship as Ever Present Past*. Lim has written widely on comparative histories of nationalist movements, the socio-cultural history of Marxism in East Asia and Eastern Europe and issues of memory, colonialism and dictatorship in East Asia in multiple languages. He is currently writing a monograph on the transnational history of 'victimhood nationalism' and co-editing (with Paul Corner) the forthcoming volume 'Handbook of Mass Dictatorship'.

Hiroko Mizuno is Associate Professor at Osaka University, Japan. She received her Ph.D. from University of Graz, Austria, in 2000 and has written widely on Modern and Contemporary History of Austria and Europe. She is the co-editor (with Jun Kono, Shuichi Iwasaki and

Atsushi Otsuru) of *A History of the Habsburg Monarchy and Its Legacy* (Kyoto: Showado, 2013) (in Japanese). Currently she is co-editing (with Takuya Ozawa and Satoshi Tanaka) *A World History from 1945 to the Present* (in Japanese).

Naoki Sakai is Goldwin Smith Professor of Asian Studies who teaches Comparative Literature, Asian Studies and History at Cornell University. He has published in a number of languages in the fields of comparative literature, intellectual history, translation studies, the studies of racism and nationalism and the histories of textuality. His publications include *Translation and Subjectivity; Voices of the Past; Japan/Image/the United State – The Community of Sympathy and Imperial Nationalisms; The Stillbirth of the Japanese as a Language and as an Ethnos* and *Hope and the Constitution*. He has edited and co-edited a number of volumes, including *Trans-Pacific Imagination 2012; Translation, Biopolitics, Colonial Difference Vol. 4* and *Traces: A Multilingual Series of Cultural Theory and Translation*, 2006; *Deconstructing Nationality*, 1996. Naoki Sakai served as the founding editor for the project TRACES (http://traces.arts.cornell.edu), a multilingual series in five languages – Korean, Chinese, English, Spanish and Japanese (with German to be added in 2013).

Michael Schoenhals is a professor of Chinese at Lund University, Sweden. He has published extensively on society and politics in the People's Republic of China, including *Mao's Last Revolution* (Harvard University Press, 2006, co-authored by Roderick MacFarquhar), a major history of the Cultural Revolution. His most recent book entitled *Spying for the People: Mao's Secret Agents, 1949–1967* (Cambridge University Press, 2013) tells the story of domestic agent and operational work by Mao's state security organs at the height of the Cold War.

Barbara Walker teaches in the History Department at the University of Nevada, Reno. She has published extensively on the history of Russian and Soviet intellectual life, with a special focus on its economic foundations and culture. Her work has appeared in journals such as *Slavic Review, The Russian Review, Kritika: Explorations in Russian and Eurasian History, Cross Currents, Comparative Studies in Society and History, Contemporary European History* and *Novoe literaturnoe obozrenie*. She published the monograph *Maximilian and the Russian Literary Circle: Culture and Survival in Revolutionary Times* in 2005, and chapters in edited volumes such as *Personenkulte im Stalinismus/Personality Cults in Stalinism* (2004), *Imagining the West in Eastern Europe and the Soviet Union* (2010) and *The Russian Experience: Americans Encountering the Enigma*

1917 to the Present (2012). Her work has been supported by the National Endowment for the Humanities, the Thomas Watson Foundation, the International Research Exchange, the Hoover Institution, the Institute for Advanced Study, Princeton and others. Her current project explores the transnational relations of Soviet and American 'information experts' in the Cold War.

1
Introduction: Coming to Terms with the Past of Mass Dictatorship

Jie-Hyun Lim and Peter Lambert

Coming to terms with past tyranny in the ancient democracy of Athens entailed the employment of a rigid strategy. Individual citizens were in fact forbidden to recall the past. Legally enforced amnesia became the tool for guaranteeing reconciliation among citizens and thus enabling them to live together again as a political community.[1] But amnesia is not thus privileged in contemporary democracies. Adam Michnik's slogan of *'amnestia tak, amnesia nie'* ('"yes" to amnesty, "no" to amnesia') represents one current of thought in coming to terms with the past of communist dictatorship.[2] The 'Truth and Reconciliation Commission' in South Africa tried to preserve memory of the apartheid regime at the expense of what might have seemed to some to be justified retribution – by offering perpetrators 'amnesty' in return for their confessions. Such confessions were seen as acts of atonement. The Stockholm Declaration of 2000 made teaching the Holocaust obligatory among EU member countries, while the 'Platform of European Memory and Conscience' was established in 2011 as an educational project about the crimes of totalitarian regimes. Indeed, the politics of memory pervade the global community; in Continental Europe, Asia, the Middle East, Africa and Latin America, they revolve above all around colonialism, dictatorship, genocide, mass killing and the many other forms of oppression that have left deep scars on the societies that they afflicted. For now, at least, it would seem that the memory of mass dictatorship is an ever present past in this global culture of memory.

Thus, the memory of mass dictatorship has become a fundamental political issue in its own right. The realm of this type of memory throughout the world is full of tensions and conflicts: between justice and reconciliation, revenge and forgiveness, the radical solution and the compromise, religious sin and legal culpability, innocence and guilt,

1

remembering and forgetting; between actors and bystanders, passive victims and active perpetrators; and finally, between dissident politicians and post-dictatorial political clients. If there is a single theme uniting the essays collected in this book it is that while the politics of remembering past mass dictatorships seek to push people into making simple binary choices, the historical realities of mass dictatorships are inevitably too complex to be thus accommodated.

The essays that follow also reveal the centrality of the problem of complicity in the politics of remembering mass dictatorship. They reveal how readily political actors have made claims to the status of victimhood in order to circumnavigate potential or actual charges of complicity with 'mass' dictatorships. They are enabled in this strategy by the fact that it is easy to blame dictatorial structures for mass suffering and death. Yet structures do not kill. It is individuals who kill. Whole social groups fearing the accusation of complicity have employed similar strategies: in embracing victimhood status, they have sought to evade such accusations, and sometimes also a sense of their own guilt or responsibility. One result of these strategies is to multiply the layers of political, legal and moral complexity surrounding the politics of remembering mass dictatorship. The morally grounded accusations of circumstantial victims may result in discomfort for self-proclaimed victims without actually leading to legal trials. Allegations of complicity may also relate to behaviour in the aftermath of the demise of a dictatorship in the form of charges of collusion in covering up the crimes of the past. Then many collaborators and individual perpetrators, who had lived in hiding behind the cover of the victimised nation, unveil themselves.

Politicians, historians and others have reconstructed the past, realigned their memories, and selectively 'forgotten' their complicity, employing strategies that may initially have served the purposes of easing legal or moral recrimination, even perhaps securing public sympathy in the place of opprobrium. These strategies contrast painfully with the true sufferings of Holocaust survivors, for example, who bear unending guilt for their survival while those around them died in vast numbers. Such a comparison may lead us to ask whether complicity and guilt are not indeed simply part of the human condition, and the inescapable consequences of survival under any circumstances. If that is so, then their occurrence and characteristics during and after the experience of mass dictatorship are only heightened versions of ineluctable phenomena.

Two otherwise seemingly unconnected 'witness statements' on victimhood and perpetration may shed light on the interplay between them in those particular historical conditions. Writing in November

1945, George Orwell reflected on the fact that whenever he encountered phrases like 'war guilt trials', 'punishment of war criminals', and so forth, they triggered 'the memory of something' he had witnessed 'in a prisoner-of-war camp in South-Germany' earlier that year. He and another journalist had been shown round the camp 'by a little Viennese Jew who had been enlisted in the branch of the American army which deals with the interrogation of prisoners'. His guide was 'an alert … rather good-looking youth of about twenty-five, and politically so much more knowledgeable than the average American officer that it was a pleasure to be with him'. The guide took him to a group of SS officers who had been segregated from the other prisoners. 'That's the real swine!' he said, indicating 'a man in dingy civilian clothes who was lying with his arm across his face and apparently asleep'. Then, 'suddenly he lashed out with his heavy army boot'. He then explained to Orwell that it was 'quite certain' that the prone man 'had had charge of concentration camps and had presided over tortures and hangings. In short, he represented everything we had been fighting against during the past five years'. Orwell, not in the least inclined to doubt his guide, carefully scrutinised this perpetrator of murder and victim of a well-aimed kick.

Had the Viennese Jew gained anything from his act of petty vengeance? Orwell asked himself. There was, he immediately concluded, no enjoyment for the young man, who was rather '*telling* himself that he enjoyed' his newfound power, and 'behaving as he had planned to behave in the days when he was helpless'. Orwell attached no blame to his guide: to do so would have been 'absurd' and considered the strong probability that 'his whole family had been murdered; and, after all, even a wanton kick to a prisoner is a tiny thing compared with the outrages committed by the Hitler regime'. A few years earlier Orwell would surely 'have jumped for joy' himself at the prospect 'of seeing SS officers kicked and humiliated'. The vision was attractive only for as long as one did not have the power to realise it; 'when the thing becomes possible, it is merely pathetic and disgusting'. Nowhere does Orwell's text suggest that he had sought to intervene when confronted with this case of the inversion of victim and perpetrator.

Yet 'this scene' was perfectly comparable with 'much else that [Orwell] saw in Germany'. Perhaps he may have felt deprived of any morally justifiable course of action. Whatever he may have felt about his own role as passive bystander in this one instant, he certainly did own to feeling the unease attendant to sharing a collective British complicity. For the 'big public' in Britain was 'responsible for the monstrous peace settlement now being forced on Germany', and 'we' – the British – had 'acquiesced in crimes like the expulsion of all Germans from East Prussia'. Thus Orwell, the consistent anti-Fascist and propagandist for the 'People's War' against Nazi Germany, sought to come to terms with his own vengeful past desires which, once put into practice, he experienced only as 'pathetic and disgusting'. His close inspection of the roles of perpetrator and victim was as sensitive to their instability as it was fully alert to the disproportionality between the SS man's past commission of violence and present suffering from it. He could even empathise with a bullied and humiliated SS man, a 'monstrous figure' who had 'dwindled to this pitiful wretch' in need not of 'punishment' but of 'psychological treatment'. He could do so without blinding himself to the far greater injustice suffered by the Jew who had bullied the SS man. And Orwell rigorously avoided the easy option of ascribing all guilt to the defeated Germans and a clean bill of moral health to a victorious democratic Britain.[3]

As the longstanding Czech human rights activist and president of post-Communist Czechoslovakia Vaclav Havel confessed, his own experience as a dissident taught him that the dividing line between the innocent and the guilty can be much more blurred than was – and very frequently still is – thought to be the case. Thus, according to Havel, 'the line of conflict runs *de facto* through each person, for everyone in his or her own way is both a victim and a supporter of the system'.[4] Nobody was simply a victim; everyone was in some measure co-responsible. If everyone is co-responsible, the question of who should be put on trial is much less clear. Havel's implicit answer is everyone, and therefore no one.[5] The firm stance Havel took against the 'lustration' process as a way of overcoming the communist past should be understood in this context.

Havel's insightful argument is related to guilt and innocence, perpetration and victimhood in the context of a dictatorship that, though it had evolved out of Stalinism, was not programmatically murderous. No longer seeking to instil ideological fervour in the population in order to drive forward a utopian agenda, the 'normalised' regime in Czechoslovakia after the Prague Spring was content with a mere show of public approval, and with the maintenance of its power for power's own sake. It made few demands on its citizens beyond the appearance of buying in to a handful of slogans that were the flotsam and jetsam of a wrecked Marxist-Leninist project. It might rather be described – to borrow Martin Sabrow's telling description of the German Democratic Republic at a comparable point in its evolution – as a 'soft dictatorship' as well as a 'consensus dictatorship'.[6] The 'social contract' that the regime offered and the people accepted was in its own way no less morally corrosive for *both* partners: the rulers and the ruled. The mass dictatorship hypothesis, which posits the collusion of the many in the construction of dictatorship over themselves and others, and which refers to dictatorships that certainly *were* programmatically violent and ideologically driven,[7] is nevertheless consonant with Vaclav Havel's self-reflective position. Here, the moralist dualism that posits a few vicious perpetrators and many innocent victims is called into question because it facilitates the displacement or denial of the historical responsibility of ordinary people.

The dictum according to which 'structures do not kill, but individuals do' points to the culpability of large numbers of historical actors. Given its stress on agency, the concept of mass dictatorship does not exonerate ordinary people from historical responsibility and juridical culpability. Indeed, the ranks of mass killers contained not only crazy psychopaths but, crucially, also ordinary human beings – that is to say, normal people. This reality of the 'banality of evil' and even the 'pleasure of evil' breaks through the moral comfort zone that the image of criminally insane perpetrators brings to us. When Raul Hilberg asked the question, 'wouldn't you be happier if I had been able to show that all perpetrators were crazy?', his implication was that history brings no comfort because those perpetrators are just like us.[8] Most recently, perceptions of war criminals in the former Yugoslavia have confirmed this insight. Neighbours remember those war criminals as good people who would never have hurt a fly.[9]

This 'Mass Dictatorship' volume explores the memory politics involved in 'coming to terms with the past' of dictatorship on a global scale. In keeping with the others in the series, the present volume is an experiment in trying to present entanglement – in this case, the entangled pasts of dictatorships viewed in a global perspective. It goes beyond a mere compilation of separate national histories. Instead, it poses a question: can the social framework of memory be global? Remembering is more than a personal act. People construct the memory of inter-subjective pasts through their relations with others as members of society.[10] Memory depends on collective forms of perception, dominant discourses, cultural practices and a variety of other social factors. A growing sense of global connectivity and global human rights politics has brought a profound change to the memory landscape. That has not necessarily meant a de-nationalisation of memory, however. The global public sphere of memory is tense and unstable, marked by competition between de-territorialising and re-territorialising memories. The contributions to this volume combine to present an overview of the landscape of the global public sphere of memory in which the loci of various national memories are confirmed.

Three themes recur with particular persistence in these chapters, though they discuss diverse kinds of memory of modern dictatorship in different places and at different times.

First, there is a shared engagement reflected in the title of the first part of the volume: 'Entangled Memory and Comparative History'. Both synchronic and diachronic comparisons are applied here, at the level of national memories and within the nation-state framework. This approach allows us to challenge the notion of an absolute binary divide between victim and perpetrator of violence as it has been transposed to the collective level of victimised and victimising nations, and thus to the dynamics of victimhood nationalism. The synchronicity of entangled memories invites exploration of transnational aspects of the production of social memory. Here, the configuration of memory in one nation state is intertwined with that of another, whether friend or foe. The diachronicity of entangled memories implies continuities and discontinuities between mass dictatorship and democracy, and between colonial and post-colonial regimes. National memories of mass dictatorship intersect with memories particular to gender, class and other collectives. Memories are shared, transferred and entangled. The entanglement of memories is the theme of the first part of this volume.

Sebastian Conrad's chapter deals with highly selective readings of the past. His chapter not only compares West German with Japanese historiographical reflections on Nazism, fascism and imperialism in the years immediately after the end of the Second World War, but shows the way in which each was marked not only by indigenous traditions and impulses, but crucially also by American influences, whether proscriptive or prescriptive. In each case, narratives of victimhood – whether framed in class terms as in the case of Japanese Marxist historians, or in national terms – played a significant part.

Jie-Hyun Lim's contribution deals with the meeting-point of two elements, namely memories revolving around victimhood and revised versions of nationalist ideologies. Lim calls the highly combustible outcome of their synthesis 'victimhood nationalism'. All nationalisms begin with definitions of 'the Other' – with the generic characterisation of foreigners, aliens, those who do not belong, simply because they are easier to identify than the assumed shared characteristics of one's own nation. 'Victimhood nationalism' does this in spades. For the victims in question are of course not the casualties of natural disasters, but of human agency, so that every identity based on victimhood is predicated on the prior initiative of the bully and persecutor. There are two obvious difficulties with this Manichaean worldview. First, not all victims had exemplary pasts. Second, victims can exhibit an alarming capacity to study and then put into practice their oppressors' strategies. This is the logic that produced cycles of purges and rehabilitations that originated within dictatorial regimes but outlived them.

Hiroko Mizuno's study of the functioning of 'People's Courts' in Austria after 1945 simultaneously exemplifies this process and shows its relevance to 'victimhood nationalism'. As Mizuno notes, the very name 'People's Courts' had disquieting echoes of the legacy of Nazism with which the new institutions were designed to settle accounts. The *Volksgerichtshof* was a creation of the Third Reich, and the most notorious of the Nazis' distortions of legal process. Yet contemporary objections to the recycling of the nomenclature were overridden. And, just as the Nazi *Volksgemeinschaft* ('community of the people') had been based on an exclusionary vision, so too was the nascent Austrian nation the 'People's Courts' were supposed to help define.

A second theme that emerges is addressed in particular in Part II: 'The Dialectical Interplay of History and Memory'. We explore such issues as how mass dictatorial regimes and movements appropriated images of the past, how the images and fragments of the past were actually (re) produced and distributed by the dictatorial actors, and how they were consumed by the masses. The influx of contested memories triggered by the dismantling of the Cold War is also at issue. In the context of coming to terms with the past of communist regimes, a new historiography, including that of textbooks, is shattering the 'righteous memory' produced in the Cold War era. This new situation is ambivalent: while it contributes to deconstructing the simplistic binary of the good and bad, it tends to disarm the certainties of legal positivism by frequently blurring the dividing line between victims and perpetrators.

Another kind of ambivalence is also interrogated in this context. There has been an extraordinary increase in the volume of work dedicated by academic historians to critically engaging with memory in recent years.[11] Sometimes, historians may even be found complaining that memory is the enemy of history, and history infinitely preferable to memory. Thus, in his brilliant study of Europe since 1945, Tony Judt maintained that 'Unlike memory, which confirms and reinforces itself, history contributes to the disenchantment of the world. Most of what it has to offer is discomforting, even disruptive'.[12] Eric Hobsbawm, convinced that in the twenty-first century, 'for the first time, we have an adequate framework for a genuinely global history', mused to similar effect: 'More history than ever is today being revised or invented by people who do not want the real past, but only a past that suits their purpose. Today is the great age of historical mythology. The defence of history by its professionals is today more urgent in politics than ever.'[13]

Historians should perhaps be more wary of seeing themselves as standing in aloof judgment, or of claiming a sort of inbuilt moral and intellectual superiority for our profession. Academic historians have been deeply implicated in the construction of politically and socially convenient myths about the past. As Volodymyr Kravchenko, Naoki Sakai, and Peter Lambert's essays show, historians have helped to legitimate mass dictatorships and, in post-dictatorial societies, have often been complicit in generating partial amnesia about, and distorted images of, the dictatorships they had themselves experienced. Kravchenko's study of post-communist Ukraine does acknowledge that historians play a relatively modest part in the construction of social memory. It does not, however, follow that the 'community' of academic historians in the Ukraine ought – at least as it is currently constituted – to enjoy a more authoritative, let alone the leading, position in articulating memory. Professional historians are divided among themselves; many retain the institutional and ideational marks of the Communist regime under which they had forged their careers; others are constrained by their positivism and resistance to methodological innovation. In Lambert's account, academic historians working in the Third Reich may have combated one set of Nazi myths, but did so largely by condoning and even heightening another.

Perhaps, however, and given the left-of-centre politics (and views on historical methodology) of each, Judt and Hobsbawm may really have meant to counter-pose only 'critical' historiography to memory. But even to do no more than that would not only be to dismiss many (and probably most) academic historians from their own professional field. It would also give too much credit to 'critical' historians themselves. Naoki Sakai opens his argument by pointing out that left-wing Japanese historians in the 1960s tended deeply to misunderstand Nazism. They failed to grasp its racial definition of the nation because of their own experiences of Japanese fascism, but also of post-1945 Japanese society. The post-war democracy in Japan was inclined to democratise, rather than problematise, the nation. Notably, the Japanese translation (and Korean translation too) of 'national socialism' has been always 'state socialism' because the left-wing historians are determined to protect the sacred meaning of nation from the suspicion of fascism. In these respects Sakai's chapter echoes Conrad's, which points to a range of other manifest misapprehensions about the Japanese past with which the work of Japanese Marxist historians was riddled.

In all these disparate cases, writing history (whether 'critical' or not) and contributing to social memory went hand in hand. Thus, and given the fact that all but one of the contributors to this volume are themselves professional historians, we have no desire to claim a monopoly on 'righteousness' for our own discipline, or simply to juxtapose 'history' (understood as the 'objective' work of a trained and expert university-based few) to 'memory' (excoriated as the uncritical rummaging in memory-banks of the partisan, untrained and inexpert many). Rather, it obligates us to attempt a critical coming to terms with the past of our own discipline.

Once righteous memory is put into question, memories of mass dictatorship become less homogenous. The third part of the book is therefore dedicated to the investigation of 'Pluralising Memories: Fragmented, Contested, Resisted'. The coexistence of a multiplicity of memories implies fragmentation, contestation and dissidence in producing and consuming the 'collective', or rather social memory. Various political actors and social agents deploy different politics of memory in their attempts to influence or control the discourse of memory. 'Official' memory-cultures carried by institutions did not entirely eradicate alternative memories within mass dictatorships. In post-dictatorial societies, their ability to mould memories is far more constrained.[14] The engagement of empathies and emotional feelings such as guilt, shame and atonement in the process of the formation of social memory adds to the complexity. The visual representation of the past as formed by films, dramas and other performances enhances and deepens the emotional dimension of coming to terms with the past.

The common thread running through this book is a search for historical accountability among the post-war generations. They are of course not directly responsible for the atrocities of the mass dictatorial regimes, but are nevertheless connected to them by ties of collective identity, whether freely chosen or imposed from without. This book moves beyond the simple assignations of responsibility so often perpetrated through the politics of memory, to a deeper understanding of mass dictatorship and of the profound historical consequences for all touched by it. To do that is not in the least to diminish the pain of those who suffered such violence as incarceration, torture, enslavement, rape or genocide as a consequence of mass dictatorship. Nor is it for a moment to deny that many of those victims – Jewish victims of the Holocaust or those who died in consequence of the Nazis' murderous pursuit of eugenic goals – were indeed victims *tout court*. Constituting what might be called an 'ethical turn', however, the quest for transnational and trans-temporal responsibility in post-war memory affords new prospects of going beyond what has become a cliché-ridden and unthinkingly and too generally applied binary of perpetrators and victims. That binary is perhaps *especially* pernicious where it is conceived of in wholly national terms.

Suk-Jung Han's contribution addresses Manchuria as a territory in which Koreans' role had been subject to a kind of official amnesia in South Korea and a simultaneous official commemoration in the North, both of which contributed to a variety of often grotesque misrepresentations of Manchuria's complex past. Han argues that transnational approaches do indeed appear the only ones capable of doing justice to a messy regional history. Poststructuralist sensibilities have in fact helped to (re-)open Manchurian history, this time to a more sensitive and nuanced discussion. According to Han, the Manchurian experience was vital to state formation in both Koreas. The leaders of the South and North Korean regimes, who started their careers respectively as a collaborator and as a resistance fighter in Manchuria, were so heavily influenced by their experiences there. At once shared and opposed, their memories of Manchuria helped each in the construction and maintenance of a dominant, oppressive, but simultaneously popular regime.

A disconcerting phenomenon that emerges from the contributions to this volume is a sometimes startling kinship between narratives and themes of victims and perpetrators. Thus, purges are capable of being linked to redemption. The connection can pertain at the collective level. In the Maoist case, as discussed by Michael Schoenhals, it does so for the ruling Party and regime. In Communist and post-Communist countries it can hold also for an entire society as it undergoes a cyclical experience of purges, rehabilitation and renewed purges. Manifestly, the connection is just as readily discernible in an individual. The concept of a purge can relate to the body, of course. It may be understood as a medicinal procedure, or more broadly as a process of cleansing, or 'cleaning out the system'. Some of the dissidents Barbara B. Walker discusses in the context of the Soviet Union expressed a sense of contamination by their past associations with the regime. They had, in their own view, been sullied. In Mao's rhetoric, too, dirt was ultimately a visible sign of corruption. Washing was one remedy he offered. It took on ritual connotations, and symbolic associations with decontamination and purification.

'Cleansing' and 'purification' were routes to redemption. Here, discourses of health and hygiene give way to those of religiosity: of sins wiped out, or at least of guilt assuaged; of spiritual rebirth through good deeds (but sometimes also through acts of self-abasement); of feelings of elation once someone has returned to a state of grace. In this, too, the role of memory is pivotal. The intellectual in the Soviet Union's post-Stalinist society could, having become a dissident, recover an identity, a sense of self that had been fragmented, disrupted, and almost lost while she or he enjoyed the benefits and privileges (and endured and internalised the hypocrisies) of living as 'insiders' in the dictatorship's functional elite. In breaking out of that morally ruinous trap the intellectual may, Walker indicates, have reconnected not only to her or his early memories and once innocent self but also to the social memory of a traditional (pre-Communist) and altruistic community. In at least one of its guises, that community had been constitutive of the modern Russian intelligentsia.

The final contribution to this volume is Jörg Gleiter's study of recent initiatives in commemorative practices in Germany. That the traditional monument has a limited functional lifespan seems abundantly clear. For all the initially dramatic impact grand monuments may at first have had on passers-by, they all tend to lose meaning and become familiar but neglected features of landscapes. Perhaps generational shifts and an increasing distance from the past of dictatorships *may* accelerate the process. Certainly, Tony Judt held that, by the present century, this was becoming true of Europe. Its 'barbarous recent history, the dark "other" against which post-war Europe was laboriously constructed, is already beyond recall for young Europeans. Within a generation the memorials and museums will be gathering dust – visited, like the battlefields of the Western Front today, only by aficionados and relatives'.[15] Gleiter, however, argues that a new generation of approaches to commemoration may escape the fate of increasing neglect and eventual oblivion. Unconcerned with making aesthetic statements, perhaps particularly of the kind one associates with 'high art' forms, the new monuments are really 'anti-monuments', designed not to dominate, but to dissolve into everyday life, or to 'be disappeared' by the active if low-key involvement of the citizens who encounter them, or to be (literally) stumbled over, so that the physical jolt may spur a reflective one.

The contributors to the present volume have wrestled with two focal points in coming to terms with the past of mass dictatorships. The first is a 'spatial turn' in the collective memory that transcends ethnic and national boundaries. Much attention was paid to the transnational themes dominant in the memories of mass dictatorship, though global or transnational memory is not always a substitute for national memory. Transnational memories contest, oppose, overlap and cohabit with national memories. The rise of a global public sphere has created a space for the contestation of conflicting national memories, and the trajectories of transnational memory are very often tainted with re-territorialised memories. The second point is a tension between the politics of memory and practices of remembering. Memory cannot simply be imposed on the public by high politics, for it is the individual who remembers. Thus memory at the collective level can manifest itself only when it produces new forms of subjectification by articulating and inscribing particular hegemonic discourses on the individual. Thus, coming to terms with the past of mass dictatorship in the space of transnational memory often overlaps with a subjectification of the individual as a remembering actor through the politics of memory.

Notes

1. David Cohen, 'The Rhetoric of Justice: Strategies of Reconciliation and Revenge in the Restoration of Athenian Democracy in 403 BC', *European Journal of Sociology* vol. 42, no. 2 (2001), 341–42.
2. Adam Michnik, 'Rozmowa z Vaclavem Havelem', *Gazeta Wyborcza* (30 November 1991).
3. George Orwell, 'Revenge is Sour' in *Tribune*, 9 November 1945, reprinted in *The Collected Essays, Journalism and Letters of George Orwell* vol. 4: *In Front of Your Nose 1945–1950* (Harmondsworth: Harvest/HBJ Books, 1968), pp. 19–22.
4. Vaclav Havel, 'The Power of the Powerless', in John Keane (ed.), *The Power of the Powerless: Citizens against the State in Central-Eastern Europe* (London: Hutchinson, 1985), p. 37.
5. Timothy Garlton Ash, *History of the Present* (New York: Vintage Books, 2001), p. 264.
6. Martin Sabrow, 'Dictatorship as Discourse: Cultural Perspectives on SED Legitimacy', in Konrad H. Jarausch (ed.), *Dictatorship as Experience: Towards a Socio-Cultural History of the GDR* (New York: Berghahn Books, 1999), p. 208. The German word of 'Konsens' has a connotation of both 'consensus' and 'consent' in English. I think 'dictatorship of consent' is a better translation than 'consensus dictatorship'.
7. Cf. Jie-Hyun Lim, 'Series Introduction: Mapping Mass Dictatorship: Towards a Transnational History of Twentieth-Century Dictatorship' in *idem* and Karen Petrone (eds), *Gender Politics and Mass Dictatorship. Global Perspectives* (Basingstoke: Palgrave Macmillan, 2011), pp. 1–22.

8. Raul Hilberg, 'Significance of the Holocaust', in Henry Friedlander and Sybil Milton (eds), *The Holocaust: Ideology, Bureaucracy, and Genocide* (Millwood, NY: Kraus International Publication, 1980), p. 101.
9. Slavenka Drakulić, *They Would Never Hurt a Fly: War Criminals on Trial in The Hague* (London: Abacus, 2004).
10. Barbara Misztal, 'Collective Memory in a Global Age: Learning How and What to Remember', *Current Sociology*, vol. 58, no. 1 (January 2010), 27.
11. A good recent overview of a now voluminous literature is Geoffrey Cubitt, *History and Memory* (Manchester and New York: Manchester University Press, 2007).
12. Tony Judt, *Postwar. A History of Europe since 1945* (New York: Penguin Press, 2005), p. 830.
13. Eric Hobsbawm, *Interesting Times. A Twentieth-Century Life* (London: Allen Lane, 2002), p. 296.
14. Cf. Richard Ned Lebow, 'The Memory of Politics in Postwar Europe' in *idem*, WulfKansteiner and Claudio Fogu (eds), *The Politics of Memory in Postwar Europe* (Durham: Duke University Press, 2006), pp. 1–39; p. 10.
15. Judt, *Postwar*, p. 830.

Part I
Entangled Memory
and Comparative History

2
The Predicaments of Culture: War, Dictatorship and Modernity in Early Post-War West Germany and Japan

Sebastian Conrad

After defeat in 1945, both Germany and Japan witnessed fundamental transformations in the interpretation of their histories. The national past – in both countries – became a casualty of the lost war, the abdication of the fascist regimes, unconditional surrender, and the loss of the vast empires both nations had assembled. The need to come to terms with the recent past, felt urgently among critical intellectuals in both countries, was further underscored by the Allied occupation that called for a thorough repositioning of both nations vis-à-vis their histories.

It has long been held that the process of coming to terms with the past in both countries was essentially flawed. In Germany, received wisdom has it that the discussion over the history of the recent past was characterised by what philosopher Hermann Lübbe called 'a certain silence'. Today there is a general consensus that in the early post-war decades, a critical debate over the history of the Third Reich and a scholarly examination of German guilt barely got off the ground. For this reason, scholars speak of the 1950s in terms of the 'repression' of the National Socialist era.[1] Likewise, in Japan, the discussions on the criminal character of Japanese expansion policies (the Nanking Massacre, forced prostitution, bacteriological warfare, etc.) in the post-war period are usually referred to as partial and highly selective, resulting in a virtual amnesia with regard to the wartime past.[2]

This failure to engage in a critical examination of the recent past should not suggest that National Socialism and Japanese fascism remained a historical *terra incognita* and were entirely ignored. In both countries, there was indeed a lively discussion about the wartime past – even if some of the sensitive topics, judging retrospectively, were eschewed. On closer examination, therefore, the widespread concepts of 'repression' and of

the 'second guilt' (Ralph Giordano) or of *sengo sekinin* – an alleged refusal
to critically come to terms with the past – seem able to only partially
capture early post-war reality. This paradigm has led historians to stress
'deficits' and 'lacks' and to ignore what was actually said and discussed.
In what follows, we will look at the debates more closely.[3] In both
countries, discussions focused on the nature of the war, on the characteristics of fascism and on the historical origins of dictatorship. At
the same time, however, more was at stake than a re-interpretation of
the recent past. We can read the historians' debates in both countries
as part of a larger endeavour to come to terms with the trajectories of
modernity. It is important to stress, however – and with this we will
begin – that debates about the past in both countries did not only
evolve internally but rather were situated in a trans-national context.

Entangled memories

A condemnation of the recent past began in Western Germany and
in Japan immediately after the end of the war and was the common
point of departure of almost every scholarly interpretation. A glance at
public statements from this time shows that West German historians
readily concurred on the negative quality of the National Socialist era.
Only the causes and deeper reasons for the 'catastrophe' remained
controversial. From one day to the next, a positive or even apologetic
view of National Socialism had become virtually unthinkable. Japanese
historians went even further in their outright condemnation of fascism. Immediately following Japan's surrender, scholars who had been
critical of the regime and who had lost their jobs during the war were
rehired. Particularly the Marxist historians who had faced state repression in the years before soon dominated the new intellectual climate.
In scholarly discourse, the rejection of the preceding 15 years was
absolute.[4]

For both countries, it is possible to speak of a discursive break that
produced a whole new arsenal of concepts, images and conventions
of enunciation, which regulated how the recent past could be legiti-
mately interpreted. However, these changes did not occur out of the
blue. On the one hand, the transformations need to be situated in a
framework in which the politics of the American occupation helped
define the parameters of enunciation. On the other hand, they linked
up with alternative traditions within Germany and Japan that until
1945 had played only marginal roles. Characteristically, these two
trajectories overlapped, and frequently the American initiatives rested

on the insights offered by these alternative perspectives, while at the same time the transnational pressures helped legitimate the claims of hitherto marginal approaches.

To begin with the first point: unconditional surrender and military occupation contributed in different ways to limiting the range of possible statements on the past in different ways. These interventions assumed a variety of forms. The unprecedented and highly publicised war crime trials held in Nuremberg and Tokyo were among the more direct interventions, with the side-effect of producing an authoritative master narrative of the war. In both cases, the political and military leaders were severed from the larger population and held responsible for expansion and atrocities.[5] On a more general level, the social reforms that the Americans attempted and to some extent achieved in West Germany and Japan transmitted, as a powerful subtext, an image of each country's respective past. But beyond these very general measures, the Allied interventions also assumed more concrete forms and explicitly banned certain interpretations from the field of permissible interpretations. These initiatives included purges at universities and schools,[6] and also the institution of censorship. In Japan, coverage of the atomic bomb explosions in Hiroshima and Nagasaki was largely prohibited, and photographic documentary was banned.[7] In Germany, it was the resistance movement of the 20th of July 1944 that attracted the attention of the censors. From the perspective of the occupation forces, the largely aristocratic composition of the 'July Bomb Plot' resistance group seemed to make it unsuitable as a starting point for the democratisation of German society.[8] While the bulk of American measures were prohibitive in character, there were instances of prescription as well. For example, an American version of the Pacific War was serialised in all national Japanese newspapers in the fall of 1945. It used 'unimpeachable sources' to present the 'truth' about the recent past 'until the story of Japanese war guilt has been fully bared in all its details'.[9] In Germany, films documenting the liberation of concentration camps were shown to a population that, in addition, was confronted with its genocidal past through a series of large-scale posters displayed in various German cities.[10]

These interventions into historical scholarship under the American occupation demonstrate the extent to which the project of rethinking the past needs to be placed in a transnational context. When looking closer at the discipline of history, however, it is important to recognise that what appeared to many contemporaries as a fundamental shift was not the product of external pressures alone. In fact, the caesura was partially rhetorical, obliterating the strands of continuity between wartime and post-war thinking. In many ways, the occupation's view of history owed considerably to native sources and was deeply embedded in earlier debates conducted among German and Japanese historians. For example, the views of Jewish émigrés to the United States and their narratives of German history proved to be an influential resource for occupation perspectives; the same was true for the analyses of Japanese Marxist historians that found their way into the occupation policies through the mediation of Japan specialists in the political establishment. On the other hand, pre-war interpretations and approaches could be endowed with additional prestige and credibility when supported by occupation interventions. This was obvious, for example, for sociology in Germany that had flourished in the 1920s and was now resuscitated in a new, American garb. Also, a version of modernisation theory had developed in Japan before 1945, upon which Parsonian theories of modernity were later grafted. Much of what may appear as a cultural imposition (and it certainly did to many contemporaries), reveals itself upon closer scrutiny as a complex interplay of actors linking earlier debates to a postwar setting shaped by military occupation and American hegemony.[11]

Thus, it would be an exaggeration to say, as Harry Harootunian has suggested, that in the early post-war decades, 'America's Japan became Japan's Japan'.[12] Things were more complicated, as 'American' perspectives on Japan were deeply entangled with debates among Japanese intellectuals. A similar point can be made for the case of Germany. Moreover, the transnational embeddedness of interpretations of the past in both countries cannot be reduced to a dialogue with the United States. The transnational context was never uniform. In the case of Germany, it included West-European integration, challenges by East German historians, the influence of former émigrés, the role of the Jewish Claims Conference, alongside the presence of the United States as guarantors of the Cold War status quo. In Japan, the chronology was different, as it took several decades before perspectives from the neighbouring countries in Asia emerged as an important factor in memory debates.

Culture and modernity: National Socialism and Japanese fascism

The West German historians who spoke in public about the recent past denounced the Nazi era as a massive catastrophe. The term 'catastrophe' experienced a rapid boom in the literature pertaining to the Third Reich and its position in the continuum of German history.[13] The best known and most frequently cited example of this early treatment of National Socialism was undoubtedly *The German Catastrophe* by the 84-year-old Friedrich Meinecke, published in 1946. The book was incidentally also received with great interest in Japan and was published there in a translated version in 1951.[14] In Japan, too, there was a widespread belief that fascism had plunged the country into a catastrophe – even if the expectations of how to move beyond the present predicaments differed widely across the political spectrum.[15]

Thenceforth, one of the central tasks of historical interpretation in both countries would be to understand this 'catastrophe', or 'dark valley' (*kurai tanima*) of national history and to inquire as to its origins. It is striking that the explanatory method that found the greatest acceptance in both West Germany and Japan was based on a correlation of national character on the one hand, and National Socialism and/or fascism on the other. Thus, to many commentators the recent past appeared as the product of a cultural substance – or, conversely, as the contamination of this very substance 'from the outside'. From this perspective, totalitarianism was either already present as a sort of bacillus in German and Japanese culture, or else it appeared as the result of a cultural import. Only a return to the original and pure traditions of the nation, according to the latter view, promised a fundamental 'overcoming' of this past.

In Japan, the efforts to arrive at an understanding of fascism and its cultural roots were particularly linked to the work of Maruyama Masao. Maruyama (1914–1996) had studied at the law department of the University of Tokyo and rose to assistant professor there in 1940. During the Pacific War he was stationed in Hiroshima where he also witnessed the detonation of the atomic bomb. Only 31 years old at the end of the war, Maruyama appeared in public with a series of essays over the coming years in which he presented a profound analysis of Japanese fascism. The enormous effect of his writings quickly made him into one of the leading intellectuals who sought to link the democratisation of the country with a critical re-examination of its past. Maruyama's work had a double purpose; while it was written against tendencies to bury the years of fascism as accidents of Japanese history and thus against conservative apologists, it also challenged the Marxist interpretation of fascism which began to occupy centre-stage in the first post-war years.[16]

The starting point of his analysis was the question of how to understand the formation of ultra-nationalism (*chōkokka shugi*) without succumbing to socio-economic reductionism. 'Scholars have been mainly concerned with the social and economic background of ultra-nationalism. Neither in Japan nor in the West have they attempted any fundamental analysis of its intellectual structure or of its psychological basis'.[17] Thus in his influential essay on 'The Theory and Psychology of Ultra-Nationalism', which first appeared in the journal *Sekai* in May of 1946, Maruyama undertook an analysis of the ideological aspects of fascism. For him, only a successful diagnosis of this abortive development promised a lasting transformation of Japanese society. 'Ultra-nationalism succeeded in spreading a many-layered, though invisible, net over the Japanese people, and even today they have not really freed themselves from its hold'.[18]

Maruyama referred to the ultra-nationalism of the 1930s and 1940s as 'fascism', which, however, was clearly distinguished from the analogous political formation in Europe. For in Japan, 'Fascism did not burst on the scene from below as it did in Italy and Germany'.[19] Instead, 'the fascist movement from below was completely absorbed into totalitarian transformation from above'. In Maruyama's eyes, this special form of fascism, which was not based on a revolutionary mass movement but rather incorporated fascist energies into an authoritarian regime imposed 'from above', revealed Japanese fascism's 'pre-modern character'. 'In the final analysis it was the historical circumstance that Japan had not undergone the experience of a *bourgeois* revolution that determined this character of the fascist movement'.[20]

In his historical genealogy, Maruyama emphasised the fact that – unlike in Europe – the separation of the public and private sphere never developed in Japan. That is why the responsible, free individual of modern civil society failed to emerge in Japan. Instead, an ideology defining social relationships as elements of a family structure, and which covered both the public and the private sphere, dominated all areas of society. As a consequence, morality and ethics did not develop as independent normative systems. Rather, they remained linked to the hierarchical social structure. This ideological framework stood in the way of a differentiation of the spheres of power and the rule of law; what is more, it prevented the emergence of the modern individual, simultaneously inhibiting the possibility of a political movement in a revolutionary fashion 'from below'.

This analysis, which made a world-historical deviance (the absence of a bourgeois revolution) responsible for the failure of the individual and of subjectivity to develop in Japan, was the most influential post-war attempt to locate Japanese fascism in history. It is obvious that Maruyama understood fascism as a thoroughly modern formation, which in turn assumed the existence of the modern individual and his or her autonomy and responsibility. Maruyama's studies were primarily directed against the 'repression' of recent history and its ideological roots. In contrast to the attempts to reduce fascism to the status of an 'accident' by insisting on the positive traditions of Japanese history, Maruyama suggested 'diagnosing the lack of ... psychological analyses of Japan's intellectual structure and/or behavioral forms'.[21] For him, the cultural 'legacy' was not a reservoir of Japan's pure and unspoiled qualities but was itself profoundly implicated in the ideological-social causes of the recent catastrophe.

In West Germany, by contrast, the tendency to view the nation's cultural traditions as a refuge untouched by the shocks of war and National Socialism was widespread among conservative historians. For Friedrich Meinecke, the only hope of 'renewal' in 1945 rested on the reassertion of the cultural achievements of the past: 'The places where we must resettle in a spiritual sense have been shown to us: religion and culture of the German spirit (*Geist*)'. At the same time, Meinecke felt that a cultural 'awakening' was necessary, and he recommended this be carried out by effectively subtracting the past 150 years of modern German history and picking up the threads with the German classics. 'The work of the Bismarck era has been destroyed by our own guilt, and across its ruins we must find our path back to the time of Goethe'.[22] In this way he believed that the cultural core of the nation, which threatened to be destroyed in the course of the 'catastrophe', could be preserved: 'In every German city and large town we would like to see form a community of likeminded friends of culture which I would love to give the name "Goethe Community"'. On this basis, he hoped for the 'rescue of the last remnant of German popular and cultural essence which has been left to us'.[23]

The early statements of Japanese historians contained no such vehement pleas in favour of immaculate national traditions. To be sure: in Japan, too, the idea of national uniqueness played an important role. For example, Maruyama Masao concentrated his research, as he admitted in retrospect, on the 'specific peculiarity of Japanese politics and of the cultural patterns which underlie them'. However, for him these specific qualities were not to be found in the grandiose achievements of a unique Japanese culture but rather in its deficiencies and shortcomings. Thus Maruyama spoke of his 'obsessive concern exclusively with the pathological aspects of my own society'. This preoccupation with the unique, with the nation's essence thus had its place not only in postwar West German historiography but in Japanese research as well. And yet the overall thrust could not have been more different. Maruyama linked the discovery of national peculiarities with an effort to eliminate them from Japanese society. 'It will be apparent that ... my conscious intention ... was to expose myself and the body politic of my own society to a probing X-ray analysis and to wield a merciless scalpel on every sign of disease there discovered'.[24] For Meinecke, by contrast, the historian's task lay not in extirpation but rather in preservation. As he himself put it, he was in search of the unchanging German essence, of the 'German *character indelebilis*'.[25]

This nostalgic longing for a cultural homecoming, of which Meinecke's work was a prominent expression, seemed to suggest that the collapse into barbarism could be traced back to external influences alone. For many historians, the French Revolution appeared as the historical event marking a fundamental break with tradition and whose shock waves were also palpable in German society. In his *German Catastrophe*, Meinecke reconstructed both the German and the European roots of totalitarianism and – by thus differentiating between the internal/ specific and external/modern – marked the boundaries within which the debate would continue to be conducted in the following decades. Historians frequently made use of both the arguments, which were not diametrical opposites and could be used in a complementary way. Gerhard Ritter, the powerful and influential representative of conservative historians, was among those who were particularly eager to pounce on the search for the non-German origins of National Socialism.

> Today everyone is anxious to seek out the 'roots of National Socialism' in German history. A thoroughly necessary business, indeed ... . But it would remain without result if we would limit this search to Germany. It was not some event of German history but rather the great French Revolution which decisively loosened up the firm soil of European political traditions.[26]

The recurring references to the bourgeois revolution in France were a manifestation of the deep scepticism conservative German historians felt toward modernity. As Ritter's comments illustrate, Nazism's historical origins not only appeared to lie outside Germany's borders but were also linked to the beginnings of modernity itself. The recourse to 'outside influences' was thus supplemented by what can be called a temporal argument. The French Revolution represented not only a foreign culture but also the invasion of European history by modernity with all its concomitant features. According to Gerhard Ritter, two factors came into play as consequences of the Industrial Revolution: the process of secularisation and the democratic movement. These two developments represented the repertoire to which most studies by conservative scholars referred. In Ritter's opinion, both developments in the nineteenth century already paved 'the way to the modern total state'.[27] This conservative perspective made it possible to place the emphasis at different points as needed. Historians arguing within a Catholic framework particularly emphasised the consequences of secularisation and saw Nazism as the logical outcome of a 'century without God'. By contrast, the Lutheran Protestant Ritter aimed his argument against the imposition of democratic government. In democracy, he asserted, the will of the people is sovereign, incontestable, and thus total. Democracy, he believed, already bore the seed of totalitarianism within it.

Nazism as a product of the modern age – that was the counter-position to an interpretation (such as Maruyama's analysis of Japanese fascism), which interpreted dictatorship as a result of structural shortcomings of culture. It is interesting to see, however, that the anti-modern perspective of many German historians continued to describe the imposition of 'modernity' by using the metaphor of invasion.[28] Localising the origins of modernity in the French Revolution, therefore, appeared to be a matter not only of chronology but also of geography. If National Socialism could be viewed as a product of modernity, then as a result, its roots had to be sought outside of German history. Gerhard Ritter was among those highlighting the European (i.e., non-German) character of the dangers that modernity allegedly brought with it. For instance, racism had been founded 'by the Frenchman Gobineau'; and even Hitler himself had been an immigrant.[29] For Ritter (and not only for him), the contamination of German political culture followed the logic of importation. 'Deep down in its core', Ritter concluded, 'National Socialism was in no way an original German growth'.[30]

In Japan, as we have already seen, Maruyama's emphasis of fascism's internal cultural roots had a broad public impact. But in Japan, too, approaches emerged that sought to understand the negative aspects of the country's own history as a consequence of foreign influence. One proponent of this theory of imported militarism was the conservative historian Tsuda Sōkichi (1873–1961). Tsuda dedicated himself to the reconstruction of indigenous Japanese popular culture, which in his view rested on the uniform ethnic basis of the nation. His interpretation diverged from the imperialist ideology of the war years, which had depicted the Japanese as a mixed population (a position that was instrumentalised to legitimate claims on territories in Korea or China). For Tsuda, Japan had been a homogeneous nation from the beginning.

This ethnic homogeneity had also been the reason why Japanese history was not characterised by subjugation and repressive policies but rather had progressed in an inherently peaceful fashion. As an island people (*shimaguni*), the Japanese had only maintained limited relations with other peoples, and thus had not developed any expansionist intentions. Tsuda saw the Tennō as the incarnation of the Japanese nation's peaceful character.[31]

It is important to recognise, however, that posing a dichotomy between the peace-loving Japanese people and an aggressive culture imported from abroad (China) was not just a conservative strategy. Indeed, it emerged as an integral part of Marxist discourse as well. Particularly following what can be termed the nationalist turn of Marxist history writing around 1950–1951, the thesis of a suppressed, neo-colonised Japanese people gained new currency. Against the backdrop of the Korean War and the rearmament plans of the government, Marxist historians translated their political opposition into a search for the peaceful and anti-militarist traditions of Japanese history. In a study on ancient Japan, Toma Seita described a homogeneous people, which had developed peacefully and rejected all expansionist inclinations. Only under the influence of cultural imports from China, which the rulers had instrumentalised to suppress the people, did Japan also develop militaristic, expansionist policies. After 1951, the absolute dichotomy between the people and their rulers, as well as between Japan and China – a dichotomy long employed by conservatives like Tsuda Sōkichi – became an integral part of Marxist discourse as well. This binary opposition tended to support the argument that the cultural roots of militarism and the Second World War came from China and not from Japan itself.[32] In the search for the causes of National Socialism and Japanese fascism, the cultural paradigm thus played an important role. This explanatory model could be instrumentalised by historians of various orientations in different and contradicting ways.

Victims of the war

Running through the post-war analyses of National Socialism and Japanese fascism, there was a pattern of argumentation that was easily reconciled with the cultural paradigm (particularly the interpretation of fascism as a product of a foreign cultural legacy). Both in West Germany and in Japan, there was an almost universal notion that one's own nation should be viewed as the real victim of the recent epoch of totalitarianism. Thus in studies written on contemporary history, the gap between the people and the government played a central role as it seemed to prove that the nation's integrity was not fundamentally affected by the events of the recent past. In nascent form, these interpretations fed into what Jie-Hyun Lim, in his contribution to this volume, has called 'victimhood nationalism'. It was to become a salient feature of Japanese, and also West German, post-war discourse.

The distinction between an innocent people and a criminal clique of militarists – a dichotomy that was reinforced by the war crimes trials in Nuremberg and Tokyo – was a common assumption across the board of different schools and factions of West German and Japanese historical studies. For example, Gerhard Ritter insisted on the distinction 'between the German people and its National Socialist leadership, between a better past and a present which has been profoundly contaminated by the revolution of 1933'.[33] The argumentative structure employed in Japan followed a similar logic.[34] The official language of the American occupiers spoke of 'crimes committed by the militarists against the Japanese people', whose greatest victim had been the integrity of the Japanese nation.[35] That a clear line be drawn between purportedly vast numbers of victims and the allegedly few perpetrators rapidly became the consensus among both conservative and critical historians. Particularly in the Marxist camp, the Japanese were soon stylised as an oppressed people who were thus validated as the subject of Japan's future history. The 'entire Japanese people', Inoue Kiyoshi declared, was 'locked ... in a giant military prison by the military apparatus'.[36]

In West Germany, the focus on German victimhood was also a reaction to a public debate. One thrust of scholarly study of the Second World War aimed at taking the wind out of the sails of revisionist memoirs. During the 1950s, a number of memoirs appeared in which leading officers addressed the public with their own versions of the war in order to provide a retroactive justification for their political-strategic decisions. Faced with this apologetic literature, historians attempted to counter-attack the growth of such myth-making. On the other hand, the majority of West German historians were simultaneously interested in protecting the achievements of the *Wehrmacht* and of the bulk of German soldiers from blanket condemnation – a motive that assumed particular prominence during the debate over German rearmament in the mid-1950s. This conflict of interest was best solved by analytically detaching the activities of the *Wehrmacht* from National Socialist policies, and by insisting on a dichotomy between the 'clean' army and Hitler's criminal expansionism. According to this logic, the *Reichswehr*, which had been forced into line by the Nazi leadership, almost appeared as the first victim of Hitler's policies. Most historians did not see the *Wehrmacht* as a Nazi organisation. At least, as Waldemar Besson argued, one could claim 'that the *Wehrmacht* was one factor which ... after ... many attempts on the part of the Nazis to penetrate it, still sought to retain its own spiritual face (*sein eigenes geistiges Gesicht*)'.[37] A result of this distinction was that most scholars limited themselves to the purely military aspects of the war and felt justified in ignoring its 'National Socialist' character.

This was corroborated by the fact that the main emphasis of these studies was usually not on researching the war's causes, but rather on an analysis of the defeat. West German historians rarely asked questions pertaining to the long-term and possibly structural causes of the war, which dominated the Japanese debates. For unlike the First World War, the Second World War did not 'break out' in 1939 but had been planned well in advance. Thus the widespread 'Hitler-centrism' (the product of a methodological intentionalism) allowed West German historians to ignore both long-term processes and to take the responsibility for the war from the shoulders of the German nation. Walther Hofer, whose *Unleashing of the Second World War* of 1954 quickly became a standard text, typically reduced the issue of causes to the

> riddle ... of the unfortunate and terrible personality of Hitler, without which the Second World War is unthinkable. Again and again, certain lines of development, which historians would like to trace back to their origin, get lost in decisions and evaluations which arose from the confused brain and sick soul of the German dictator. Again and again, the search for the original source of decisive and fateful decisions cannot help but land in psychological, indeed psychiatric studies.[38]

The focus on German victimhood implied that Germans as perpetrators were only marginally present in early post-war scholarship. The genocidal policy toward the Jews in particular, which a later generation came to see as the core of the Nazi reign, was largely eclipsed. In the first decades after the war, the Holocaust was not among the central themes of West German historical studies.[39] This only began to change from the 1960s. The Eichmann trial and the Auschwitz trial shoved the genocide into public consciousness, which also manifested itself in the historians' turn toward questions of racial and extermination policy. The Institute for Contemporary History regularly prepared expert reports in connection with the trials. And yet the close engagement with courtroom investigation led to a state of affairs where in historical research, too, the perpetrators stood in the centre and the victims appeared as merely marginal subjects. The category of the perpetrators was implicitly limited to a small group of 'monsters' operating in secret. The German population as a whole was rarely charged with collective responsibility. On the contrary, the German nation often appeared as a victim in its own right, and as having endured the most appalling suffering because of the genocide. Walther Hofer, for example, concluded his chapter on 'The Persecution and Extermination of the Jews' in 1957 with the following characteristic twist: 'Thanks to the immeasurable crimes of the National Socialist regime, Germany's name was desecrated and condemned like that of no other nation before'.[40]

Not only in the Federal Republic but also in Japan, the war was one of the preferred terrains of controversy. By contrast with Germany, the main targets of the debate were not military and diplomatic issues. Instead, discussion revolved around the war's historical meaning and how the interpretation of modern Japanese history was affected by the evaluation of the war. Academic scholarship explicitly concerned with the experience of war only appeared following independence, that is, after 1952. In view of the interpretational monopoly that Marxist historians exerted in the field of modern history, it is hardly surprising that the first extensive presentation of the war was written from the point of view of Historical Materialism. The Marxist historical association *Rekishigaku kenkyūkai*, under the supervision of the historian Eguchi Bokurō, organised a conference series on the history of the war, whose results were published in a large five-volume collective work under the title *The History of the Pacific War* in 1953–1954.

In the foreword (by Inoue Kiyoshi) the whole of modern Japanese history was described as a 'history of relentless wars', in which the peaceful moments between two military conflicts merely served to prepare for the next war. However, this militaristic past did not correspond to a warlike national character, for 'the Japanese people is just as peace loving as other proletarian peoples in the world'. In the same way, the argument of a fateful war, which had been forced upon Japan by the country's geographic and demographic situation, was rejected as imperialist and deterministic. Instead, the war could be explained by pointing to imperialism's social base and function: 'Japan was pulled into one war after another by the Tennō system, the semi-feudal land ownership system as well as the inextricably linked monopoly capital ... and to their advantage'.[41] In the ensuing 1300 pages readers were treated to a detailed depiction of the events from the orthodox

Marxist perspective, which was concerned with providing a broad world-historical perspective.

The main emphasis was on the war in China, which was interpreted as a conflict between the Chinese people, as represented by the Communists, and the Japanese ruling class. The war against the USA, as a result, faded into the background. From the Marxist perspective, it was not much more than a typical conflict between two imperialistic states that illustrated the instability of the capitalist system. However, despite their profound awareness of the war in China and Southeast Asia, most historians largely ignored the concrete colonial reality in the territories occupied by Japan. Just as on the domestic scene, the mechanisms of social repression were condemned in general terms but not studied empirically. The Japanese crimes on the mainland battlefields, in particular, were scarcely looked at during this period. The atrocities committed in Nanking had been an issue at the Tokyo Trials, but academic studies of this event only began in the 1970s. In fact, biological warfare and forced prostitution were not seriously studied until after 1990.[42]

Following the end of the occupation in 1952, however, there soon emerged a revisionist current, which crusaded against the coalition of Marxist and Allied historiography. Typical of this tendency was the four-volume history of the war by the former Colonel Hattori Takushirō (1910–1960). During the occupation Hattori had worked for five years in the historiographical department of the American army, which had originally commissioned him to write the work. He had access to the records of the Imperial Headquarters and used them to author a purely military history of the war. Already in the foreword, Hattori made it clear against whom this war had essentially been fought: he quoted Fichte's 'Addresses to the German Nation' at the time of the Napoleonic occupation, in which he saw an historical parallel to the American occupation in Japan. While Marxist historians specifically interpreted the war as an act of imperialistic Japanese aggression against the 'innocent' Chinese people, Hattori primarily viewed the 'Greater East Asian War' as a conflict with the United States. Out of the book's more than 1600 pages, more than 1400 were devoted to the events following the Japanese attack on Pearl Harbor in December 1941. By contrast, the colonisation of China was only dealt with in the margins, and the Rape of Nanking of 1937 was not even mentioned. This selection of what should even be considered an historical 'fact' was destined to point the interpretation of national history in a different direction – which is exactly what Hattori had intended. His interpretation emphasised the 'profound fatefulness' that characterised Japan's path to war.[43]

The common theme of the revisionist publications in the 1950s was a turn away from what was viewed as the degrading Marxist historiography and thus an alternative understanding of the nation. Typical of this approach was the emphasis on the fatefulness of Japan's modern development, from the modernising reforms forced upon it by the West to the war, which it ended up fighting against the very same West. The entire Japanese nation – including civilian and military leaders – was thus presented as a victim of world history that should be rehabilitated in toto.

Since the late 1950s, then, academic (largely Marxist) accounts, which pilloried the war as an imperialistic war of aggression, were faced with an increasingly broad range of revisionist literature. Both sides directed their argumentation at one another, but common to both sides was their joint emphasis on the war's significance for the identity of the nation. Across the political and methodological differences, all participants in the debate characterised the war as a 'national legacy'. For Marxist historians, the Japanese people – just like the suppressed peoples of Asia – were the real victims of a war perpetrated by the militaristic Japanese ruling class. The revisionist approaches did not share this division of the nation into the people and its rulers. Instead, they saw the entire nation as a unity, which was forced into war against its will. And while the Marxist historians were particularly concerned with searching for the war's socioeconomic causes, the revisionist scholars understood Japan's entry into the war as the product of historical 'fate'. This term played a decisive role in all revisionist accounts and, incidentally, bore some striking resemblances to the concept of historical 'necessity' in the Marxist discourse.

In this way, Japan appeared as both the object and the victim of world history. It was a nation under attack. According to this interpretation it was history (or fate) that had determined the decision to wage war with the United States long in advance. The philosopher Ueyama Shumpei expressed this notion clearly in an essay published in 1961. As others had done before him, Ueyama emphasised the 'unique national experience' of the war, whose historical roots he chose to locate in the period of Japan's 'opening' in the nineteenth century. He characterised the opening of the country and the ensuing modernisation as a response to the threat from outside. The turn against the 'West', for him, was already implicit in the logic of the Meiji Restoration:

> The decision to open the country implied with virtually logical necessity a course of development which could not help but lead from the dissolution of feudalism to the Industrial Revolution, and

then to the invasion of underdeveloped countries all the way to the collision with the advanced powers.

Thus, for Ueyama, every criticism of the 'Greater East Asian War' was also a criticism of the foundation of modern Japan, namely the Meiji Restoration. If Japan did not want to lose its sovereignty back then, 'then there was no other path than that of war'.[44]

Conclusion

Both in Germany and Japan, historians in the early post-war years dealt with the recent history of war and dictatorship in an attempt to position their own nation in a context of military defeat and occupation. In both countries, we can observe an immediate distancing from the recent past – which is all the more striking considering the fact that the post-war purges did not essentially alter the composition of the discipline. At the same time, however, there emerged in both countries a form of victim consciousness that essentially cast the own nation as the prime victim of the war, of the years of authoritarian government, and occasionally of foreign occupation.

These similarities notwithstanding, there were striking differences in the way the past was appropriated and interpreted – both between the two societies and within them. The central matrix within which the recent history of fascism and war was explained was constructed along two interpretative axes, making reference to backwardness versus modernity on the one hand, and to foreign import versus internal development, on the other. There was a tension, in other words, between views that identified fascism/National Socialism with the modern age (with mass society, secularism, democracy, etc.) on the one hand, and those that held fascism to be the result of a failed, truncated modernity. This dichotomy was articulated with a logic of inside versus outside, according to which the cultural and structural deficits of society were either the result of cultural borrowing and import, or the effect of internal, and fundamentally flawed, social dynamics.

The result was a heterogeneous field of competing enunciations. Each in its own way linked assumptions about culture and modernity. Both in Germany and in Japan, historiography was not monolithic. Different groups and milieus competed with each other for the appropriate interpretation of history, and frequently the competing versions of the past were invested with meanings and interests derived from the present. Historiography of the recent past, in particular, was a highly contested field.[45] It is therefore difficult to generalise and to speak of 'German' and 'Japanese' approaches toward the past. For comparative purposes, however, and glossing over many of the differences and peculiarities, one can say that in West Germany, the conviction that fascism was a deviation from national traditions was hegemonic, and historians attempted to prescribe elements of the cultural legacy of the nation as a cure. In Japan, however, many historians suggested a purging of national traditions in order to fall in line with the universal process of modernisation.

It is important to recognise, finally, that these different trajectories of debate were due both to dynamics internal to each society and to the larger transnational context within which they unfolded. Debates about the past bore the traces of a globalising world, which were deeply engraved in what is often still perceived as the realm of the uniquely national, of a peculiar mentality and mindset. The various exchanges and interventions across national boundaries introduced multiple temporalities into an arena where these conflicting narratives of the past were negotiated. At times, interventions from without delimited the discursive space within which the past could be remembered; in many instances, however, they helped to de-centre dominant narratives of a nationalised history and thus contributed to a pluralisation of the past. Thus, any assessment of the different forms of public memory in post-war Germany and Japan needs to be situated in this context of the Cold War and American Occupation.

Notes

1. Cf. Ralph Giordano, *Die zweite Schuld oder Von der Last Deutscher zu sein* (Hamburg: Rasch und Röhring, 1987).
2. Cf. Ian Buruma, *Wages of Guilt. Memories of War in Germany and Japan* (London: Jonathan Cape, 1994).
3. Much of the following argument relies on Sebastian Conrad, *The Quest for the Lost Nation: Writing History in Germany and Japan in the American Century* (Berkeley: University of California Press, 2010).
4. For an overview of German and Japanese post-war historiography, see Winfried Schulze, *Deutsche Geschichtswissenschaft nach 1945* (München Dt. Taschenbuch-Verl., 1993); Tōyama Shigeki, *Sengo no rekishigaku to rekishi ishiki* (Tokyo: Iwanami Shoten, 1968).
5. On the effects of the American occupation in Germany see Walter L. Dorn, 'Die Debatte über die amerikanische Besatzungspolitik für Deutschland (1944–1945)', *Vierteljahrshefte für Zeitgeschichte*, vol. 6 (1958), pp. 60–77. For Japan, see Richard H. Minear, *Victors' Justice. The Tokyo War Crimes Trial* (Tokyo: Tuttle, 1972); Awaya Kentarō, *Tokyo saibanron* (Tokyo: Ōtsuki Shoten, 1989).
6. For Germany, see Schulze, *Geschichtswissenschaft*, pp. 121–30; for Japan, see Yamamoto Reiko, *Senryōka ni okeru kyōshoku tsuiho. GHQ, SCAP monjo ni yoru kenkyū* (Tokyo: Meisei Daigaku Shuppanbu, Heisei 6, 1994).

34   *Mass Dictatorship and Memory as Ever Present Past*

7. John Dower, *Embracing Defeat: Japan in the Wake of World War II* (New York: W.W. Norton & Co., 1999), pp. 405–40; Monica Braw, *The Atomic Bomb Suppressed: American Censorship in Occupied Japan* (Armonk, NY: M.E. Sharpe Inc., 1991); Horiba Kiyoko, *Genbaku. Hyōgen to kenetsu* (Tokyo: Asahi Shinbunsha, 1995).

8. See Peter Steinbach, Widerstand im Dritten Reich – die Keimzelle der Nachkriegsdemokratie Die Auseinandersetzung mit dem Widerstand in der historischen politischen Bildungsarbeit, in den Medien und in der öffentlichen Meinung nach 1945, in: Gerd R. Ueberschär (ed.), *Der 20.Juli 1944. Bewertung und Rezeption des deutschen Widerstandes gegen das NS-Regime* (Köln: Bund-Verlag, 1994), pp. 79–100.

9. GHQ (General Headquarters United States Army Forces, Pacific), Historical Articles on the War in the Pacific, GHQ/SCAP-Records in the National Diet Library Tokyo, Sheet No. CIE (D) 05235, 05236, Box No. 5869, Classification No. 840, 800, 000 & No. 000, 840, 1.

10. Cornelia Brink, *Ikonen der Vernichtung. Öffentlicher Gebrauch von Fotografien aus nationalsozialistischen Konzentrationslagern nach 1945* (Berlin: Akademie, 1998).

11. On the wartime origins of Japanese theories of modernisation, see Nakano Toshio, *Ōtsuka Hisao to Maruyama Masao. Dōin, shutai, sensō sekinin* (Tokyo: Seidosha, 2001).

12. Harry D. Harootunian, 'America's Japan/Japan's Japan', in Masao Miyoshi/Harry D. Harootunian (eds), *Japan in the World* (Durham: Duke University Press, 1993), pp. 196–221.

13. Cf. Schulze, *Geschichtswissenschaft*, p. 47.

14. Friedrich Meinecke, *Die deutsche Katastrophe. Betrachtungen und Erinnerungen* (Wiesbaden: E. Brockhaus, 1946). The translation by Yada Toshitaka was titled 'The German tragedy' (doitsu no higeki).

15. Franziska Seraphim, 'The Debate about War Responsibility', in Early Postwar Japan (ed.) Masters Thesis (New York: Columbia University, 1992), unpublished.

16. On Maruyama's biography and works cf. Rikki Kersten, *Democracy in Postwar Japan: Maruyama Masao and the Search for Autonomy* (London: Routledge, 1996); Ishida Takeshi, *Nihon no shakai kagaku* (Tokyo: Tokyo Daigaku Shuppankai, 1984); Andrew E. Barshay, *The Social Sciences in Modern Japan: The Marxian and Modernist Traditions* (Berkeley: University of California Press, 2004), pp. 197–239.

17. Maruyama Masao, 'Theory and Psychology of Ultra-Nationalism', in Maruyama, *Thought and Behaviour in Modern Japanese Politics* (London: Oxford University Press, 1963), p. 1.

18. Ibid., p. 1.

19. Maruyama Masao, 'The Ideology and Dynamics of Japanese Fascism', in Maruyama, *Thought and Behaviour*, pp. 25–83, quote: p. 82.

20. Maruyama Masao, 'Thought and Behaviour in Modern Japanese Politics', in Maruyama, *Thought and Behaviour*, pp. 72, 80.

21. Quoted from Wolfgang Seifert and Wolfgang Schamoni, Vorwort, in Maruyama Masao (ed.), *Denken in Japan* (Frankfurt: Suhrkamp, 1988), pp. 7–19, quote: p. 13.

22. Meinecke, *Katastrophe*, pp. 164, 168.

23. Meinecke, *Katastrophe*, p. 8.

24. Maruyama Masao, 'Author's Introduction', in Maruyama, *Thought and Behaviour*, pp. v–ix, quotes: pp. xiv, xi, xii.

25. Meinecke, *Katastrophe*, p. 176.

26. Gerhard Ritter, *Europa und die deutsche Frage. Betrachtungen über die geschichtliche Eigenart des deutschen Staatsdenkens* (Munich: Münchner Verlag, 1948), p. 51.

On Ritter, see Christoph Cornelißen, *Gerhard Ritter. Geschichtswissenschaft und Politik im 20. Jahrhundert* (Düsseldorf: Droste Verlag, 2001).

27. Ritter, *Europa*, p. 43.

28. For a general treatment of German historians and their concept of 'modernity', see Jin-Sung Chun, *Das Bild der Moderne in der Nachkriegszeit. Die westdeutsche 'Strukturgeschichte' im Spannungsfeld von Modernitätskritik und wissenschaftlicher Innovation 1948–1962* (Munich: Oldenbourg, 2000).

29. Ritter, *Europa*, pp. 115–17.

30. Gerhard Ritter, *Geschichte als Bildungsmacht. Ein Beitrag zur historisch-politischen Neubesinnung* (Stuttgart: Deutsche Verlags-Anstalt, 1946), p. 32.

31. 'Kadowaki Teiji, Tsuda Sōkichi, in Kano Masanao and Nagahara Keiji (eds.), *Nihon no rekishika* (Tokyo: Nihon Hyōronsho, 1976), pp. 165–74.

32. Toma Seita, *Nihon minzoku no keisei* (Tokyo: Iwanami Shoten, 1951). Cf. Oguma Eiji, Wasurerareta minzoku mondai. Sengo Nihon no 'kakushin nashionarizumu', *Sōkan shakai kagaku*, vol. 5, (1995), pp. 30–48; Curtis Anderson Gayle, *Marxist History and Postwar Japanese Nationalism* (New York: Routledge Curzon, 2003), p. 87–92.

33. Ritter, *Europa*, p. 7.

34. For a general account, see James J. Orr, *The Victim as Hero: Ideologies of Peace and National Identity in Postwar Japan* (Honolulu: University of Hawai'i Press, 2001).

35. GHQ, Historical Articles, pp. 1, 2.

36. Inoue Kiyoshi, 'Bōkansha to giseisha. "Shōwa no seishinshi" hihan', *Shisō* vol. 386, (1956), pp. 895–906, quote: p. 897.

37. Waldemar Besson, 'Zur Geschichte des nationalsozialistischen Führungsoffiziers (NSFO)', *Vierteljahrshefte für Zeitgeschichte* vol. 9 (1961), pp. 76–116, quote: p. 79.

38. Walther Hofer, *Die Entfesselung des Zweiten Weltkrieges. Eine Studie über die internationalen Beziehungen im Sommer 1939* (Stuttgart: Deutsche Verlags-Anstalt, 1954), p. 11.

39. Cf. Nicolas Berg, *Der Holocaust und die westdeutschen Historiker. Erforschung und Erinnerung* (Göttingen: Wallstein, 2003).

40. Walther Hofer, (ed.), *Der Nationalsozialismus. Dokumente 1933–1945* (Frankfurt: Fischer Bücherei, 1957), p. 276.

41. Rekishigaku kenkyūkai, *Taiheiyō sensō shi*, vol. 5 (Tokyo, 1953/1954), Quotes from vol. 1, p. 1, 2.

42. Cf. Joshua Fogel (ed.), *The Nanjing Massacre in History and Historiography* (Berkeley: University of California Press, 2000); Sheldon Harris, *Factories of Death. Japanese Biological Warfare and the American Cover-up* (London: Routledge, 1994); Yoshimi Yoshiaki, *Comfort Women. Sexual Slavery in the Japanese Military During World War II* (New York: Columbia University Press, 2000).

43. Hattori Takushirō, *Daitōa sensō zenshi* (Tokyo: Hara Shobō, [1953] 1993), p. 3.

44. Ueyama Shumpei, *Daitōa sensō no shisōshiteki igi*, *Chūō kōron*, vol. 76 (September 1961, pp. 98–107), quotes: pp. 100, 106, 106.

45. For a good analysis of the heterogeneity of actors and voices, see Franziska Seraphim, *War Memory and Social Politics in Japan, 1945–2005* (Cambridge: Harvard University Press, 2006).

3
Victimhood Nationalism in the Memory of Mass Dictatorship

Jie-Hyun Lim

The nationalist sublimation of victimhood

With the advent of a global public sphere, a shift from heroic martyrdom to innocent victimhood has begun to manifest itself in the construction of collective memories. It is difficult to pinpoint the precise moment of this shift, but it can be argued that as the space of global memory has expanded, its changing topography has contributed to the emergence of a discourse of victimhood. The rise of global human rights politics, the politics of apology among great world powers, ethnic cleansing and genocide in former Yugoslavia and Rwanda as they have been conjured out of the history of totalitarianism, the transposition of Holocaust memories onto contemporary sensibilities about genocide, the institutionalisation of cosmopolitan memories, the democratisation of the narrative with its increasing concern about the victim's voice and testimony and the process of coming to terms with the memories of mass dictatorships in the post-totalitarian era: all of these phenomena have made a global civil society more receptive to the discourse of victimhood.[1] A 'spatial turn' in global history finds its parallel in global collective memory, which transcends ethnic and national boundaries. Around the globe, transnational themes dominate the emergence of memories of mass dictatorship.

However, global or transnational memory is not a substitute for national memory. Transnational memories contest, oppose, overlap and cohabit with national memories. Transnational memory does not necessarily guarantee the de-territorialisation or de-nationalisation of collective memories. The rise of a global public sphere has created a space for the contestation of conflicting national memories, and the trajectories of transnational memory are very often tainted with re-territorialised memories. For instance, the cosmopolitanisation of Holocaust memories often results in the re-territorialisation or (re-)nationalisation of memories, as non-European victims of colonialism begin to equate themselves with Holocaust victims in the processes of decolonisation and nation-building. To many a postcolonial regime, Israel has become a reference point as 'a little Great Power'.

Thus, victimhood nationalism is a vital element of transnational memory. Increasing global concern about the victims of genocide has been appropriated by nationalist discourses. Given that the global public sphere tends to be sympathetic to innocent victims, nations have been increasingly engaged in 'a distasteful competition over who suffered most'.[2] In a global confessional culture, victimhood narratives can promote national identification that cannot be achieved in other ways. As Walter Benjamin wrote, 'death is the sanction of everything that storyteller can tell'.[3] Victimhood nationalism, in other words, is the offspring of an international competition for victimhood. The dichotomy of victimising nation/victimised nation, then, articulates the transnationality of nationalism for a transnational memory space.

But memory cannot simply be imposed by high politics on the public, for it is the individual who remembers. Thus memory at the collective level can manifest itself only when it produces new forms of subjectivisation by articulating and inscribing particular hegemonic discourses on the individual. In other words, institutional memory as a discourse of power can enjoy a hegemonic effect only when it is accommodated in the public memory as an aggregate of individually perceived memories. 'Victimhood nationalism' has a hegemonic impact only when collective suffering can be inscribed on the individual memory through a perception of 'hereditary victimhood'. This is the point at which the particular subject of victimhood nationalism comes into being.[4] But victimhood per se does not inspire nationalism. The sublimation of innocent victims into sacrifices committed for the sake of a national community galvanizes the development of nationalism. Once individual victims can be perceived as having performed ritual sacrifices on the altar of the nation, nationalism begins to attract citizens of the nation in question. This political religion has often appealed to a cult of fallen soldiers for the purpose of constructing the national subject.[5]

There are a few discursive sets to shape the social, political, cultural and historical configuration of victims and victimisers into victimhood nationalism. Firstly, the epistemological binary of collective guilt and innocence has facilitated the nationalist sublimation of victimhood. In the categorical thinking of collective guilt, 'people supposedly are guilty of, or feel guilty about, things done in their name but not by them'.[6] Along with the collective guilt of the rival nation, the collective innocence of the national self contributes to building a strong solidarity among the self-proclaimed victims. The muscular ties of victimhood community seem to be a central theme in postwar collective memory. I would like to suggest the term 'victimhood nationalism' as a tool to explain the competition of national memories in coming to terms with the dictatorial past.[7] Without a reflection on the interplay of the collective guilt and victimhood nationalism on the transnational scene, the post-war *Vergangenheitsbewaeltigung* cannot be properly grasped. A transnational history of 'coming to terms with the past' would show that victimhood nationalism has been a rock to any historical reconciliation effort.

Second, what is the most stunning facet of victimhood nationalism is its magical metamorphosis of the individual victimiser into collective victim in memory. It is through this magic that individual perpetrators can be exonerated from their criminal doings. Polish history offers a vivid example in the Laudański brothers' successive self-exonerations. As the only living individuals convicted of genocide in the Jedwabne pogrom, they defined themselves as 'the victims of fascism, of capitalism, of the *Sanacja* regime' in the era of People's Poland. After the 'Fall' of 'real existing socialism', capitalism and the *Sanacja* regime as the impersonal victimisers were replaced by socialism and People's Poland in the Laudański brothers' memories. Perpetrators changed, but their position as victims remained the same: 'like the whole nation we suffered under the Germans, the Soviets, and the People's Republic of Poland'.[8] Thus, individual victimisers became collective victims by hiding themselves behind the memory wall of national victimhood. Similarly, Korean perpetrators in the service of the Japanese imperial army, classified as B and C class war criminals and executed for their atrocities and brutalities in treating the POWs, were thought to be innocent in the collective memory of postcolonial Korea. It was believed that they should be indulged because of their Korean nationality, which had been repressed under Japanese colonial rule. What is underlying in this metamorphosis is the obsession with collective innocence and victimhood.[9]

Third, victimhood nationalism has the sacralisation of memories as its epistemological mainstay, particularly when sacralised memories effectively block the skeptical and critical eyes of the outsiders on 'our own unique past'. Perhaps a certain degree of sacralisation of memories is inevitable for individuals, as it transforms the past into a unique event that is incommensurable with the experiences of other human beings. However, collective memory comes into being through communication, education, commemoration, rituals and ceremonies among the masses. Once evoked, it tends to become fixed in a stereotype and to install itself in the place of raw memories.[10] By nature, such a collective memory cannot be sacralised. Rather, it is an arena of political contestation. Yet the discourses of victimhood nationalism have enabled such sacralisation of collective memories. By disavowing any possibility that outsiders may understand 'our own unique past', sacralised memories enable a monopoly control over the past. In this unique past, nationalists can build a mental enclave of moral self-righteousness, very often disregarding the fact that these heirs of yesterday's victims may have become today's perpetrators. The colloquial argument that 'you foreigners can never ever understand our own tragic national past' protects victimhood nationalism from historical scrutiny.[11] Once exposed to the light of comparative analysis, however, sacralised memories are opened up to public discussion, and the seemingly solid victimhood nationalism has the potential to melt away into the air.

Fourth, along with the task of desacralising national memories, the transnationality of victimhood nationalism demands a multilayered *histoire croisée* approach to comprehend the entangled past of the victimised and victimisers. For instance, victimhood nationalisms among the victimised in Poland, Israel and Korea should be examined with a focus on the interplay of perpetrators and victims, collective guilt and innocence. Without Nazi Germany and colonial Japan, victimhood nationalisms in these three countries are not imaginable. The entangled past of the victimised and victimisers is more complicated than has been previously thought. Surprisingly enough, it is not difficult to find the outcry of victimhood nationalism among victimisers in Germany and Japan, which in turn strengthens victimhood nationalism among victimised nations. Indeed, victimhood nationalism has been nourished by the 'antagonistic complicity of nationalisms' in East Asia.[12] One should recognise the asymmetry between victims in the victimised/ colonised nation and victims in the victimising/colonising nations, but the vicious circle of victimhood nationalisms should not be excused by that asymmetry of the historical position.

Finally, that asymmetry manifests itself in a distinction between the over-contextualisation and decontextualisation of the past. Victimhood nationalism among the victimised nations tends to over-contextualise the past, which provides the morally comfortable position of historical victims, while victimhood nationalism among the perpetrating nations is inclined to decontextualise historical victimhood to ignore its past crimes and sins. If the over-contextualisation negates the coexistence of perpetrators and victims within the victimised nation, the decontextualisation conceals the past of perpetrators who became victims under certain circumstances. In stark contrast with the tendency toward over-contextualisation found in the Polish debates on Jedwabne, Israelis' memory of the Holocaust, and Korean discourses on the comfort women, it is the drift toward decontextualization that dominates German expellees' memories of the defeat of World War II, and Japanese discourses of the atomic bomb. Remembering and forgetting as opponent memory politics are also closely interrelated with this division. Arguably, a multilayered *histoire croisée* analysis would reveal the messy complexities of collective memory as perceived reality. This essay attempts to lay the foundations of a transnational history of victimhood nationalism as it has criss-crossed through Korea, Japan, Poland, Israel and Germany in the memory of mass dictatorship.

Hereditary victimhood: Korea, Israel and Poland

In January of 2007, Yoko Kawashima Watkins's autobiographical novella *So Far from the Bamboo Grove* brought Korean mass media and the intellectual world to a vociferous turmoil.[13] Major newspapers in Korea covered this novella for more than a month. This *Bildungsroman* tells how the narrator, a 11-year-old Japanese girl, and her family were faced with threats against their lives, hunger and fear of sexual assault on their way home to Japan from Nanam, a north Korean town, upon Japan's defeat in World War II. Based on her own experience and memory, this story describes vividly the ordeal Japanese expellees had to go through. No fewer than 3 million Japanese expellees from Manchuria and the north Korean region are said to have encountered similar fates on their way back home, an East Asian version of the East European '*wypędzenie-Vertreibung*'. Yoko Kawashima Watkins's memoir belongs to a genre of stories produced in post-war Japan detailing these expellees' ordeals, called 'repatriation narratives' (*hikiage-mono*, 引揚: withdrawal). *So Far from the Bamboo Grove* was not the first Japanese *hikiage* memoir translated into Korean; another *hikiage* memoir by Fujiwara Tei, *Nagareru hoshi wa ikiteiru* [Wandering stars are still alive], 1949, was translated into Korean during the Korean Civil War in 1951 and remains one of the 50 bestselling books in Korea since 1945, perhaps because it resonated with Koreans who were suffering from the civil war.[14]

Translated into Korean in 2005, Yoko Kawashima Watkins's novella enjoyed a positive, though lukewarm, response from the Korean mass media. Reviews of this book were neither enthusiastic nor critical. On 13 May 2005 *Yonhap News* reviewed it as 'an autobiographical novella describing the story of Japanese expellees upon Japan's defeat'. *The Chosun-Ilbo* published a book review on 6 May 2005 that reads: 'Leaving aside the nationality (of the author), it can be evaluated as a *Bildungsroman* to describe in serenity how war can bring a whole family into an ordeal'. *So Far from the Bamboo Grove* did not seem to make much of an impression on book reviewers. It was not a commercial success either: fewer than 3000 copies were sold in the first year and a half after its publication. Seemingly, Yoko Watkins's book was doomed to be forgotten by Korean readers, but suddenly this novella was caught in the cross-fire of four major Korean newspapers and one news agency on 18 January 2007, followed by a series of further attacks. The social pressure was so enormous that the Korean publisher *Munhakdongne*, having tried to defend the book in vain, had to make a quick decision to withdraw all copies from the bookstores.

It is almost impossible not to detect a sort of orchestration in this simultaneous discharge by the Korean mainstream media. It seems not a coincidence that the Korean consul in Boston sent a protest letter to the Massachusetts state Department of Education on 16 January 2007. Given the difference in local time between Boston and Seoul, there was virtually no time lag between the Korean consul's protest in Boston and mass media coverage of *So Far from the Bamboo Grove* in Seoul. According to a report from the *Boston Globe*, the main point of contest was that Yoko Kawashima Watkins's novella describes Koreans as evil perpetrators while the Japanese remain innocent victims.[15] The Korean consul expressed its deep concern that young Americans would be tempted by a distorted and false past of East Asia if they read *So Far from the Bamboo Grove* in schools. An archaeological excavation of this strange uproar reveals that Parents for an Accurate Asian History Education (PAAHE) was working behind the scenes, initiating this tsunami of long distance nationalism. This group consists of Korean Americans in the New York City and Greater Boston areas, many of whom are well-educated medical doctors and lawyers.[16]

It was these Korean Americans of the PAAHE who took the initiative in the trans-Pacific criticism of the *So Far from the Bamboo Grove*. They were furious that Yoko Kawashima Watkins's book, which, they said, portrays Koreans as evil perpetrators and Japanese as innocent victims, was widely read in schools by American school children who are largely ignorant of East Asian history. The wording of their criticism sounds very positivistic: the PAAHE is seeking an 'accurate Asian history' whose clear-cut accuracy does not allow for complexity and ambiguity. Phrases like 'distortion of truth', 'fabrication of facts', 'historical lies' are used repeatedly in the statement.[17] It is due to the initiative of the PAAHE that the Korean press turned its negligent eyes to *So Far from the Bamboo Grove* in January of 2007. As it crossed the Pacific to Korea, the accusation snowballed: Yoko Kawashima Watkins was suspected as a daughter of a Japanese war criminal, 'presumably' an officer of Unit 731 infamous for its bio-warfare experiments. Soon enough, she was branded as such without any evidence. Despite the PAAHE's obsession with 'accurate' history, their suspicion that Kawashima Watkins is the daughter of a Japanese war criminal has yet to be proven. This suspicion in itself, however, was enough to give the impression that as the daughter of a Japanese war criminal, she could not possibly be an innocent victim. This sort of positivistic criticism seems very vulnerable to the historical reality that clearly shows the suffering of the Japanese expellees from Manchuria and Korean peninsula in the summer of 1945.

What made the PAAHE members most impatient is the reversed order of victims and victimisers. In the schematic dichotomy of collective guilt and innocence, the Japanese as an absolute category becomes a uniform mass of victimisers. The bitter experience of the Japanese expellees as individuals stands no longer as a fact under the abstract category of the Japanese as perpetrators. The schematic dichotomy of collective guilt and innocence in terms of the nation, deeply rooted among Korean Americans, seems to reinforce the ethnocentric self-identity among them. What is at issue is the Korean Americans' parental concern for their children. They assumed their children would be subject to bullying by their schoolmates just because they are ethnic descendents of Koreans like the terrible victimisers depicted in *So Far from the Bamboo Grove*. Perhaps the Korean American readers' reaction to *So Far from the Bamboo Grove* was complicated by the imbalance of sensitivity toward one historically persecuted group (Jewish suffering in the Holocaust) versus another (Korean persecution under Japanese colonial rule).[18] The PAAHE's criticism might rather have targeted the Eurocentrism that dominates the American perception of historical suffering. Unfortunately, however, the PAAHE's perspective failed to problematise that Eurocentrism and could not escape from the schematic dichotomy of Japanese victimisers and Korean victims. This type of reasoning, inherent to collective guilt, shows how these parents are caught up in a hegemonic ethnic nationalism of Korea that seems not to recognise that Korea has become a more multinational and multicultural country since their emigration. Ethnocentrism in the emigrants' long distance nationalism is, in many ways, stronger than that of homeland nationalism in Korea. This farcical tumult shows us a vivid, though not 'accurate', example of how victimhood nationalism is nourished by long distance nationalism and vice versa. Indeed the victimhood comes into relief in the transnational space more than the national one. The transnationality of victimhood nationalism in relation to Kawashima Watkins's story can be seen as well in the frequent emphasis on historical parallelism between Jews and Koreans as victims. One customer review of *So Far from the Bamboo Grove* by a Korean American on Amazon.com reads:

> It is completely distorting the truth about the Japanese WW2 aggressions and atrocities. It makes as if atrocities were committed by the victims rather than the aggressor ... If Anne Frank were a German and she were still alive to this day and if she wrote about the mindless rapes committed by Jewish resistance fighters and Jewish-American soldiers after WW2 and no mention was made about the Holocaust during WW2. Wouldn't you think that is a DISTORTION of history?

Another customer review reads similarly:

> This book is akin to an escape narrative of an SS officer's family running away from Birkenau Auschwitz concentration camp while the heroine daughter of the Nazi officer is running away from cruel and dangerous Jews freed from concentration camps and Poles. Such a narrative is morally irresponsible and disgusting material to force upon innocent children.[19]

These customer reviews can be read as a criticism of the decontextualisation of colonial history in the novella.

One more interesting point in these customer reviews on Amazon.com is the use of historical parallelism between Jews and Koreans. Basically it seems a narrative tactic to convince American readers that the victims are not the *Japanese*, but rather, the *Koreans*. This is nothing new: historical parallelism between Jews and Koreans was rampant in Korean nationalist discourse throughout 1960s and 1970s, but it focused on heroism rather than victimhood. In the era of development dictatorship under Park Chung Hee, Israeli Zionism was a role model to be followed by Koreans. The impressive victory of Israel in the

Six Days' War, supposedly unexpected, was hailed as the victory of patriotism among young Israelis. Korean newspapers were filled with stories of American Jews who volunteered for Israel's army at the cost of comfortable lives, honeymooners who came back to the front after cancelling their honeymoons; they were cast as self-sacrificing heroes rather than passive victims. In Korea, leaders of the 'New Village Movement' and 'industrial warriors' were trained regularly on a collective farm called 'Canaan'. President Park himself visited the farm several times since 1962 and held in high esteem the 'anthropological revolution' (*ingan hyŏkmyŏng*) or 'anthropological reformation' (*ingan kaecho*) he saw there. Anthropological revolution as a project to create new human beings of hard working, industrious and community-bound morality was the first step to making the self-mobilisation system of mass dictatorship in South Korea. It was not passive subjects, but heroic agency that would meet the demands of self-mobilising mass dictatorship.[20] A brief look at post-colonial Korean historiography reveals that heroism goes hand in hand with victimhood in the nationalist discourse.

Contrary to common belief, it is also not victimhood but heroism that was dominant in Jewish public memory from its inception. Werner Weinberg – whose classification shifted from that of a liberated prisoner to a displaced person, to a survivor – writes that a survivor appeared to himself and others as 'a museum piece, a fossil, a freak, a ghost'.[21] In the fall of 1945, after his visit to the DP camps in Germany, David Shaltiel – Ben Gurion's personal envoy to Western Europe – said bluntly, 'those who survived did so because they were egotistical and cared primarily about themselves'.[22] The slanderous belief of the 'survival of the worst', though it faded with time, was widespread among the worldwide Jewry immediately after the war, when victims were victimised again by their compatriots. Referred to often within Zionist literature as 'factors' or as 'human resources', Holocaust survivors were subject to objectification and instrumentalisation in Zionist discourse.[23] It was the *Yishuv* heroes who were immortalised in Zionist literature of Exodus, while Jewish refugees bore the burden of the clandestine immigration campaign on their shoulders.[24] The discourse of Zionists in Palestine regarding the Diaspora Jews was suffused with a rhetoric of pity and paternalistic patronising. A love sermon to the coming Jewish refugees, 'My Sister on the Beach' by Yitzhak Sadeh, the first commander of the legendary Palmach, tells a story of 'male power ... in the strong, rooted and brave Israeli Zionism facing a defeated, despairing Diaspora longing to die'.[25] What prevailed in this dichotomy of Hebrew heroism in Eretz Israel versus Jewish humiliation in exile was 'a sexist reconstruction of history' to feminise the survivors.[26] In this dichotomy, survivors remained passive objects deprived of agency. Masculine war heroes were the approved ideals of American Jewry too. Toward the end of World War II, John Slawson, the chief executive of the American Jewish Committee, said explicitly that '[Jewish organisations] should avoid representing the Jew as weak, victimised, and suffering ... There needs to be an elimination or at least a reduction of horror stories of victimised Jewry ... War hero stories are excellent'.[27] Belonging to the race of victors instead of victims was a cultural code shared widely by the American Jewry. Compared with today's exceptionalist discourse of the Holocaust as historically unique, it is a striking contrast to discover that leaders of the Anti-Defamation League were critical of an ADL film strip 'The Anatomy of Nazism' for its too-narrow focus on Jewish suffering.[28] The hero cult in the aftermath of World War II was dominant, and then the Cold War inclined the American Jewry toward relative indifference to the Holocaust. Under Cold War pressure, it was more urgent for Jewish organisations in the US to combat the Jew-Communist equation. As far as policy-makers in Washington were concerned, with Germany only as a bulwark against Bolshevism, American Jews were encouraged to have a realistic attitude rather than a punitive and recriminatory one against West Germany. The emphasis was put on Soviet anti-Semitism rather than the Holocaust. The Prague trial in 1952, which signalled the Stalinist purge of veteran Jewish communists from the Czechoslovakian leadership, was thought to have dissociated Jews from Communism in the minds of the American public.[29] The fact that Stalinist-Communists persecuted Jews would belie the stereotype of Jewish-Communists. The 'realistic' attitude of the American Jewry was not far from Ben Gurion's calculation that Israel needed to keep a close relationship with France and Germany to join the 'Western bloc'.

As long as 'historiographical triumphalism'[30] dominated the historical discourse in Israel, the Holocaust was not a popular theme for discussion. When the Holocaust was discussed, it was structured by a dualism focusing on the activist response of the ghetto fighters and questioning the role of Jewish leadership in the ghettoes. It was only in 1959 that the observation of a Holocaust memorial day became mandatory. Even then, the Holocaust commemoration remained focused on heroic fighters in the Ghetto Uprisings as we can see in the official references to the commemoration of 'the Holocaust and the Ghetto Uprisings', 'the Holocaust and Heroism' or 'the Martyrs' and Heroes' Remembrance'. While the Ghetto fighters were addressed as 'Zionist' or 'Hebrew youth', other Holocaust victims were referred to as 'Jews'. Israeli youth often described the Jewish victims' behaviour as 'going like sheep to the slaughter'.[31] In this historiographical heroism, the Masada fighters, ancient Hebrew warriors of national liberation, were glorified as a counter-model to the Holocaust victims.[32] Michel Warschawski remembers Israel of the 1960s, where weakness was still considered a flaw and a 'savonette' was the designated term for a person who was not tough enough.[33]

The Eichmann trial signifies a turn toward victimhood in the collective memory of Holocaust. With the trial, 'a process of identification with the suffering of victims and survivors' occurred among Israelis.[34] Awakened by the riot of the Sephardic Jews in 1959, immigrants mostly from Morocco, Israeli leaders badly needed a patriotic national catharsis for national unity. When the hegemony of the Ashkenazic establishment was threatened, the Eichmann trial was deemed to educate these Oriental Jews who did not really know what happened to Ashkenazy Jews in the Holocaust. It was the Six Days' War of 1967 that then ratcheted up victimhood nationalism. A young soldier's recollection of the war indicates that 'people believed we would be exterminated if we lost the war. We got this idea – or inherited it – from the concentration camp. It's a concrete idea for anyone who has grown up in Israel ... Genocide – it's a real possibility'.[35] It is not a surprise, then, that close to 80 per cent of teachers' college students identified Israeli identity with 'Holocaust survivors' in a 1992 survey.[36] Thus victimhood became hereditary.

But it would be naive to say that victimhood nationalism repelled Yishuv heroism and victor's nationalism. Victimhood nationalism linked the righteousness of little David, an eternal victim of all the Goliaths of human history, to a sense of omnipotence and invincibility. And subsequently, the images mutually interpenetrated one another in a vision of 'Yishuvist and Shoah-centric narrative'. In this self-contradictory narrative, victimhood nationalism did not necessarily mean to pay homage to concrete victims. What is at issue is not the agony and anguish of concrete victims but the idea of abstract victimhood. The victimhood cult went together with the biographical forgetting of the Holocaust victims who were mostly assimilationists in pre-War Europe. The Holocaust, a catastrophe for the assimilationists, seemingly justified the Zionists' desire for an independent state for Jews, and the defeat of assimilationism seemed to endorse the ethnocentric perception of the nation and history in Israel.[37] Holocaust exceptionalism, then, reinforces the ethnocentric nationalism of these righteous victims. To Ben Gurion, the Holocaust was 'a unique episode that has no equal ... has no parallel in human history'. Universalising the Holocaust can thus be seen as plundering the 'moral capital' that Jews had accumulated. Menachem Begin responded to the international criticism of Israel's invasion of Lebanon with the Holocaust discourse: 'After the Holocaust, the international community had lost its right to demand that Israel answer for its actions'.[38] Beyond doubt, the Holocaust is in many crucial aspects an unparalleled or singular event, but this does not mean it is unique or cannot be subject to comparative analysis.[39]

Victimhood nationalism cannot stand alone. Just as victimhood nationalism has been nourished on the 'antagonistic complicity of nationalisms' in East Asia, anti-Semitism has fed victimhood nationalism in Israel. As Golda Meir said at the beginning of the 1970s: 'too much anti-Semitism is not good because it leads to genocide; no anti-Semitism at all is also not good because then there would be no immigration (to Israel). What we need is a moderate anti-Semitism'.[40] The Jewish stereotype of Polish anti-Semitism that 'Poles sucked anti-Semitism with their mothers' milk' evokes the Polish stereotype of 'Żydokomuna' that justifies Polish anti-Semitism. The Polish self-image of the 'crucified nation' as the eternal victim of the neighbours to the East and West cannot accommodate the image of bystanders, let alone victimisers, as shown by the Laudański brothers, victimisers of their Jewish neighbours in Jedwabne, who define themselves as victims by sharing the collective memory of victimhood in Poland.

Indeed, in a poll held in early April 2001, 48 per cent of those surveyed did not believe that Poles should apologise to the Jewish nation for the pogrom of Jedwabne, while 30 per cent stood for the apology. 80 per cent did not feel any moral responsibility for Jedwabne, while only 13 per cent felt such a responsibility. Still 34 per cent believed that the Germans were solely responsible for the crime, 14 per cent that Germans and Poles were jointly responsible, and 7 per cent that Poles were solely responsible. Public opinion did not change much even after the publication of the report of the IPN (Instytut Pamięci Narodowej) to evidence the Jedwabne massacre by Poles.[41] Jan Gross summarises the dominating debate in Poland on Jedwabne in the following terms:

> an outpouring of thoughtful and searching articles about the need to rewrite Poland's twentieth-century history; about facing up to the larger consequences of anti-Semitism that gave rise also to complicity

with Nazi crimes against Jewish neighbors; about the responsibility for misdeeds so difficult to contemplate in a community that was itself victimised by outside oppressors.[42]

But one cannot fail to detect the Poles' perplexity at finding themselves not victims, but victimisers.

Undeniably, Poland was one of the most devastated countries during World War II. Poland lost about more than 5 million inhabitants including 3 million Polish Jews, which amounts to more than 20 per cent of the total population. And it was the elites who suffered most. Less than half of the country's lawyers survived the war. Poland lost two fifths of its medical doctors and one third of its university professors and Roman Catholic clergy. It would be unfair to bring an accusation of genocide against the Polish victims. As Rabbi Byron L. Sherwin declared, 'the tendency among Jews to stereotype Poles as the perpetrators of the Holocaust not only distorts but obscures the enormous suffering of Poles during the Nazi occupation'.[43] Certainly, it would be much worse to shift the overwhelming responsibility for the genocide away from the Nazis by emphasising the secondary responsibility and complicity of Poles, but this criticism of the Jewish stereotype of anti-Semitism in Poland does not automatically justify the Polish obsession with innocence, and therefore victimhood nationalism in Poland, which believes Auschwitz was a place primarily of Polish martyrdom. The 'anti-Semitism without Jews' in today's Poland, though not dominant, should not be ignored either.[44]

Czesław Miłosz's insight that 'the Party descends directly from the fascist Right' adumbrates the public memory of the Holocaust in People's Poland.[45] The Party shared the Polish nationalists' dream of an ethnically pure state, and it was the nationalist vision that has dominated the official Party historiography. In a way, the socialist ideal of the ethical and political unity of society reinforced the primordialist concept of the nation, a way of seeing the nation as an organic community and even as a family community.[46] It is no wonder that World War II has been remembered as a matter between Poles and Germans, with the Jews marginalised in the public memory of Poland.[47] In the era of Stalinism, the memory of the Holocaust was repressed and marginalised since it did not fit in the Soviet narratives of the antifascist front of the working class and of the Great Patriotic War.[48] As Michael Steinlauf puts it, 'In the essential communist narrative, the Holocaust became an object lesson in the horrors of the last stage of monopoly capitalism … The site of Auschwitz-Birkenau … became a monument to internationalism and commemorated the "resistance and martyrdom" of "Poles and

... other nationalities", among whom, alphabetically and therefore "democratically", Żydzi came last'.[49] With the rise of the national communist faction, the genocide of Polish Jews was made an integral part of the ethnic Polish tragedy. The widely held historical statement that 'six million Poles died during the war' promoted the victimhood fantasy that Poles had suffered the most. Jews, therefore, were integrated into the Polish nation only on the politics of numbering Polish citizens as victims. The Holocaust had been interpreted as a German-Jewish conspiracy against Poles to minimise Polish wartime martyrdom and suffering. The Moczar-led partisans launched an attack on *Wielka Encyklopedia Powszechna* (*WEP*) in 1967. The division of 'concentration camp (*obozy koncentracyjne*)' and 'extermination camp (*obozy zagłady*)' in the *WEP* was criticised as a bias against Polish martyrdom in favour of the suffering of Jews. The Jewish editor went into exile in Sweden, which was followed by the anti-Zionist campaign in 1968. In the public memory fabricated by the Party, it was the Poles who were sentenced to annihilation by Nazis while the Jews were relocated. The Warsaw Ghetto Uprising was seen as 'a specific kind of fighting of the Polish underground'.[50] Witold Kula, a prominent Polish economic historian, remarked on Polish victimhood nationalism sarcastically: 'In the past the Jews were envied because of their money, qualifications, positions ... today they are envied because of the crematoria in which they were burned'.[51]

It was the essay 'Biedny polacy patrzą na getto (poor Poles look at ghetto)' by Jan Błoński in 1987 that brought the repressed memory of the Holocaust to life in the public memory. Błoński's seminal essay raised the question not of culpability for what they did, but of sins for what they did not.[52] It upgraded the Polish discussion on the Holocaust beyond legal positivism to ontological ethics. The debate revealed a deep trauma among those Poles who felt the guilt of being helpless witnesses to atrocity. Błoński's essay was then followed by Jan Gross's book *Neighbors*. In the words of Hanna Świda-Ziemba, what Jedwabne taught her was that 'only a thin layer of ice separates innocent prejudices from crime'.[53] Despite Jan Gross's calm appreciation of the Polish response to his book, the reluctance to admit to guilt is found rampantly among Poles. To Cardinal Józef Glemp, the Primate of Poland, Gross's book was a commissioned work. In his opinion, Jews were disliked for 'their pro-Bolshevik attitude and odd folk customs',[54] and the Jedwabne mayor was unable to persuade the townspeople to name the local school after Antonina Wyrzykowska, who rescued seven Jews during the massacre. Stanisław Stefanek, the Bishop of Łomża, spoke of an organised campaign to extract money from the Poles.

The collective memory of apologetic victimhood had no room to accommodate such a drastic transformation from innocent victims to the 'Homo Jedvanecus'. Paradoxically enough, Poland suffered the consequences of not having had a Quisling-like collaborationist puppet regime during the Nazi occupation. If it had, anti-Semitism would have remained as a compromised collaborationism.[55] But because Poland was not compromised by a collaborationist regime, it was less susceptible to a consciousness of guilt for the Holocaust, and anti-Semitism remained a requisite of patriotism. That complexity is rooted in 'a singularly Polish paradox' in the words of Adam Michnik, where a person could be an anti-Semite, a hero of the resistance and a saviour of Jews all at once, since the Polish nationalistic and anti-Semitic right did not collaborate with the Nazis.[56] When the news of Kielce pogrom spread in 1946, Polish workers were unwilling to condemn publicly the perpetrators of the Kielce pogrom and opposed an anti-pogrom resolution. The Polish Workers' Party (PPR) had difficulty with the anti-pogrom propaganda, and workers perceived the PPR as 'Jewish' in their opposition to the workers.[57] Victimhood nationalism as such frames the coming to terms with the past into an either/or question: victims or victimisers. The fury of some Poles against Jan Błoński and Jan Gross resonates with the anger some Jews express toward Hannah Arendt for erasing the comfortable dichotomy of the purely innocent victims and totally evil victimisers by stressing complexity and ambiguity. Indeed historical fantasy is a crucial factor in the creation of a nation, which is why progress in historical studies often constitutes a danger for the principle of nationality. To put this fantasy world of 'hereditary victimhood' under historical scrutiny remained, remains and will remain a blasphemy to some.

Apologetic victimhood: Japan and Germany

Ernest Renan's insight that 'shared suffering unites people more than common joy, and mourning is better than victory for the national memory'[58] is not confined only to victims. Victimisers suffered too when they lost the war. The most paradoxical facet of coming to terms with the past might be that victimhood consciousness among the victimisers in Japan and Germany was seemingly stronger than that among victims in China, Poland and Israel. While these victims of the war of aggression, massacres and genocide were celebrating liberation and victory, the Japanese and Germans were mourning their defeats and war suffering. Paradoxically, victimisers more urgently sought to explore the experience of being victimised, as if the transgressions of the victims exonerated the crimes of victimisers. For instance, the atrocities committed by the Japanese against the POWs of Western allies were thought to be coun-terbalanced by the suffering and massive death of Japanese POWs in the Siberian gulags. The killing of innocent German civilians in the Allied bombing and suffering of German expellees from the East have been emphasised in the same vein. But victimhood is unequal and asymmetri-cal between Germans, Jews and Poles, and between the Japanese, the Chinese and Koreans. This may explain why victimhood nationalism in Japan and Germany is more complicated, sophisticated and embarrassing. The rise of victimhood nationalism among victimisers was possible because of the magic of historical decontextualisation.

Compared with Germany, Japan as 'the only nation ever to have been atom-bombed' (*yuiitsu no hibakukoku*) may enjoy a privileged position in the competition for victimhood. Decontextualised from the history of the 'fifteen-year war', 'this declaration is replete with the single-minded assertion that the Japanese were the victims of the atomic bomb', in the words of Imahori Seiji.[59] American writers' frequent remarks about 'Auschwitz and Hiroshima as terrible twin symbols of manmade mass death', especially after the Soviet Union's acquisition of the first nuclear weapon, seemed to evidence Japanese victimhood.[60] Radhabinod Pal, an Indian judge at the Tokyo trial, confirmed Japanese victimisation by the atomic bomb by suggesting that the American use of the bomb might be deemed to be the closest counterpart to Nazi atrocities in the war.[61] In the public memory of post-war Japan, however, it was Japanese military leaders who victimised the innocent Japanese even before the A-bomb. Fire bombings, the repatriation of Japanese civilians from Manchuria and Korea and wartime sufferings such as hunger and mili-tary oppression on the home front have also been stressed to emphasise Japanese victimhood. Citing John Dower, 'it became commonplace to speak of the war dead themselves – and indeed, of virtually all ordinary Japanese – as being victims and sacrifices'.[62]

The public memory of war that mythologises ordinary Japanese people as the innocent victims of a system rather than as the accomplices of war atrocities was not just self-generated. The Supreme Commander for Allied Powers (SCAP) fanned this morally comfortable tale the other way round. The SCAP worked on the assumption that Japanese people had been slaves of feudal habits of subservience to authority. A secret report by the Psychological Warfare Branch of the US Army reads:

The Japanese personally have contributed their full measure to the war effort and fulfilled their obligation to the Emperor. All their effort is to no avail because their military leaders have betrayed them. The people are not to be blamed for their suffering ... The military clique has practiced false indoctrination.[63]

By thus patronising the Japanese people, the SCAP's Orientalist view exempted ordinary Japanese people from war culpability and guilt. The ordinary Japanese individuals paid in their own agency in return for this discursive amnesty. Deprived of agency, the ordinary Japanese became a passive subject blindly loyal to authority, thereby making them innocent of the nation's various transgressions committed in their names, and with their participation. Victims deprived of agency cannot be held accountable for the misuse of power. Both left-wing activists and right-wing politicians appropriated Japanese victimhood in their own way. It was a useful device for them to be able to either blame the Cold War US-Japan security alliance or to detach themselves from the legacy of militarism and war responsibility.[64]

The term 'Pacific War' imposed by the SCAP was another deliberate conceptual tool to waive Japanese war responsibility toward its Asian neighbours. The SCAP substituted the term 'Pacific War' for the 'Great East Asia War', which paired with the 'Greater East Asia Co-Prosperity Sphere' had been designated by the Japanese total war system to legitimatise the Japanese invasion to its Asian neighbours. With its focus on the conflict between America and Japan, the term 'Pacific War' downplayed Japanese military aggression against its Asian neighbours. That term brought into relief Japanese aggression against Americans or Europeans such as the maltreatment of Allied POWs. Japanese military transgressions such as Unit 731's biological warfare, forced labour mobilisation through Asia, comfort women and other violations of human rights in Asia, all fell into oblivion. That partly explains why 'the Japanese people don't have much consciousness of having invaded China and have a tendency to emphasise only the suffering they bore in the Pacific War'.[65] Doubtlessly that exemption of the Japanese people from war guilt contributed to building victimhood nationalism in post-war Japan.

It was in anti-nuclear pacifism that Japanese war victimhood was most easily detached from Japanese wartime atrocities. Atomic bomb exceptionalism ('the only nation ever to have been atom-bombed') decontextualised this traumatic tragedy from its historical background. All the anguish and agony that Japanese people suffered was to be epitomised in Hiroshima and Nagasaki. Hiroshima as an absolute evil was often compared with the Holocaust. A popular novella singled out the Japanese and Jews as the archetypal victims of white racism.[66] But the public memory of the atomic bomb in Hiroshima and Nagasaki had been repressed by the censorship of the SCAP. By the early 1950s, it had been treated more or less as an unexpected natural calamity. It was only through the Lucky Dragon Incident of 1 March 1954, when a Japanese fishing boat was exposed to radiation from a U.S. thermonuclear device test and the entire crew suffered from acute radiation poisoning, that atomic victimhood developed into victimhood nationalism with a pacifist tint. Thus, 'Hiroshima became an icon of Japan's past as innocent war victim and a beacon for its future as pacifist nation'.[67] Perhaps the victimhood narrative of *hikiage* including Yoko Kawashima Watkins's memoir had the anti-war pacifist movement as its cultural matrix of collective memory. As the 'Yoko Story' controversy shows, in the historically structured antagonistic complicity of nationalisms in East Asia, Japanese obsession with the victimhood of the A-bomb spurs on victimhood nationalism in Korea and 'a distasteful competition over who suffered most' seemed inevitable.

Although Japanese wartime aggression was totally forgotten in the victimhood discourse, Japanese conventional war atrocities seemed relatively insignificant in comparison to the apocalyptic hell of Hiroshima and Nagasaki. The story of the aesthetic origins of the Hiroshima Peace Memorial Park is very intriguing in this respect. The design for the Hiroshima Peace Memorial Park, selected through a public competition in 1949, shares a nearly identical ground plan with the Commemorative Building Project for the Construction of Greater East Asia projected in 1942 as a grandiose Shintoist memorial zone to be built on an open plain at the foot of Mount Fuji. In fact it was Tange Genzō, a world-renowned architect, who created both designs. The striking parallels between the imperial project commemorating the Great East Asia Co-Prosperity Sphere and the Hiroshima memorial site for peace and mourning of the victims of the atomic bomb is symptomatic of the Japanese apologetic memory based on the shift from victimisers to victims.[68] It is also noteworthy that Yamahata Yosuke, who became world famous for his picture of a child victim of the Nagasaki A-bomb, campaigned with the Japanese Army in China as a war photographer during the 'Fifteen-Year War' and took lots of photos of innocent Chinese children smiling with Japanese soldiers.[69]

In the turbulent memories of the Nazi past in Germany, it is not clear yet whether Germans were Hitler's first or last victims. Perhaps Willy Brandt's widow Brigitte Seebacher's thesis of 'Hitler's first victims' may be more problematic as Germans ought to compete with Austrians for the position of Hitler's first victims. But the 'Hitler's last victims' thesis, represented by Oliver Hirschbiegel's film *Der Untergang*, is no less problematic. In this deeply problematic film, 'perpetration and victimhood are played out within the national collective, between evil Nazis and good Germans, thus (almost) excluding memory of Jewish suffering'.[70] The sudden emergence of the discourse of German suffering through Allied bombing and expulsion was possible thanks to the fall of the Berlin Wall, which made it possible for Germans to confront the complicated past free of the ideological constraints of the Cold War.

Guenther Grass's novella *Im Krebsgang* represents this new current. While the novella focuses on the tragic fate of about 8000 German civilian refugees on the *Wilhelm Gustloff*, which was torpedoed and sunk by a Soviet submarine, it never fails to contextualise the disaster by alluding to the history of the ship in service of the Nazi's 'Strength through Joy' campaign, the Nazi career of its dedicatee, and the presence of non-civilians on board.[71] This novella depicts the thousands of German victims on board the *Wilhelm Gustloff* in consideration of their roles as Nazi collaborator-victimisers. The historical meandering implied in the title, 'Crabwalk', warns against the naïve dichotomy of victimisers and victims at both the abstract level and in absolute terms. Grass's balanced contextualisation of the tragedy of the *Wilhelm Gustloff* does not necessarily endorse the over-contextualisation of colonial history to negate any suffering of the ordinary Japanese on the ground that she/he belongs to the Japanese nation. Grass's tale of the victimised victimisers is immeasurably more balanced than Yoko Kawashima Watkins's decontextualised saga that seems immune to history.

Indeed, Grass's cautious handling of contextualisation distinguishes itself from Joerg Friedrich's account of the Allied bombing, which relativises the Holocaust by comparing the suffering of the German civilians with the suffering of European Jews through linguistic association. As Stefan Berger points out, 'Friedrich refers to Bomber Command 5 as "task force (Einsatzgruppe)"; cellars and bomb shelters are described as "crematoria" and the bombing victims are being "exterminated (vernichtet)" '.[72] What is evident in the victimhood narrative by Joerg Friedrich is the seemingly intentional decontextualisation, through which Friedrich produces the metaphorical effect of equating the Allied bombing victims with the Holocaust victims. The historical contextualisation, as shown in *Im Krebsgang*, means not to justify the Allied bombing as a punishment for historical culprits but to reveal historical complexity and ambiguity beyond the dichotomy of absolute good and evil.

Victimhood nationalism is *a*historical since it dwells in the realm of over-contextualisation and decontextualisation. If the over-contextualisation inherent to historical contextualism gives rise to historical conformism of whatever happened in history, the decontextualisation results in *a*historical justification of the historical aftermath. Very often being *a*historical is vulnerable to politicisation. Thus victimhood had been selective in both Germanys. In West Germany the suffering of expellees from Eastern Europe and German POWs imprisoned in the Soviet Union was collectively mourned. Their private memories structured the public memory of Communist brutality and the loss of the German East. The 'Documents of Expulsion' was full of countless reports of terror, rape, plundering, separation of families, forced deportations, starvation, slave labour and killings. According to Robert G. Moeller, 'the editors of documentation projects [the 'Documents of Expulsion'] claimed that what Germans had suffered under Communists was comparable in its horror only to what Jews had suffered under Nazis'.[73] Discursively it was in the vein of Goebbels's attempts to orientalise Russians as subhuman Asian hordes. In East Germany the expulsion of Germans from the brotherly Communist countries was never questioned. Discussing the rape of German women by the Red Army soldiers was taboo. Instead of criticising the heroic Red Army, the Allied bombing of East German cities such as Dresden was selected as a devious plan to sabotage the socialist building in the GDR (German Democratic Republic). GDR citizens had been primarily victims of the criminal Allied bombing. At times the suffering of the bombing victims in the GDR area was equated with the suffering of the Jews in the Holocaust.[74]

With the unification of Germany, German victims in the two politically differentiated historical memories were unified too. Tensions then grew over the position of victimhood between the unified Germany and its Slavic neighbours. And 'a distasteful competition over who suffered most' has become more heated between Germans and its Slavic neighbours as the German expellee organisations demand compensation for their wartime losses. Under the post–Cold War circumstances the leaders of the expellee organisations appealed to the Polish court to return their properties confiscated by the Communist regime. The vociferous outcry was heard that Free Poland should not advocate the oppressive policies of the Communist regime of Poland.[75] Erika Steinbach, the president of 'Der Bund der Vertriebene (BdV)', has been more aggressive in her assertion. She urged the German government to set the annulment of the Beneš Decree as the precondition of Czech and Poland's entry to the European Union. Steinbach is not reluctant to describe the intern camp of German expellees in Czech and Poland by using the terms of 'forced labor, extermination camp and genocide (Zwangsarbeits- und Vernichtungslager, Genozid)'. 'Genocide of more than 15 million people' was her estimation of the victimhood of German expellees. In fact she equated the suffering of German expellees with the suffering of Jews in Holocaust.[76] In other words, Poles and Czechs who victimised these expellees were equated with the Nazi perpetrators. Indeed Steinbach compared the rightist Polish government with the neo-Nazis in Germany for its indifference to the question of expulsion in an interview with 'Passauer Neue Presse' in March 2007.[77]

It is undeniable that Germans were victimised by Poles and Czechs upon their defeat in World War II. On 30 June 1945, twenty-two Sudeten Germans and one Czech woman were shot by Czechs in the Czech town of Teplice (Wekelsdorf). In the graveyard of Lambinowice (Lamsdorf), the bodies of 1137 Germans, mostly women, children and the elderly, were consecrated in September 2002. They died of starvation and hard labour in a work camp run by Poles with Soviet permission. On 31 July 1945 Czech militia and civilians threw more than fifty Germans into the river and opened fire on them in Ustí nad Labem (Aussig). The German victims are too many to enumerate here. But it is also true that these German expellees were hardly innocent of responsibility for Nazism. For example the Sudeten Germans were strong Nazi supporters who voted for the Nazi-style Sudeten German Party with an absolute majority of 90 per cent. The decontextualisation of German victimhood by Steinbach & co. has given rise to a furious response from their counterparts who were also victims of Nazism. Poles and Czechs are responding to the decontextualisation of German victimhood with over-contextualisation, which would seemingly excuse their own vengeful actions against the German expellees by citing their suffering under Nazi rule. What is left, again, is 'a distasteful competition over who suffered most' and the antagonistic complicity of victimhood nationalisms.

Indeed, the spectres of decontextualisation and over-contextualisation hover over the controversy in regard to victimhood, which has made historical reconciliation vulnerable to politicisation. It is true that the Japanese expellees became victims of Koreans, and German expellees were victimised by Poles and Czechs upon defeat in World War II. But it is also true that both the Japanese and German expellees were not innocent of responsibility for atrocities committed under colonialism and Nazism. With its unilateral emphasis of victimhood, decontextu-alisation by Japanese and German victimhood nationalism gives rise to a furious response from their counterparts who were victimised before World War II. These respond to the decontextualisation of the Japanese and German victimhood nationalism with over-contextualisation, which would seemingly justify their acts of violence against the civilian expellees of Japan and Germany. The competition for exclusive claims to victimhood between opposing victimhood nationalisms is geared up. What is left is the antagonistic complicity of victimhood nationalisms among unequal victims.

Responsibility: From whom to whom?

Collective memories are not fixed, but rather float in the continuous negotiations between available historical records and current social and political agendas. Historical responsibility does not float, however. If one refers to English dictionaries, s/he may find an interesting synonym for responsibility—namely, 'answerability', an ability to answer. Indeed 'Verantwortung', 'odpowiedzialność', 'responsibilité' as equivalents of the 'responsibility' in other European languages have the same connotation. The word answerability sounds very casual. But if the question of 'answerability to whom?' arises, this word suddenly becomes very heated. Answerability presupposes listening to the voices of others. If we remind ourselves of Derrida's remark that 'the Other is my justice', then listening to others is a substantial part of my justice and yours. The voices of others are very often dissenting. Listening to those outrageous, distressing, moaning voices is very often disturbing and painful. Fulfilling historical responsibility, then, entails listening and answering to the voices of others who passed away in the brutal past.

Ontologically, one can be neither blamed nor convicted for what one did not do. One can be responsible only for what one did oneself. In other words, only the murderer is responsible for the murder. Collective guilt or innocence will not help us to come to terms with the brutal and tragic past of mass dictatorship. It would only encourage people to perceive reality by way of thinking in national terms and thus to justify victimhood nationalism. The perpetrators' principle of 'a reductive selectiveness' would remain intact. It would signify a posthumous victory for the oppressors. However, to deny collective guilt does not equal denying the 'cultural collective' constructed out of a sense of participation in a common past spanning over a period of many generations.[78] Adam Michnik's confession is intuitive in that sense: 'I do not feel guilty for those murdered, but I do feel responsible ... I feel guilty that after they died they were murdered again, denied a decent burial, denied tears, denied truth about this hideous crime, and that for decades a lie was repeated'.[79] If responsibility means answerability to the others' voices and pains, historical responsibility equals the responsibility for the present memory of the past. We historians are responsible for the apologetic memory of victimhood nationalism, as memorial collective is still in the making, with each of us doing our parts.

Notes

1. See Daniel Levy and Natan Sznaider, *The Holocaust and Memory in the Global Age* (Philadelphia: Temple University Press, 2006); Barbara Misztal, 'Collective Memory in a Global Age: Learning How and What to Remember', in *Current Sociology* vol. 58, no. 1 (January, 2010); Jean-Marc Drefys and Marcel Stoetzler, 'Holocaust Memory in the Twenty-First cCentury: Between National Reshaping and Globalisation', in *European Review of History* vol. 18, no. 1 (February 2011); Andrzej Paczkowski, 'Czy historycy dokonali "obrachunku" z PRL?' in Joanna Łukasiak-Mikłasz, *Ofiary czy Współwinni* (Warszawa: Volumen, 1997), pp. 13–29.
2. Antony Polonsky and Joanna Michlic, 'Introduction', Polonsky and Michlic (eds.), *The Neighbors Responded: The Controversy Over the Jedwabne Massacre in Poland* (Princeton: Princeton University Press, 2004), p. 9.
3. Walter Benjamin, 'The Storyteller', *Illuminations: Essays and Reflections*, Hannah Arendt (ed.) (New York: Schocken, 1968), p. 94.
4. I borrowed the term of 'hereditary victimhood' from Zygmunt Bauman. See *Modernity and Holocaust* with a new afterword by the author (Ithaca: Cornell University Press, 2000), p. 238.
5. George L. Mosse, *Fallen Soldiers: Reshaping the Memory of the World Wars* (New York: Oxford University Press, 1991), pp. 70–106.
6. Hannah Arendt, *Eichmann in Jerusalem: A Report on the Banality of Evil* (New York: Penguin Books, 1994), p. 278.
7. See Lim Jie-Hyun, 'Hŭisaengja Ŭisik Minjŏkjuŭi' [Victimhood Nationalism], *Bip'yŏng* [criticism], vol. 15 (Summer, 2007), pp. 154–76; 'Victimhood Nationalism: Compelling or Competing?', *The Korea Herald* (9 April 2007).
8. Anna Bikont, 'We of Jedwabne', in Polonsky and Michlic (eds.), *The Neighbors Responded*, pp. 268, 294.
9. In the turbulent debates on Jewish massacres in Jedwabne, a 70-old ordinary Pole admitted that, 'we were taught as children that we Poles never harmed anyone. A partial abandonment of this morally comfortable position is very, very difficult for me.' See A. Polonsky and J. Michlic, 'Introduction', in Polonsky and Michlic (eds.), *The Neighbors Responded*, p. 1. Leon Kieres, the first president of the Institute for National Memory (Instytut Pamięci Narodowej), confessed that 'it was persistently hard for me to believe in that crime perpetrated by the decisive participation of the people speaking Polish like me.' See Leon Kieres, 'Przedmowa,' in P. Machcewicz and K. Persak (eds), *Wokół Jedwabnego. Tom I: Studia* (Warszawa: IPN, 2002), p. 7.
10. Primo Levi, *The Drowned and the Saved* (New York: Vintage Books, 1989), p. 24.
11. I have encountered this colloquial thesis most frequently from ordinary Poles in street. It is intriguing that many a 'Western' historian of Korean history shares a similar experience in Korea in which they were dissuaded from studying Korean history.

12. Jie-Hyun Lim, 'The Antagonistic Complicity of Nationalisms-On Nationalist Phenomenology in East Asian History Textbooks', in Steffi Richter (ed.), *Contested Views of a Common Past: Revisions of History in Contemporary East Asia* (Frankfurt: Campus Verlag, 2008), pp. 205–22.

13. Yoko Kawashima Watkins, *So Far from the Bamboo Grove* (New York: Beech Tree, 1994). Korean translation *Yoko-Iyagi* (Seoul: Munhakdongne, 2005).

14. Yoon Sang-In, 'Sunandamŭi Yuhok', *Bipyung*, vol. 15 (Summer, 2007), pp. 197–98.

15. http://www.boston.com/news/globe/west/2007/02/korean_official.html.

16. http://issue.chosun.com/site/data/html_dir/2007/02/15/2007021500361.html.

17. The protest emails from members of the PAAHE to my column on victimhood nationalism in *The Korea Herald* taught me the importance of historical facts and accurate history for historical study.

18. A history of perceiving East Asian history in the American context may justify their worry partly. See Lisa Yoneyama, 'Asiagye Mikukin gwa Ilboŭi Jŏnjaengbŏmjoi', paper presented to the 4th Symposium of Korean-Japanese Solidarity 21 (14 July 2007). Carter Eckert's insistence on the necessity of proper historical annotation on Japanese colonial rule in Yoko Kawashima Watkins's novella can be understood in a similar context. He also recommends reading Richard Kim's *Lost Names* along with Yoko Watkins, which depicts a Korean boy's hardship under the Japanese colonial rule. See Carter Eckert, 'A matter of context', *The Boston Globe* (16 December 2006).

19. http://www.amazon.com/review/product/0844668109/ref=cm_cr_dp_all_helpful?%5Fencoding=UTF8&coliid=&showViewpoints=1&colid=&sortBy=bysubmissionDateDescending.

20. See Jie-Hyun Lim, 'Heroship, Victimhood and Nation-Building: Imagining Israel in the Postcolonial Korea', paper presented to 'Everyday Coloniality' workshop held at RICH, Hanyang University on 2 and 3 November 2012.

21. Werner Weinberg, *Self-Portrait of a Holocaust Survivor* (Jefferson, N C: Mcfarland, 1985), p. 152.

22. Quoted in Idith Zertal, *From Catastrophe to Power: Holocaust Survivors and the Emergence of Israel* (Berkeley: University of California Press, 1998), p. 217.

23. Zertal, *From Catastrophe* ..., p. 216; Tom Segev, *The Seventh Million: The Israelis and the Holocaust,* trans. by Heim Watzman (New York: An Owl Book, 2000), pp. 43–44, 109.

24. *Ibid.*, p. 221.

25. *Ibid.*, p. 263.

26. Ilan Pappe, 'Critique and Agenda: The Post-Zionist Scholars in Israel', *History and Memory*, Special Issue: Israel Historiography Revisited. vol. 7, no. 1 (1995), p. 72. It is noteworthy that a sexist reconstruction of history can be found also in the Korean nationalist discourse of the comfort women.

27. Quoted in Peter Novick, *The Holocaust and Collective Memory* (London: Bloomsbury, 2001), p. 121.

28. *Ibid.*, p. 116.

29. *Ibid.*, pp. 92–98, 116, 121 and passim.

30. Dan Diner, 'Cumulative Contingency: Historicising Legitimacy in Israeli Discourse', *History and Memory*, Special Issue: Israel Historiography Revisited. vol. 7, no. 1 (1995), p. 153.

31. Yael Zerubavel, 'The Death of Memory and the Memory of Death: Masada and the Holocaust as Historical Metaphors', *Representations*, vol. 45, no. 1, (Winter, 1994), pp. 80–81.
32. Dan Diner, *op. cit.*, pp. 74–78.
33. Michel Warschawski, *On the Border*, English trans. Levi Laub (Cambridge, MA: South End Press, 2005), pp. 153–54.
34. Tom Segev, *The Seventh Million*, p. 361.
35. Quoted in Tom Segev, *The Seventh Million*, p. 389. It should be also noted that in the international arena Israeli officers and American Jewish political activists tried to enhance public awareness of the Holocaust in order to generate sympathy and support for Israel. See Novick, *op. cit.*, pp. 156–57.
36. Segev, *op. cit.*, p. 516.
37. Diner, *op. cit.*, pp. 155–57.
38. Novick, *op. cit.*, 156; Segev, *op. cit.*, pp. 399–400.
39. For the excellent analysis of the uniqueness discourse, see Alan S. Rosenbaum (ed.), *Is Holocaust Unique?: Perspectives on Comparative Genocide* (Boulder, Colorado: Westview Press, 2001).
40. Quoted in Michel Warschawski, *op. cit.*, p. 154.
41. A. Polonsky and J. Michlic. 'Introduction', p. 39; Jan T. Gross, *Neighbors: The Destruction of the Jewish Community in Jedwabne, Poland* with a new Afterword (New York: Penguin Books, 2002), p. 120.
42. Gross, *Neighbors*, p. 123.
43. Quoted in 'Introduction' in Joshua D. Zimmerman (ed.), *Contested Memories: Poles and Jews During the Holocaust and Its Aftermath* (New Brunswick, NJ: Rutgers University Press, 2003), p. 9.
44. It is striking that 40 percent of respondents in a nationwide survey of public opinion in 2004 declared Poland is still being governed by Jews. See Jan T. Gross, *Fear: Anti-Semitism in Poland after Auschwitz* (New York: Random House, 2006).
45. Quoted in *Ibid.*, p. 243.
46. See Jie-Hyun Lim, 'Nationalist Message in Socialist Code: On Court Historiography in People's Poland and North Korea', in Solvi Sogner (ed.), *Making Sense of Global History* (Oslo: Universitetsforlaget, 2001), pp. 373–80.
47. Barbara Engelking-Boni, 'Psychological Distance between Poles and Jews in Nazi-Occupied Warsaw', p. 48.
48. It is symptomatic that it has not been allowed to publish the Polish version of Wladyslaw Szpielman's *Pianist* in the ear of People's Poland.
49. Michael Steinlauf, 'Teaching the Holocaust in Poland', in Zimmerman (ed.), *Contested Memories*, p. 264.
50. *Ibid.*, pp. 265–66.
51. Quoted in A. Polonsky, 'Introduction', p. 9.
52. Jan Błoński, *Biedny Polacy Patrzą na Getto* (Kraków: wydawnictwo literackie, 1996). Originally published in 'Tygodnik Powszechny', 11 January 1987.
53. Hanna Świda-Ziemba, 'The Shortsightedness of the Cultured', in Polonsky and Michlic (eds.), *The Neighbors Responded*, p. 103.
54. 'Interview with the Primate of Poland, Cardinal Józef Glemp, on the Murder of Jews in Jedwabne, 15 May 2001', in Polonsky and Michlic (eds.), *The Neighbors Responded*, p. 167.

55. Jan Gross, *Fear*, p. 130.
56. Adam Michnik, 'Poles and Jews: How Deep the Guilt?', in Polonsky and Michlic (eds.), *The Neighbors Responded*, p. 435.
57. *Ibid.*, p. 120–22.
58. Ernest Renan, *Qu'est-ce qu'une nation?* Korean translation by Shin Haeng-sun (Seoul: Chaeksesang, 2002), p. 81.
59. Quoted in James J. Orr, *The Victim as Hero: Ideologies of Peace and National Identity in Postwar Japan* (Honolulu: University of Hawai'i Press, 2001), p. 1.
60. Peter Novick, *The Holocaust and Collective Memory* (London: Bloomsbury, 2001), p. 112.
61. John W. Dower, 'An Aptitude for Being Unloved: War and Memory in Japan', in Omer Bartov *et al.* (eds), *Crimes of War: Guilt and Denial in the Twentieth Century* (New York: The New Press, 2002), p. 226.
62. Dower, 'An Aptitude', p. 228.
63. Quoted in Orr, *The Vicitm as Hero*, p. 16.
64. Orr, *The Victim as Hero*, pp. 7, 14, 15, 32 and passim.
65. Quoted in Orr, *The Victim as Hero*, p. 32.
66. Ian Bruma, *The Wages of Guilt: Memories of War in Germany and Japan*, Korean translation by Chung Yonghwan (Seoul: Hangyoreh Shinmun, 2002), pp. 119–26.
67. Orr, *The Victim as Hero*, p. 52.
68. Lisa Yoneyama, *Hiroshima Traces: Time, Space, and the Dialectics of Memory* (Berkeley: University of California Press, 1999), pp. 1–3.
69. Tessa Morris-Suzuki, *The Past Within Us: Media, Memory, History*, Korean translation by Kim Kyoungwon (Seoul: Humanist, 2006), pp. 127–33.
70. Bill Niven, 'Introduction', in Bill Niven (ed.), *Germans as Victims* (Houndmills: Palgrave Macmillan, 2006), p. 16.
71. Guenther Grass, *Im Krebsgang*, Korean translation by Chang Hee-Chang (Seoul: Minumsa, 2002).
72. Stefan Berger, 'On Taboos, Traumas and Other Myths', in Niven (ed.), *Germans as Victims*, pp. 219–20.
73. Robert G. Moeller, 'War Stories: The Search for a Usable Past in the Federal Republic of Germany', *American Historical Review* vol. 101, no. 4 (October 1996), pp. 1013, 1017, 1027 and passim.
74. Berger, 'On Taboos, Traumas and Other Myths', p. 215.
75. Bartosz T. Wieliński, 'Czego żąda owiernictwo pruskie', *Gazeta Wyborcza*, (19 December 2006).
76. Jan M. Piskorski, *Vertreibung und Deutsch-Polnische Geschichte* (Osnabrueck: Fibre Verlag, 2005), pp. 37, 42, 43.
77. It is intriguing to see that her interview in such a small local newspaper became news in the Polish media. 'Steinbach: Polski rząd jak niemieccy neofaszyści', *Gazeta Wyborcza*, 7 March 2007.
78. David Engel, 'Introduction to the Hebrew Edition of *Neighbors*', in Polonsky and Michlic (eds.), *The Neighbors Responded*, p. 413.
79. Michnik, 'Poles and Jews: How Deep the Guilt?', p. 435.

4
Creating a Victimised Nation: The Politics of the Austrian People's Courts and High Treason

Hiroko Mizuno

Introduction

In 1945, Austria was liberated from Nazi rule and re-established as an independent nation state. It was over seven years after the 'Anschluss', or annexation of Austria by Hitler's Germany in March of 1938. Karl Renner, the first Chancellor of the First Republic that was established in 1918–1919 as a result of World War I, was given a second chance to form a provisional state government. He was now responsible for re-founding an Austrian (but no longer 'German') nation state for the Austrian people and proclaiming it an independent state.[1]

The Austrian provisional state government headed by Renner soon set about the unfinished national project, based on an interpretation of the annexation of Austria by National Socialist Germany (NS Germany) as an imposed action and therefore 'null and void'. This argument originated in the so-called 'Moscow Declaration on Austria', published in 1943 by the Allied Powers. This Declaration claimed that

> [t]he Governments of the United Kingdom, the Soviet Union and the United States of America are agreed that Austria, the first free country to fall a victim to Hitlerite aggression, shall be liberated from German domination. They regard the annexation imposed upon Austria by Germany on March 15, 1938, as null and void.[2]

Relying upon the so-called *Opfertheorie*, or theory of Austria as a victim of German aggression, Austrian political elites not only attempted to win international support for Austria's independence but also began to frame a revised conception of the Austrian people that denied German national consciousness as a component of the Austrian nation state.

From a historical perspective, however, there was little reason to consider Austria's separation from Germany as the only legitimate way to reconstruct the devastated land. One of the most significant obstacles that post-war Austria encountered was the national question concerning relations with Germany. It dated back at least to the late nineteenth century, when, confronted with national demands from the other ethnic groups, German-speaking people had laid the foundations of their (imagined) national community within the multi-linguistic monarchy. This gave rise to a significant lack of 'Austrian national' consciousness, which – compounded by the defeat of World War I and the breakup of the monarchy – prevented a sense of belonging (to the Austrian nation state during the interwar period) from strengthening among Austrian citizens. This situation had ultimately contributed to the annexation by NS Germany in 1938. Austria had seemed to be doomed to join World War II on the side of NS Germany.

In addition to the national question, Austria's claim to sovereignty was made more difficult by its participation in World War II and Nazi atrocities. The question of how to reframe a people who had been used to defining themselves primarily as part of a German cultural nation as an Austrian nation was therefore closely connected with how clearly the Austrian people (as victims) could differentiate themselves from the National Socialist German nation (as perpetrators). Yet even the Moscow Declaration contains ambivalent language regarding Austria's responsibility for joining World War II: 'Austria is reminded, however, that she has a responsibility which she cannot evade for participation in the war on the side of Hitlerite Germany, and that in the final settlement account will inevitably be taken of her own contribution to her liberation'.[3] The Austrian self-definition as 'victims' indeed hardly conformed to historical realities; many Austrian people had supported the NS regime during the 'Anschluss' period, even if they were motivated by varied reasons and circumstances.

To resolve the national question, on the one hand, and to evade the consequences of participating in the war, on the other hand, Austrian political elites quickly initiated an attempt to reintegrate the populace into the Austrian national framework, in accordance with the theory of Austria as a victim of German aggression. This national reintegration policy, however, was especially challenged by the existence of war criminals, since these people could neither be counted as a part of a nation of 'victims' nor did they share Austrian national consciousness. It was widely believed that the war criminals, due to their support for the Nazi Regime, and their stronger National Socialist and German identification, should bear the most responsibility for the consequences of NS rule. In this sense, they were considered not only perpetrators of, or collaborators with NS German brutality in Austria, but even 'national traitors' against the Austrian nation state. Therefore, the Austrian political elites decided to establish a special judicial system called 'People's Courts' to prosecute domestic war criminals (including the national traitors).

The People's Courts were (at first) expected to enable the exclusion of major former Nazis from the process of building an Austrian nation, thus settling political demarcations between those who were to be included in and those who were to be excluded from an Austrian nation. The political landscape in Austria changed drastically, however, as the Cold War progressed in the form of domestic and international political struggles. Former Nazis who had once been prosecuted for high treason would soon be rehabilitated, whereas Austrian communists would be marginalised and, instead, branded as 'national traitors'. As pressure to abolish the People's Courts and to reduce the prosecution of high treason to a formality gained momentum, the problems of wartime Nazi collaboration and national identity would be subsumed into the problem of the Cold War ideological conflict. Finally, the demarcation lines of Austrian nationality came to be redefined in terms of Austria as a victimised nation, which in turn was now based on anti-communism.

The aim of this chapter is to answer the question of how the Austrian people tried to overcome their Nazi past by focusing on the policies of reintegrating former Nazis. For this purpose, it will explore how the Austrian political elites dealt with 'national traitors' in the People's Courts, successfully reintegrating them into a reframed Austrian nation.[4] Against this background, it will also focus on how they succeeded in avoiding the problem of war and Nazi responsibility. Secondly, this chapter will also consider the deliberations involved in resolving the national question. In so doing, it will not only try to set the policy of the People's Courts in the context of coming to terms with the past ('Vergangenheitsbewältigung') in terms of a new European norm, but it will also investigate these policies as part of the reconstruction process of an Austrian nation, thus casting a new light on Austrian studies.[5]

The scope of war crimes and limits of an Austrian nation

'War Crimes' in terms of National Socialist Prohibition Act of 1945

The politics of war criminal prosecution were initiated by the Renner provisional state government, which was formed in Soviet-occupied Vienna. As had already been proclaimed on 15 May 1945, the Renner government – defining itself as the concentration government made up of all three 'anti-fascist' political parties – was determined to fight against fascist elements. The anti-fascist parties participating in the Renner government were the Socialist Party of Austria (SPÖ), the Austrian People's Party (ÖVP), and the Communist Party of Austria (KPÖ). Some of the most important political measures taken by the Renner government to demonstrate anti-fascist attitudes were two basic pieces of legislation that were enacted very quickly: The National-Socialist Prohibition Act of 1945 (Prohibition Act, enforced as of 8 May 1945) and the War Criminals Law (enforced as of 26 June 1945), on the basis of which the Renner government embarked upon extensive judicial investigations of the suspected war criminals, collaborators as well as former Austrian Nazis. And for precisely this purpose, the Prohibition Act provided for the establishment of the People's Courts.[6]

The Prohibition Act was enacted to dissolve the National Socialist German Workers' Party (NSDAP) or the Nazi Party and to prohibit National Socialist activities, focusing primarily on how to deal with the 'lesser' or 'petty' Nazis, but it also contained some important regulations that obliged the People's Courts to purge 'national traitors'. The category of 'high treason' included those who had belonged to the Nazi Party or its organisations prior to the annexation of Austria by Nazi Germany in March 1938. These were defined as 'illegal Nazis', since in Austria the Nazi Party was banned between 1934 and 1938 by the so-called Austrofascist regime. Differentiated from other Nazis, the 'illegal Nazis' were made vulnerable to the charge of high treason on the grounds that they had acted against the Austrian nation state by committing themselves to German National Socialism. In this sense, the penal code would have been applied individually to them on a charge of 'treachery'. In view of the number of those to be charged, however, Adolf Schärf (SPÖ) suggested that 'illegal Nazis' should instead be collectively punished on the basis of their political attribution or social status, incurring penalties of lesser severity.[7] As a result of Schärf's consideration, 'illegal Nazis' would incur penalties of five to ten years of severe imprisonment, provided that the Austrian government found that the former 'illegal Nazis' had reverted to National Socialism or acted against the Austrian nation state and determined that such a penalty was necessary.[8] If the 'illegal Nazis' had been of higher social status or their behaviours in the Nazi movement were inhumane, they were to be tried individually. For such cases Article 11 of the Prohibition Act prescribed the application of penalties of ten to twenty years' severe imprisonment and confiscation of property. 'High treason' was thus defined by Articles 10 and 11 of the Prohibition Act as a criminal act to be punished by the People's Courts.

'War Crimes' as defined in the War Criminal Law – War/Nazi crimes and high treason

While the Prohibition Act targeted 'lesser' Nazis in general, the War Criminal Law provided the legal foundations for prosecuting so-called 'greater' Nazis; some of these were suspected as principal offenders against the laws of war and others were deemed to be mainly responsible for Holocaust massacre, and the People's Courts would bring them to trial if necessary. But it is worth noting that the War Criminal Law included additional provisions for those accused of 'high treason' that differ from those defined by both Articles 10 and 11 of the Prohibition Act, namely the Article 8 citation of 'high treason against the Austrian people'.

It was the Austrian communist, Ernst Fischer, who exerted the greatest pressure on the Renner government for sweeping punishment of war criminals. He had already asserted in a cabinet meeting on 12 June 1945 that the government had to punish 'greater' Nazis with severity.[9] It is noticeable that the communists' demand for strict punishment of 'greater' Nazis was closely connected with the politics of the speedy reintegration into the Austrian nation of 'lesser' Nazis. For Fischer, it would be better if these people were acquitted of charges of misdeeds under the Nazi regime.[10]

Renner, however, adopted a more moderate standpoint. In his opinion, it was almost impossible to differentiate acts of violence in wartime (which would incur punishment through special laws) from crimes determined by conventional laws, 'since war itself was nothing but violence'. As for the relationships with the Allied Powers, moreover, Renner insisted that there was no good reason to tolerate sterner measures against Austrian citizens than those the Allies would take against the war criminals of Germany.[11] In the end, however, Fischer seems to have persisted in his opinion, and war criminals were defined not only as those who violated international laws and the laws of war but also as those who had agitated for war or committed outrages against humanity. These definitions of war criminals are the categories of criminal acts on which most previous studies of the People's Courts have concentrated their attention.

It is also important, however, to take into consideration the political debates over 'high treason against the Austrian people'. The incorporation of this crime into the War Criminal Law contributed to the delineation of an Austrian nation. Capital punishment was expected for such a crime on the grounds that political responsibility for the catastrophe under the

Nazi regime was to be ascribed primarily to those who had once denied and challenged the existence of the Austrian nation state. Besides the general validity of Article 8 ('high treason against the Austrian people'), the most intensely discussed questions in cabinet meetings were who fell into this category, what kind of penalties should be adopted and, whether political and social position had an impact on how broadly inclusive the article should be.

Opinions of the three ruling parties varied on defining 'high treason against the Austrian people'. The People's Party advocated that the government limit the scope of who or, better yet, *which position* fell into this category to the minimal extent, only applying Article 8 to the ministers of the cabinets that promoted the annexation of Austria by Nazi Germany.[12] The Socialists also required circumspection and insisted on not treating war/Nazi criminals and offender of 'high treason against the Austrian people' equally solely based on the high-ranking positions of the latter group.[13] But these rather moderate concepts met with strong opposition from the Communist Party. The Communists insisted upon rigid terms for the treatment of high-ranking persons, including the members of the Reichstag in the Nazi period and the judges of the Nazi People's Court. As all of them were looked on as a part of the NS machinery, they deserved, in the eyes of the Communists, to fall into the category of 'high treason against the Austrian people', equal to war/Nazi criminals. As for penalties, the Communists demanded no less than the application of capital punishment under Article 8.[14]

Ultimately the Communists' opinions were taken into account to the extent that the War Criminal Law included Article 8, which prescribed that a person who, for instance, helped the political takeover of Austria by the Nazis or collaborated with a person in a position of authority to change the political regime of Austria in favour of Nazi Germany by force was to be prosecuted for 'high treason against the Austrian people'. Those who held leading positions in National Socialist organisations such as the SS (Schutzstaffel or protection force) did not fall into the category vulnerable to the punishment required by Article 8, however; they were rather classified as war criminals. And despite the Communists' demands, the same applied to the members of the Reichstag in the Nazi period, even though capital punishment was to be applied in this case, as well. When considering the inclusion of Article 8 in the drafting of the War Criminal Law, it seems obvious that, at this point in time, the strict Communists' opinions were very influential.

As we have already seen, the War Criminal Law contained stipulations on war and Nazi criminals. It seems no less important, however, that it also included the category of 'high treason against the Austrian people'.[15] Considerably influenced by the Communists' opinion, the War Criminal Law can be characterised by its wide scope covering a variety of offences ranging from war crimes through Nazi atrocities to 'high treason against the Austrian people'. In this sense, the basic concept of punishing those who were thought of as most responsible for Austria's involvement in the war and the violent Nazi regime suggests that the War Criminal Law defined the demarcation lines of the Austrian nation. In 1945, immediately after World War II, the people who were judged to be guilty based on Article 8 of 'high treason against the Austrian people' were destined to be eliminated from the future Austrian nation. The criminal category of 'high treason against the Austrian people' reveals the limits of an Austrian nation designed by the political elites in 1945.

Communists' influence over the politics of the war criminals trials

Why did the Austrian Communists have such a powerful voice within the government in the politics of war criminal trials? As already mentioned earlier, the Renner government was formed under and with the support of the Soviet occupation, while the three other Allies acknowledged the Renner government much later on the premise of the first general election held in November 1945. But the support of Soviet power alone does not seem to justify the Communists' influential position. The Communists in Austria could, first of all, take advantage of their achievements in the wartime resistance against the NS regime. Secondly, they had the upper hand over the other two ruling parties in the national project of building an Austrian nation. It was the Austrian Communists who, in the 1930s, had already attempted to develop their own theoretical concept for the Austrian nation on the premise of Austria's independence from Germany.[16] They had never tended toward the idea of a 'Greater Germany', and consistently fought against the NS regime for a free and democratic Austria. Therefore, they could proudly speak of their great contribution to Austrian independence after World War II, and their historical continuity from the interwar period helped the Communists to claim the right to their presence in the government. In this sense, they were justified in appealing to the public as well as to the Allies, especially regarding the national project of building a new Austrian nation. Insofar as the Communists' demand for stern punishment of the 'greater Nazis' originated from their strong anti-Nazism, their very concept of re-establishing an independent Austrian state and building an Austrian nation seemed legitimate and convincing.

As far as the concept of the Austrian nation was concerned, both the People's Party and the Socialist Party were forced to play second fiddle to the Communists. The former stemmed from the Catholic-conservative Christian Socialist Party in the interwar period, which was characterised by the idea of a federation of Danubian states based on legitimism as well as the concept of a second German state in connection with Austrofascist corporatism of the 1930s. The Socialist Party too, originating in the Social Democratic Party in the interwar period, had ever sought to realise a union between Germany and Austria after World War I in the pursuit of internationalism. Even Renner had little authority to strongly object to the Communists, due to his approval of the annexation of Austria by NS Germany in 1938. Thus, the Communist Party in Austria had clearly gained a strong political foothold for the first time in this country, and the category of 'high treason against the Austrian people' was incorporated into the War Criminal Law at their urging.

The forgotten experience of Austrofascism and the limits of an Austrian nation

As mentioned earlier, the Renner government consisted of three 'antifascist' parties, but it is difficult to determine the meaning of such words as 'antifascist' or 'antifascism'. It cannot be ignored that these words were actually used equally to mean 'anti-Nazism'. In fact, those who were to be charged based on the Prohibition Act or the War Criminal Law were limited to war/Nazi criminals. The same can be said for the crime of 'high treason against the Austrian people' that was to be applied to those who had something to do with National Socialism. Thus the rhetorical use of the word 'antifascism' in place of 'anti-Nazism' made it possible to lay aside historical responsibility for the 'Austrofascist' regime in the 1930s. In cooperation with Mussolini, Engelbert Dollfuss and his follower Kurt Schuschnigg had attempted to change Austria into an authoritarian state based on corporatist ideas. Leaning toward the political right, Dollfuss had shut down the national parliament and suppressed the political left. To those suppressed, the Dollfuss-Schuschnigg regime had been fascist. Nevertheless, those who mattered to the Renner government and the federal governments that followed in Austria in terms of 'fascism' were, in fact, only those responsible for the Nazi regime, and not the 'fascists' of the Dollfuss-Schuschnigg regime. In this way, the responsibility of the Austrofascist regime was forgotten. Thus, in 1945, the scope of the Austrian nation as determined by the Prohibition Act and the War Criminal Law ranged widely from the Communists and the Socialists through the Austrofascists to the 'lesser' Nazis, while the 'greater' Nazis like war criminals or persons to be charged with 'high treason against the Austrian people' (national traitors) were to be excluded. A wide range of Austrian people seemed very likely to be soon reintegrated into an Austrian nation.

The trials of national traitors by the people's courts

The Austrian People's Courts

Before we look into the trials of national traitors, it might be helpful to consider briefly the organisation and composition of the People's Courts in Austria.

The Austrian People's Courts were characterised by their structure. A people's court was composed of two professional judges and three laymen chosen from the 'people' with a majority. The laymen were recommended by each ruling party at the early stage of formation of the People's Courts. This recommendation system must have had great value in enabling the ruling parties to show the public that the People's Courts would represent and reflect public opinion, which, in turn, helped to assert their own legitimacy (and of course, the legitimacy of the Renner government). Indeed, given that a general election had still not been held since the end of World War II, the legitimacy and the very existence of the political parties concerned were susceptible to doubt. To demonstrate their toughness and to lay such doubt to rest, they sought quick decisions, so the accused usually had no possibility of appealing to a higher court.

There were serious debates over the name of this special trial system, because the German original words for People's Courts, 'Volksgerichte', could easily be associated with the Nazi People's Court. But Josef Gerö, the State Secretary of Justice of the Renner government, especially insisted upon this name, strongly emphasising its importance in demonstrating to the public that this trial system would be the 'people's court', proper.[17]

The People's Courts were thus to be set up as courts responsible for war crimes trials based on the Prohibition Act and the War Criminals Law. The first to take up its task was the People's Court in Vienna, where the Renner government had been given authority by the occupying Soviet forces to initiate legislation from the beginning of the post-war period. According to documents summed up by Marschall, an official from the Ministry of Justice, 202 persons in 1945[18] and 1326 in 1946[19] were convicted at the People's Court in Vienna. In the other regions occupied by the western Allies (Great Britain, the United States and France), the People's Courts were introduced in 1946, after the governments of the Allied occupation authorities had officially rec- ognised the Renner government. A People's Court was set up in Graz in January 1946, mostly covering the regions of Styria and Carinthia under the British occupation. By 1946, 390 persons had been convicted on the basis of the War Criminal Law or the Prohibition Act in Graz.[20] The People's Court in Linz was mainly in charge of the regions that were occupied by US forces with some branches in Upper Austria and Salzburg. By August 1946, the People's Court of Linz had convicted no more than 201 persons.[21] The People's Court in Tyrol was obliged to try the suspected persons in the regions the French forces occupied, only taking up its tasks very slowly. One of the common reasons for getting off to a slow start in these regions occupied by the Western Allies was a shortage of personnel appropriate for the duties of the People's Courts, since many legal professionals had Nazi pasts.[22]

The first case brought to trial in Vienna on August 1945 dealt with mass murder in Engerau/Petržalka (Slovakia). Drawing considerable attention from the public, the People's Court in Vienna sentenced those accused to the death penalty. On March 1946, the first sentence handed down by the People's Court in Graz was to those accused of war crimes committed within the military on the Italian front.[23] The People's Court of Linz, which dealt with cases of the crime of information (or 'tipping off') in the early stages of the politics of the war crimes trials, was criti- cised for not applying the death sentence although it was not expected for this crime. It was not until one year after initiating its activities that, amidst intense pressure from the public, the People's Court of Linz sentenced any offenders to death (in a murder case, for example).[24] In Innsbruck there were no records of any death sentences.

Whereas the Communists' demand for severe punishment was more or less incorporated into the laws concerned in theory; in practice, the People's Courts seem uneven region by region. Keeping these conditions in mind, how did the People's Courts work in the cases dealing with national traitors or high treason? Let us look at some examples of the two categories of high treason; the first is 'high treason against the Austrian people' based on Article 8 of the War Criminal Law, and the second, high treason based on Articles of 10 and 11 of the Prohibition Act.

High treason trials by the People's Courts based on Article 8 of the war criminal law

There were only three cases in which it mattered whether Article 8 was to be applied or not, but they attracted much attention from the public, dealing as they did with the Ministers at the time of the annexation of

Austria by NS Germany, Rudolf Neumayer (Minister of Finance), Anton Reinthaller (Minister of Agriculture) and Guido Schmidt (Minister of Foreign Affairs of the Schuschnigg government).[25] As all three were perceived as being the people most responsible for the annexation, they were accused of 'high treason against the Austrian people' on the basis of Article 8 of the War Criminal Law. Neumayer, sentenced to life imprisonment and confiscation of property, was released in 1949 due to illness and was given presidential amnesty for the unserved portion of his sentence in 1951. And in 1957, his conviction was annulled.[26] Reinthaller was sentenced to prison for three years in 1950 after his imprisonment by the US forces. Soon thereafter, he would become the leader of the Austrian Freedom Party that originated from the League of the Independent, which had been founded in 1949 as an electoral basis for the former Nazis.[27]

It was Schmidt's case, however, that caused considerable public concern at the time. In 1945, Schmidt was accused for his conciliatory attitude toward Nazi Germany, which, it was thought, facilitated the annexation policy. His case, which had come to trial 49 times by 1947, assumed the characteristics of a show trial, and was regarded as a place – to borrow the expression found in the final decision – 'of political justice'.[28] Schmidt's case, which ended with a declaration of innocence, seems to show two important aspects of the People's Courts. First, it revealed the difficulty of prosecuting high treason. It is true that one of the main reasons for the decision of innocence was 'insufficient evidence', but even more importantly, the People's Court provided a clear judicial judgement against the retroactive prosecution of a person who had held a key position in the government based solely on his high position.[29] This judgement was far from the initial policy of rigid prosecution aimed for by the War Criminal Law under the influence of the Communists.

Secondly, Schmidt's case helped to propagate the official position that the annexation of Austria by NS Germany was totally unjustified. Over the course of the trial, not only was Schmidt's role in foreign policy with regard to the annexation demonstrated to be harmless, the People's Courts, which had been expected to punish national traitors without mercy, became instead a tool for spreading the belief in their victimisation among the Austrian people. The appearance in court of ÖVP politician and Federal Chancellor, Leopold Figl (who followed Renner after the general election of 1945) and many other politicians in power must have helped to inspire more and more confidence in the theory of Austria as a victim of German aggression among the public when they testified in favour of the accused, Schmidt, while making it much easier to drop the matter of Austria's war and NS responsibility. Leopold Figl was nothing but a representative figure of victims because he had even been imprisoned in a Nazi concentration camp. There is little doubt that there was a highly political calculation in this vision of the victimisation of the Austrian people that underlay the judgement of Schmidt's innocence. The People's Courts were thus transformed from a tool of conviction to that of acquittal.

High treason trials based on Articles 10 and 11 of the Prohibition Act

The high treason trials based on Articles of 10 and 11 of the Prohibition Act were numerous, and according to the documentation published by Karl Marschall, 1435 individuals were convicted according to the terms of the War Criminals Law, and 2358 were convicted on the basis of the Prohibition Act by 1947.[30] Approximately half of all 3793 convictions were made in terms of high treason, namely on the basis of Articles 10 and 11 of the Prohibition Act, while the other half resulted from punishments for the war and Nazi crimes. It is obvious that the People's Courts had to deal with a large number of cases of high treason under Articles 10 and 11 of the Prohibition Act.

Of course, we should think of other potential factors that may not be reflected in these data. For example, the attitude of laymen sitting on People's Courts toward the suspect was one important factor that might have influenced these results. As a study by Garscha and Kuretsidis-Haider of the People's Court of Linz shows, there were considerable numbers of unprofessional judges who hesitated to punish the former Nazis accused of high treason.[31] This suggests that the Communists' intention to punish the national traitors as severely as war and Nazi criminals was not necessarily shared by those leading the People's Courts. This might be unsurprising if we consider the political influence of the three ruling parties on the selection process of unprofessional judges. So we should be careful in judging the historical meanings of the punishment of national traitors in the People's Courts by their numbers.

Another factor we should take into consideration in analysing the Schmidt case is its general influence on Austrian society. Soon after Schmidt was found innocent, he was qualified to get his suspended pension.[32] Since he was released and completely rehabilitated, it is little wonder that the 'lesser' Nazis who were charged with high treason began to appeal for retrial. For instance, a National Socialist district leader of the city of Linz had been prosecuted and sentenced to ten years' imprisonment by the People's Court in 1946. But only two years later, he was retried and his sentence mitigated to 18 months' imprisonment (the retrial began in 1946[33]). This mitigation meant the cancellation of almost the whole of his sentence; it is not too much to say that this was equal to an amnesty through the People's Courts.[34]

As the Schmidt case shows, the political agreement reached by the three ruling parties in 1945 on Article 8 of the War Criminal Law was unlikely to be carried out in practice. Although the real practices of punishment based on Articles 10 and 11 of the Prohibition Act concerned half of all cases dealt with by the People's Courts, the results were no less ambivalent than the high treason trials through Article 8 of the War Criminal Law, taking into account the possibilities of retrial or of the questionable attitudes of unprofessional judges.

At any rate it is worth noticing that, after reaching the peak number of convictions in 1948 (3908), the number of convictions by the People's Courts steadily decreased: there were 1696 convictions in 1949, 666 in 1950 and 263 in 1951.[35]

The changing limits of an Austrian nation: The rehabilitation of 'Lesser Nazis' and marginalised Communists

Around 1949, when the number of convictions by the People's Courts started to decrease drastically, the re-alignment of political constellations began to occur domestically as well as internationally. By 1948, most former 'lesser Nazis' were amnestied and could vote in 1949, when the second general election after World War II was called. Whereas most 'lesser' Nazis were being integrated into a new Austrian nation, the political influence of the Communists was decreasing.

As outlined earlier the Renner government planned for a new Austrian nation that would include 'lesser Nazis'. But this national project developed differently than originally planned, insofar as in the course of amending the Prohibition Act the Allied Council demanded considerable modification of the original bill drafted by the Figl government, through which most of the 'lesser' Nazis were finally deprived of their civil rights and accordingly excluded from the reintegration process in the early stages. Therefore, the Figl government had to struggle with the rehabilitation of these 'lesser' Nazis, seeking amnesties for them in various ways, before it could begin to revise the politics of the People's Courts as a whole. For this purpose, the Figl government made skilful use of the theory of Austria as a victim of German aggression as an important tool to reintegrate 'lesser' Nazis. The Figl government considered even the 'lesser' Nazis victims of Nazi rule, relying upon the idea of a 'victimised Austrian nation', into which they were to be reintegrated. By 1949 various amnesties were approved by the Allies, and the problem of 'lesser' Nazis could be considered settled.

On the other hand, the Communists, who were the driving force of the politics of the People's Courts in the first moments after World War II, were losing their political influence. Accordingly, the politics of the People's Courts had been changing, as we will investigate next. The first remarkable sign of the weakening of the Communists appeared in 1945, when they suffered a crushing defeat in the first general election in the post-war period. While the People's Party won 85 seats in the National Council and the Socialist Party won 76 seats, 49.8 per cent and 44.6 per cent of votes, respectively, the Communist Party gained only four seats for 5.4 per cent of the votes.[36] This result revealed unmistakably that the Communists had little popular support in Austria. The disastrous defeat had serious consequences for the Communist Party, and though they narrowly remained in the government, they received only one post (Minister of Electricity and Energy) in the new cabinet (headed by Figl). As Karl Altmann, who had been appointed to this last *portfolio*, resigned his post in 1947 in protest of the acceptance of the Marshall Plan, the Communists went into complete opposition. From that time on, the influence of the Austrian Communists diminished steadily, and they were marginalised in the internal political sphere. The original project of the Communists to seize the initiative in creating an Austrian nation by way of the politics of war crimes trials in the early post-war period had failed to bear fruit.

Along with the changing political constellations outlined earlier, the politics of integrating the nation were also adjusted at this time. From 1949 on, indeed, it showed a marked change, tending to reintegrate the former Nazis and excluding the Communists. With these tendencies strengthening, the People's Party and the Socialist Party began to change direction in the politics of the war crimes trials. This struggle began in the form of revising the politics of the high treason trials, where the national question and that of war and NS responsibility found confluence. Furthermore, it aimed for winning the support of the former Nazis, at the same time taking on the new form of anti-communism.

Toward the end of the politics of the war crimes trials – creating a new image of national traitors and the internal cold war

Soviet interference and the failure to abolish the system of People's Courts

On the initiative of the Ministry of Justice, Josef Gerö, the reorientation of the politics of the People's Courts began. He who, aside from the Communists, had demanded the harshest treatment of war/Nazi criminals through special laws, now seemed to have radically changed his mind. In mid-1948, as the People's Courts made accelerated progress with their trials, Gerö mentioned publicly that he would allow all war crimes trials by the People's Courts to be finished by the end of the year.[37] As early as November 1948, the National Council started to deliberate on abolishing the system of People's Courts in the form of 'normalising' the judicial system by shifting the former to the jury system. Gerö made public that, for the sake of attaining this end, he would introduce an amendment soon and entered into the negotiations with the Allied Council for permission, without which neither the Prohibition Act nor the War Criminal Law could be revised.[38]

But the negotiations with the Allied Powers did not go smoothly at all. As tensions between the Soviets and the Western Allies rose, the Soviet occupation authority began to criticise the Austrian government for failing to deal with the NS problem, especially focusing on the politics of the war criminal trials. As Figl put it in a report for the cabinet, he was blamed by the Soviet envoy, Alexej Scheltow, for facilitating National Socialist politics by means of the generous treatment of NS collaborators. Figl tried to explain that this inaccurate information originated from the Communist Party, but his explanation did not satisfy Scheltow at all. Therefore, Figl thought that the situation would allow little room for optimism.[39]

Even after giving permission for the amnesty of 'lesser' Nazis in 1948, the Allies – especially the Soviets – continued to criticise the Austrian government for insufficient punishment of war criminals. Although the Figl government attempted to prevail on the Soviets to give permission for an amendment bill, Soviet interference prevented the Austrian government from abolishing the system of People's Courts. In 1950, the National Council passed a bill to abolish the People's Courts, but it could not be enforced owing to a lack of permission from the Allies. Ultimately, the system of the People's Courts continued to exist until Austria recovered full sovereignty in 1955.

An attempt to make the system of People's Courts less effective by reducing the range of national traitors

Soviet interference halted the attempt of the Austrian government to abolish the system of the People's Courts, but the political struggle to reintegrate those accused by the People's Courts into the Austrian nation continued, as proponents sought to employ a variety of different strategies. As early as April 1948, some representatives of the National

Councils from the People's Party and the Socialist Party united to demand legislation of an amnesty for the 'greater' Nazis. They intended to revise the Prohibition Act especially by amending it to reduce the range of national traitors charged under Articles of 10 and 11.

In 1949, the People's Party again asked for an amnesty for the 'greater' Nazis, on the grounds that there was no necessity for further measures against former National Socialists given that the 1948 amnesties for 'lesser' Nazis had enabled most former Nazis to turn away from National Socialism and successfully reintegrate themselves. Figl also expressed this view.[40] But the attempt to pass such a bill failed because the three parties facing the next general election planned in 1949 were unable to reach an agreement.

While struggling for an amnesty for 'greater' Nazis became a central strategy of the People's Party, what did the Socialist Party do? They, too, sought to pardon the former Nazis charged with high treason, but preferred the idea of a presidential amnesty.[41] The Minister of Justice, Gerö, followed the bureaucratic procedures to grant presidential amnesty to a number of former Nazis charged with high treason. Officially, this was supposed to be carried out individually, but it was in fact an attempt to pardon them collectively. The Allies including the Soviets raised objections to Gerö's plan, so it had to be discontinued.[42] Although from 1950 the two main parties attempted to narrow the range of those charged with high treason through an amnesty, it was never permitted by the Allies.

In May 1954, Gerö began renewed efforts to tackle the NS problem, with a view to abolishing the system of People's Courts once and for all. For this purpose, he sent the heads of all of the highest provincial courts an official notice containing two directives. The first, which concerned those charged with high treason under Articles 10 and 11 of the Prohibition Act, was to conclude all open cases by applying an amnesty as quickly as possible. The second concerned those who were to be prosecuted for crimes defined by the War Criminals Law, aiming to bring their incomplete cases to an end due to the impossibility of an amnesty.[43] By November 1955, almost all of the 13000 people who had been convicted by the People's Courts were rehabilitated; only 14 remained in prison.[44] After ten years' existence, there was indeed no longer any reason for the People's Courts. At the end of 1955, soon after Austria won full sovereignty and was released from Allied occupation, the National Council passed a bill abolishing the system of the People's Courts by more than a two-thirds majority, while the Communists voted against it.[45]

Reversing roles during the internal cold war

As the significance of People's Courts decreased, the problem of high treason or national traitors gradually lost its meaning. However, the concept of national traitors did not disappear: it was newly interpreted and applied to another political force, namely the Communists themselves. A marked change occurred when the two ruling parties began to move toward anti-communism with the clear purpose of fully excluding the Communists from the reintegration process. In the course of this exclusion, both ruling parties strengthened their anti-communist sentiment, accusing the Communist Party of plotting with the Soviets against Austria.

And indeed, due to its loyalty to the Soviets, the Austrian Communist Party was incapable of independent political decision-making. The Party leadership consisted of those who had been in exile in Moscow during the war and included none who had struggled against NS rule in local resistance movements. This led to a situation in which the Communists often had to give Soviet interests higher priority than Austrian. For example, they had to vote against the Marshall Plan. They also had to object to the nationalisation of Austria's main industries, since it conflicted with the interests of the Soviets who intended to demand them as repatriation. That is why they were susceptible to being labelled as 'national traitors' and to being identified with Soviet interests by the non-communist forces,[46] even as the ruling parties were working to reintegrate those charged with high treason.

There was a growing spirit of anti-communism behind the politics of both ruling parties. The anti-communism of the People's Party may be easier to understand, because this party gained much of its support from the urban middle class and the Catholic-conservatives in the rural regions. Furthermore, Figl and some of the other politicians from Lower Austria were greatly concerned about communist influence because their province was under direct Soviet control. They feared in particular that Austria might be divided into East and West. As its anti-communist tendencies rose, the People's Party tried increasingly to reintegrate the former Nazis with the intention of creating a common political block against the Communists.

The anti-communism of the Socialist Party was more complicated, because it was not easy to draw a clear distinction between communism and socialism. In fact, there was a small fraction, including Erwin Scharf, with political roots in Otto Bauer's theory of 'Integral Socialism'.[47] They occupied the 'left-wing' position within the Socialist Party and tried to unite the Socialists with the Communists. But after

World War II, Renner, Adolf Schärf and Oskar Helmer of Lower Austria, all central figures of the 'right-wing' forces, dominated the party. While they had never participated in the resistance movement, they were very sceptical of Bauer's theory. Scharf, who was loyal to Bauer's theory, criticised the 'right-wing' party leaders; he argued that Schärf and Helmer were colluding with Figl and the others from the People's Party through anti-communism, leaning instead toward the West and thus against socialism.[48] As it became clear that Schärf and Helmer were abandoning internationalism, Scharf became a nuisance to the 'right-wing' Socialists.[49] He had to leave the Socialist Party in 1948 to work together with the Communists, but he also had to go on the defensive with them and was marginalised or even excluded from the new national project. On the other hand, the 'right-wing' political elites of the Socialist Party made a great effort to reintegrate the former Nazis, competing with the People's Party to win their support. It was the Minister of Interior, Helmer, who facilitated the creation of the League of the Independent as a 'fourth' party, later the Austrian Freedom Party.

In the course of pursuing the strategy of reintegrating former Nazis, both ruling parties began to reverse their conceptions of victims and perpetrators. The former Nazis who – perceived as perpetrators and collaborators of Nazi rule – had been punished by the People's Courts for illegality/high treason, were now often represented as victims of these unjustified measures. Even their families and relatives were referred to as victims of injustice. At the same time, the People's Party as well as the Socialist Party forced the Communists to take on the role of 'national traitors' that had previously been played by those former Nazis who had been punished. For example, when the Communists strongly objected to the bill abolishing the People's Courts, a representative of the Socialist Party condemned their supposed lack of Austrian national feeling, branding them 'national traitors'.[50] The positions of the former Nazis and the Communists were completely reversed, and a new image of 'national traitors' was created in the form of the Communists. The Communists, who could take reasonable pride in their own previous contribution to creating the new Austrian nation, were now excluded from the government and became the scapegoats of its new policy of reintegration.

Conclusion

As an internal Cold War developed and transformed the domestic political constellation, the demarcation lines of the Austrian nation were finally defined. Against the background of the intense anti-communism of both ruling parties, a transformation in the definition of high treason was effected. Following this changing political climate, the boundaries distinguishing those who were to be integrated from those who were to be excluded, established by the War Criminals Law and the Prohibition Act, were transformed. As the ruling parties succeeded in shifting war and NS responsibility away from many Austrians including former Nazis, and onto a small group of communists *and* the 'left-wing' socialists pursuing Internationalism, the new demarcation lines of Austrian national identity were defined in such a way as to exclude the communists as well as the 'left-wing' socialists, and to include former Nazis, Austrofascists, Catholic-conservatives and the 'right-wing' of the socialists. Needless to say, victimhood theory played a vital role in creating the foundations of Austrian national identity, but it is important to take into account the fact that a consciousness of 'victimhood', at first based on anti-fascism/anti-Nazism, was gradually transformed into a pro-Nazi/anti-communist ideology as the internal Cold War unfolded. Thus, not only the Nazi past of Austria but also the national question that so disturbed Austria in the longer term was overcome. As the Austrian nation as a whole was reconceptualised as 'victim', it was much easier for people to identify themselves with this nation, even if the means of identification varied widely. Some could feel themselves to be victims of the war; others regarded themselves as victims of the ten years' occupation by the Allied forces. The politics of the People's Court trials for war/Nazi crimes and high treasons had all contributed significantly to a process of defining the new Austrian national identity in terms of 'victimhood'. Both the post-war Austrian national question and the question of war and NS responsibility were thus successfully 'resolved'.

Notes

1. 'Proklamation über die Selbständigkeit Österreichs', in *Staatsgesetzblatt für die Republik Österreich* (StGBl.), Jg. 1945, Nr. 1, Österreichische Staatsdruckerei (ausgegeben am 1. Mai 1945).
2. 'Great Britain–Soviet Union–United States: Tripartite Conference in Moscow Reviewed work(s)', *The American Journal of International Law* vol. 38, no. 1, Supplement: Official Documents (January 1944), pp. 3–8, published by: American Society of International Law (http://www.jstor.org/stable/2214037 Accessed: 09/11/2012 05:55, JSTOR). See also *Red-White-Red-Book: Justice for Austria. Descriptions, Documents and Proofs to the Antecedents and History of the Occupation of Austria.* First Part (From Official Sources), Vienna, 1947, printed and published by the Austrian State Printing House, pp. 207–08.
3. 'Great Britain – Soviet Union – United States: Tripartite Conference in Moscow Reviewed work(s)', *Ibid.*

4. Regarding the reintegration policy of 'petty' or 'lesser' Austrian Nazis who were differentiated from those responsible for NS and war criminals, see Hiroko Mizuno, '"Die Hand zur Versöhnung ist geboten". Die Reintegration der ehemaligen Nationalsozialisten in Österreich am Beispiel der Amnestiepolitik 1945–1948', in Margit Franz u. a. (Hg.), *Mapping Contemporary History. Zeitgeschichten im Diskurs* (Wien/Köln/Weimar: Böhlau, 2008), pp. 385–400.

5. On Austrian People's Courts especially in Vienna, see Winfried R. Garscha unter Mitarbeit von Claudia Kuretsidis-Haider, *Die Verfahren vor dem Volksgericht Wien (1945–1955) als Geschichtsquelle. Forschungsprojekt des Dokumentationsarchivs des österreichischen Widerstandes* (Wien: Dokumentationsarchiv des österreichischen Widerstandes, 1993); Winfried R. Garscha/Claudia Kuretsidis-Haider, *Die Nachkriegsjustiz als nicht-bürokratische Form der Entnazifizierung. Österreichische Justizakten im europäischen Vergleich.Überlegungen zum straf-prozessualen Entstehungszusammenhang und zu den Verwertungsmöglichkeiten für die historische Forschung* (Wien: Dokumentationsarchiv des österreichischen Widerstandes, 1995); Claudia Kuretsidis-Haider/Winfried R. Garscha (Hg.), *Keine »Abrechnung«. NS-Verbrechen, Justiz und Gesellschaft in Europa nach 1945* (Leipzig/Wien: Akademische Verlagsanstalt/Dokumentationsarchiv des österreichischen Widerstandes, 1998); Heimo Halbrainer/Claudia Kuretsidis-Haider (Hg.), *Kriegsverbrechen, NS-Gewaltverbrechen und die europäische Strafjustiz von Nürnberg bis Den Haag* (Graz: Clio, 2007); Claudia Kuretsidis-Haider, 'Das Volk sitzt zu Gericht'. *Österreichische Justiz und NS-Verbrechen am Beispiel der Engerau-Prozesse 1945–1954* (=Österreichische Justizgeschichte 2) (Innsbruck/Wien/Bozen: StudienVerlag, 2006); For Austrian People's Courts in Linz, Claudia Kuretsidis-Haider/Winfried R. Garscha, 'Das Linzer Volksgericht. Die Ahndung von NS-Verbrechen in Oberösterreich nach 1945', in Fritz Mayrhofer/Walter Schuster (Hg.), *Nationalsozialismus in Linz*, Bd. 2 (Linz: Archiv der Stadt Linz, 2001), pp. 1467–1561; On Austrian People's Courts in Styria, see Martin F. Polaschek, *Im Namen der Republik Österreich! Die Volksgerichte in der Steiermark 1945 bis 1955* (Graz: LAD-Zentralkanzlei, 1998); Heimo Halbrainer/Martin F. Polaschek, 'NS-Gewaltverbrechen vor den Volksgerichten Graz und Leoben', in Halbrainer/Kuretsidis-Haider (Hg.), *Kriegsverbrechen, Ibid*, pp. 236–50. Most of these works on the Austrian People's Courts focus on the Nazi atrocities or the Holocaust and have a different approach from this chapter, which tries to more directly connect the politics of the Austrian People's Courts with the question of building an Austrian nation.

6. 'Das Verfassungsgesetz vom 8. Mai 1945 über das Verbot der NSDAP (Verbotsgesetz)', in StGBl., 1945, Nr. 13; 'Verfassungsgesetz vom 26. Juni 1945 über Kriegsverbrechen und andere nationalsozialistische Untaten (Kriegsverbrechergesetz)', in StGBl., 1945, Nr. 32.

7. Adolf Schärf, *Zwischen Demokratie und Volksdemokratie. Österreichs Einigung undWiederaufrichtung im Jahre 1945* (Wien, 1950), pp. 100–02. The NSDAP had been banned in Austria between June 1933 and March 1938, but the 'Prohibition Act' fixed the beginning of its illegality for 1 July 1933.

8. See the Article 10 of the Prohibition Act (Das Verbotsgesetz).

9. See Kabinettsratsprotokolle (KRP), Nr. 12 (12. Juni 1945), in Gertrude Enderle-Burcel/Rudolf Jařábek/Leopold Kammerhofer (Hg.), *Protokolle des Kabinettsrates der Provisorischen Regierung Karl Renner 1945, '… im eigenen Haus Ordnung schaf-fen'. Protokolle des Kabinettsrates 29.April 1945 bis 10. Juli 1945* (Horn/Wien: Verlag Ferdinand Berger & Söhne, 1995), Bd. 1, pp. 206–07. See also Hiroko

Mizuno, "Die Vergangenheit ist vergessen". "Vergangenheitsbewältigung" in Österreich. Die österreichische Amnestiepolitik und die Reintgration der ehemaligen Nationalsozialisten 1945–1957 (Graz, Univ., Diss., 1999), p. 68.

10. See Mizuno, 'Die Hand zur Versöhnung ist geboten'.
11. KRP, Nr. 12 (12. Juni 1945), p. 206.
12. KRP, Nr. 13 (19./20. Juni 1945), pp. 261–62.
13. KRP, Nr. 13 (19./20. Juni 1945), pp. 265–66.
14. KRP, Nr. 13 (19./20. Juni 1945), pp. 265–67.
15. Cf. Polaschek, *Im Namen der Republik Österreich!*, p. 14.
16. Alfred Klahr played a vital role in developing the Communist theory of an Austrian nation in the late 1930s. On Alfred Klahr's works, see *Die Kommunisten im Kampf für die Unabhängigkeit Österreichs. Sammelband* (Wien: Stern Verlag, 1955); See also Helmut Konrad, 'Die Arbeiterbewegung und die österreichische Nation', in Helmut Konrad/Wolgang Neugebauer (Hg.), *Arbeiterbewegung-Faschismus-Nationalbewußtsein* (Wien/München/Zürich: Europaverlag, 1983), pp. 367–79, especially see p. 375; Cf. Manfred Mugrauer, *Die Politik der KPÖ in der Provisorischen Regierung Renner* (Innsbruck/Wien/ Bozen: StudienVerlag, 2006), p. 87.
17. Polaschek, *Im Namen der Republik Österreich!*, s. 12.
18. Karl Marschall, *Volksgerichtsbarkeit und Verfolgung von nationalsozialis-tischen Gewaltverbrechen in Österreich. Eine Dokumentation*, 2. Auflage (Wien: Bundesministerium für Justiz, 1987), p. 40.
19. The number of those accused of high treason and neonazi activities was excluded. Marschall, *Volksgerichtsbarkeit*, p. 42.
20. The number of those accused of 'high treason!' and 'neonazi activities' was excluded. Marschall, *Volksgerichtsbarkeit*, p. 42.
21. The number of those accused of 'high treason!' and 'neonazi activities' was excluded. Marschall, *Volksgerichtsbarkeit*, p. 42.
22. On Graz, for example, see Polaschek, *Im Namen der Republik Österreich*, pp. 23–27; For the situation of Linz, see Kuretsidis-Haider/Garscha, 'Das Linzer Volksgericht', p. 1477.
23. Marschall, *Volksgerichtsbarkeit*, pp. 117–18.
24. Winfried R. Garscha/Claudia Kuretsidis-Haider, 'Legionäre, DenunziantInnen, Illegale. Die Tätigkeit des Volksgerichts Linz', in Halbrainer/Kuretsidis-Haider, *Kriegsverbrechen*, pp. 251–69. Here, see p. 261.
25. On their brief profiles, see Claudia Kuretsidis-Haider, 'Volksgerichtsbarkeit und Entnazifizierung in Österreich', in Walter Schuster/Wolfgang Weber (Hg.), *Entnazifizierung im regionalen Vergleich* (Linz: Archiv der Stadt Linz, 2004), pp. 563–601. Here see, pp. 592–93. Regarding Neumayer's trial, see also Marschall, *Volksgerichtsbarkeit*, pp. 133–35.
26. On his career, see also Kuretsidis-Haider, '*Das Volk sitzt zu Gericht*', p. 403 (Anm. 42) and http://www.nachkriegsjustiz.at/prozesse/volksg/neumayer_urteil.php: Verlag der Wiener Volksbuchhandlung, (downloaded on 25 January 2012).
27. See also Kuretsidis-Haider, '*Das Volk sitzt zu Gericht*', p. 403 (Anm. 41).
28. *Der Hochverratsprozess gegen Dr.Guido Schmidt vor dem Wiener Volksgericht. Die gerichtlichen Protokolle mit den Zeugenaussagen, unveröffentlichten Dokumenten, sämtlichen Geheimbriefen und Geheimakten* (Wien: Druck und Verlag der österreichischen Staatsdruckerei, 1947), p. 659.

29. *Der Hochverratsprozess gegen Dr.Guido Schmidt vor dem Wiener Volksgericht*, pp. 659–90.
30. Marschall, Volksgerichtsbarkeit, pp. 40–41.
31. Garscha/Kuretsidis-Haider, 'Legionäre', p. 253
32. This bureaucratic decision soon became a problem for the government, because it made it very difficult to deny any demands for paying the pensions of 'lesser' Nazis who had been convicted of high treason, once they were found innocent through retrials. Robert Knight (Hg.), *'Ich bin dafür, die Sache in die Länge zu ziehen'. Die Wortprotokolle der österreichischen Bundesregierung von 1945 bis 1952 über die Entschädigung der Juden* (Wien/Köln/Weinar,: Böhlau, 2000) (1988[1]), pp. 168–70; Verhandlungsschrift (VHS) Nr. 197 (21. März 1950), in Ministerratsprotokolle (MRP), Archiv der Republik (AdR).
33. 'Verfassungsgesetz vom 30. November 1945 über das Verfahren vor dem Obersten Gerichtshof in Volksgerichtssachen (Überprüfungsgesetz)', in *Bundesgesetzblatt für die Republik Österreich* (BGBl.), 1946, Nr. 4; Cf. Marschall, *Volksgerichtsbarkeit*, p. 13.
34. Kuretsidis-Haider/Garscha, 'Das Linzer Volksgericht', p. 1478.
35. Dieter Stiefel, *Entnazifizierung in Österreich*, (Europaverlag: Wien/München/Zürich, 1981) p. 255.
36. Rudolf Neck, 'Innenpolitische Entwicklung', in Erika Weinzierl/ Kurt Skalnik (Hg.), *Österreich. Die Zweite Republik*, Bd. 1 (Graz/Wien/Köln: Verlag Styria, 1972), pp. 149–68. Here see p. 156.
37. 'Vom Jahresende an: Naziprozesse im ordentlichen Verfahren. Noch 1500 Volksgerichtsverfahren – 260 Häftlinge warten auf Ihre Aburteilung', in *Neues Österreich* (22. September 1948), p. 4.
38. 'Parlament für Auflösung der Volksgerichte!', in *Die Presse* (10. November 1948), p. 1.
39. VHS/MRP, Nr. 114/3 (2. Juni 1948), AdR.
40. 'Figl: Volksgerichte sollen mit Ende dieses Jahres eingestellt werden', : *Wiener Kurier* (12. September 1949), p. 1.
41. *Arbeiter Zeitung* (8. Juli 1949), p. 2.
42. VHS/MRP, Nr. 178 (4. November 1949), AdR; VHS/MRP, Nr. 216 (5. September 1950), AdR.
43. Garscha/Kuretsidis-Haider, 'Legionäre', p. 254.
44. *Wiener Zeitung* (16. November 1955), p. 2.
45. *Stenographisches Protokoll. 91. Sitzung des Nationalrates der Republik Österreich:* Österreichische Staatsdruckerei (20. Dezember 1955), pp. 4497–500.
46. Anton Pelinka, 'Auseinandersetzung mit dem Kommunismus', in Weinzierl/ Skalnik (Hg.), *Österreich. Die Zweite Republik*, pp. 169–201. Here see p. 191.
47. Otto Bauer, 'Integraler Sozialismus', in Alfred Pfabigan (Hg.), *Vision und Wirklichkeit: Löcker Verlag Ein Lesebuch zum Austromarxismus* (Wien, 1989), pp. 218–34.
48. Erwin Scharf, 'Vorwort', in *Die Linkssozialisten (Hg.), Otto Bauer über Demokratie und Arbeitereinheit* (Wien: Freunde des Neuen Vorwörts-Vereinigung Fortschrittlicher Sozialisten, 1950), (pp. 3–6).
49. Pelinka, 'Auseinandersetzung mit dem Kommunismus', pp. 191–92.
50. *Stenographisches Protokoll. 34.Sitzung des Nationalrates der Republik Österreich* (22. November 1950), pp. 1341–42.

Part II
The Dialectical Interplay of History and Memory

5
Ukraine Faces Its Soviet Past: History versus Policy versus Memory

Volodymyr V. Kravchenko

Since the dissolution of the Soviet Union in 1991, Ukrainian society has remained in limbo, caught between communism and nationalism, between the former identity of Ukraine as a Soviet socialist republic and its current identity as a formally independent nation state. The conceptualisation of (post-)Soviet Ukraine appears to be an extremely difficult task. Both Ukrainian national space and time belong to several overlapping symbolic geographies and to various transnational, intertwined histories. Accordingly, they are viewed from a great variety of different research perspectives. No wonder the field of contemporary Ukrainian studies is replete with such terminology as 'contradictions', 'paradoxes', and even 'schizophrenia'. Obviously, something must be wrong either with Ukraine or with Ukrainian studies.

The inertia of the Soviet way of life in contemporary Ukraine increasingly compels some scholars to declare it a post-Soviet, neo-Soviet, or post-communist entity.[1] Stephen Kotkin describes the period 1970–2000 of Russia's history as 'an integrated whole', as 'the sudden onset, and then inescapable prolongation, of the death agony of an entire world comprising non-market economics and anti-liberal institutions'.[2] I consider his observation to be applicable to contemporary Ukraine as well. History there, as in other post-communist countries, is in no way perceived as a remote phenomenon: it is a living system of institutions, norms and values. No wonder history has turned out to be the key to the theory and practice of nation and state building undertaken in Ukraine.[3]

The impact of history on the transformation of post-communist societies has been analysed from numerous different angles.[4] Yaroslav Hrytsak, for example, emphasises 'the crucial role' that historical legacies play 'in shaping different patterns of post-communist economic, political, and cultural developments in Eastern Europe'.[5] Other historians are more cautious in their evaluations of the impact of the past on the post-communist present.[6] Recently the focus in some of the debates has shifted from 'The Past' to many 'Pasts', and toward the concept of multiple historical legacies with multiple roles in the post-communist transformation.[7]

All former communist republics, as Taras Kuzio put it, 'are in the process of searching for their "lost" history in the pre-imperial era in order to confirm that they possess "golden eras" and a workable past that can be used to legitimise their newly independent states'.[8] In other words, national historical legacies are being employed to oppose communist legacies. However, Soviet Ukraine was neither colony nor nation state sensu stricto: it was engineered as a mini-Soviet Union and has acquired both modern Soviet ideological and pre-modern Rus'-Orthodox components of the Soviet historical legacy, complementing them with its own modern national identity. Nowadays these components are institutionalised and politically articulated, laying the foundations for both Russian/Soviet and Ukrainian identities in the Ukrainian socium, with a vague 'middle ground' between the two.[9]

The combination of modern with pre-modern components makes the Ukrainian 'burden of history' extremely heavy to manage.[10] The concept of multiple historical legacies is rarely employed to analyse the Soviet past, despite a few exceptions.[11] The Soviet phenomenon is sometimes perceived as supra-national or even international in contrast to modern national or local particularism. My understanding of the nature of the Soviet epoch is different. I consider the Soviet identity to be at least two-fold, compounded of both ideological Soviet (communist) and imperial-religious Rus' (Orthodox) elements. Lenin's communist utopia and Stalin's more pragmatic blending of modern Sovietness with premodern Russianness laid foundations for the two main Soviet myths, respectively: 'The Great October Socialist Revolution' and the 'Great Patriotic War'.

Contemporary post-Soviet Ukraine is the product of a particular period of Soviet history, namely the Brezhnev epoch of the late 1960s to the early 1980s, which was the formative period for the present generation of Ukrainian politicians. This epoch was ridiculed by Soviet democratic intellectuals and despised by political dissidents as a period of 'zastoi' (stagnation), but it has come to be perceived as a Golden Age of stability and prosperity for the ordinary people.[12] From this point of view the Brezhnev epoch has in itself been turned into a kind of new historical mythology, aspiring to synthesise both Leninist and Stalinist myths in the national post-Soviet narrative.

Coming to terms with the national past is considered to be a precondition for a successful post-Communist transformation, including that of Ukraine. If so, this means that a newly created national narrative must be acceptable to all three major public actors in the realm of national public discourse: to the professional community of scholars, to the state, and to society. This in turn means that historical narrative, history policy and collective memory are all in a process of an endless negotiation, or so this chapter argues. In what follows I will try to answer three central questions: How is the recent Ukrainian past[13] being conceptualised by Ukrainian professional historians? How is it being exploited by political elites? How is this past being perceived by ordinary people? I will focus on three periods of Ukrainian history: the revolution and civil war of 1917–1920; the Stalin period; and the Brezhnev epoch, as they are all represented in post-Soviet Ukraine.[14]

Professional historical writing

Who holds the key to the Ukrainian past? Professional historians, of course, or so they think. After the disintegration of the Soviet Union Ukrainian Soviet historians were challenged by three main tasks: to reconsider their professional and personal identities; to dismantle the old and create the new historiographical canon; and to answer to up-to-date intellectual challenges in the humanities. Responding to these challenges has triggered a complex process of political, ideological and methodological differentiation within the professional community of scholars.[15]

However, post-Soviet Ukrainian historiography still resists any strict classificatory systemisation, because the vast majority of Ukrainian historians seek to avoid any methodologically articulated statement. Almost all texts produced by these professionals are highly eclectic. Sometimes it is even difficult to recognise the author's individual identity behind the agglomeration of quotations, references and factual findings. Because of this, any attempt at taxonomy must be limited. For the purposes of this chapter, I will review three central trends in contemporary Ukrainian historical writing, taking into account not only 'normative' academic texts – with their hidden or open messages – but their authors' styles of thinking and writing as well.

The first and the most influential trend or school in contemporary Ukrainian historical writing is represented by official, 'normative' texts produced by academic historians. They are a well-entrenched community of scholars, based on the unreformed Ukrainian Academy of Sciences, which in the Soviet era was embedded in the party-state bureaucratic hierarchy. Following the dissolution of the Soviet Union this school of historical writing has formally adopted the nation state paradigm as its guiding principle, but generally speaking, methodological eclecticism and the production of semi-normative texts still remain the principal features of this amorphous and contradictory academic historiography. That is why I call it 'post-Soviet' historical writing. It dominates professional interpretations of the recent Ukrainian past.[16]

The next is a national school of historical writing based on the nation state paradigm. It is represented by two main versions – a traditional one, elaborated in the first half of the twentieth century, and a second one that was modernised in the second half of the same century by Ivan Lysiak-Rudnytsky and the first generation of specialists in Ukrainian studies trained in Western Universities. The national school of historical writing seems to be less influential compared with the aforementioned post-Soviet school, in terms of institutional structure.[17] The traditional Ukrainian historical narrative is based on a semi-religious approach to the past (salvation through suffering, glorification and victimisation), a primordialist concept of nation and the idea of the '1000 years of Ukrainian state'. The modernised version of Ukrainian national history could be called revisionist, for its proponents question some of the fundamental tenets of traditional historical writing such as the continuity and discontinuity of the Ukrainian nation-building process, the colonial status of Ukraine within the Russian empire and the role of the Soviet elite in Ukrainian history.[18]

The third or modern (post-national) school of historical writing is influenced by the cultural turn in the Western humanities of the second half of the twentieth century and acts as a merciless critic of the traditional nation state paradigm of Ukrainian past. Modern Ukrainian historians are sometimes seen as mediators between the native and the Western humanities. Compared with the two aforementioned historiographical schools, this trend is the weakest, with limited institutional, normative and political influence. It is represented mostly by a comparatively few western-oriented individuals and is connected with some NGOs and new periodicals.[19]

Generally speaking, contemporary Ukrainian historiography is not yet ready for discussion and reassessment of the Soviet past at the level of modern methodology. According to Yaroslav Hrytsak, 'in itself, the unwillingness of Ukrainian historians to study this theme [of the Soviet past] is the sign of deep Sovietisation of Ukrainian society. If it would have greater resolve to get rid of the communist legacy, discussions [on this topic] would be inevitable'.[20] Instead, the majority of Ukrainian historians – being incapable of restoring their autonomous, corporative professional status within post-Soviet society – are still involved in the ideological and political struggle between the Ukrainian and Soviet/Rus' nationalisms and their respective historical mythologies.

In chronological terms the leading field of study in academic research on Ukrainian Soviet history is the Stalinist epoch.[21] After or near to it in prevalence comes the history of the revolution and civil war of 1917–1920. The second half of the twentieth century is of considerably less focus compared with the first one in terms of scientific preferences and number of publications.[22] The main interest of scholars is in the state-political and national aspects of the Ukrainian historical process, the creation and the functioning of the Soviet party-state system, and the history of elites.

The history of the revolution of 1917 and the civil war once laid the very foundation of Soviet historiography and historical mythology. Ukrainian historians are trying to re-conceptualise this historical epoch by employing the nation state paradigm.[23] They have created a concept of the Ukrainian national revolution as an integral and original phenomenon different from the Russian Revolution. However, there is a notable variation among them in approaching and interpreting the events: for example, between such a prominent scholar as Valerii Soldatenko, committed to the Soviet style of historical writing, on the one hand, and national and modern-oriented historians such as Vladyslav Verstiuk or Yaroslav Hrytsak, on the other.

The traditional nation state historiography is inclined to mythologise events in Ukraine, exaggerating the state-leading political potential of Ukrainian national leaders, emphasising for example episodes of martial glory such as the Battle of Kruty – the 'Ukrainian Thermopylae' – and interpreting them in terms of a national Ukrainian-Russian struggle. In the writings of Ivan Lysiak-Rudnytsky and his followers, along with the rhetoric of 'Soviet Russian occupation', one finds observations on the 'unreadiness' of the 'Ukrainian people' for political independence and on the 'underdevelopment' of the modern Ukrainian nation, which did not attain an appropriate 'condition' or 'maturity' until the late 1920s in the course of the communist national policy of 'Ukrainisation', only to have its development set back by the Stalinist terror of the 1930s.

Numerous efforts to 'nationalise' the Soviet paradigm of the 'Great October' in contemporary Ukraine have so far failed to offer a satisfactory explanation for why the modern project of Ukrainian national statehood came to grief; or to come up with a coherent explanation of the political chaos that prevailed in the fragmented Ukrainian territory during the disintegration of the Romanov and Habsburg empires; or to solve the problem of reconciling of competing national historical narratives – Ukrainian, Russian, Soviet, Polish and Jewish. In this regard, some of the specialists question the very applicability of the nation state paradigm to Ukrainian and Russian histories of the post-imperial period.[24] Thus, Heorhii Kasianov, who represents the modern trend in Ukrainian post-Soviet historical writing, deconstructs the phenomenon of the 'Ukrainian national revolution', emphasising that the course of events in the Ukrainian lands was determined by a variety of factions, none of which garnered notable social support.[25] By contrast, another representative of modern Ukrainian historiography, Yaroslav Hrytsak, denies the notion of the weakness of Ukrainian national movement before and during the disintegration of the Russian Empire and stresses the 'normality' of the Ukrainian national revolutionary experience in principle. Still, the poorly discussed term 'Ukrainian national revolution' looks more like rhetoric than a concept, yet in this capacity dominates professional historical writing.

In Ukrainian historiography, both Lenin's and Stalin's political regimes are considered to be the epoch of the establishment and evolution of the Soviet totalitarian system. The concept of totalitarianism has provided Ukrainian post-Soviet historiography with its basic methodological orientation in the general interpretation of Soviet history. The leading Ukrainian expert on the Soviet era, Stanislav Kulchytsky, inclines to the view that the Soviet system was totalitarian from the very beginning. Violence and state terror are considered immanent features of the totalitarian regime, to be explained by the very nature of the communist system.

The Stalin era is regarded as the apogee of Soviet totalitarianism. Ukrainian academic historiography generally describes Stalinism in the spirit and accusatory tonality of the *perestroika* period, with its characteristic emphasis on the political repression and crimes of the communist system. In the traditional national historical narrative, Ukraine appears mainly as a victim of that system. The totalitarian regime is regarded as something external, forcibly imposed on Ukraine by Russia. One of the exponents of this idea is Serhii Bilokin, a historian of the 'nation state' orientation who has written a source study of the system of political repression in the USSR (awarded the Taras Shevchenko National Prize in 2002) and depicts the Soviet period as a mere interruption in the course of Ukrainian history. Contrary to this notion, Yaroslav Hrytsak inclines to the views that even 'the Red terror was not all that great a deviation from Ukrainian history'.[26]

The Holodomor or the Great Famine of 1932–1933 is considered the apogee of Ukrainian national martyrdom in the Soviet period,[27] and the discussions surrounding it have continued unabated. Was the Famine man-made and deliberately organised, or the result of 'objective' circumstances? Did it acquire a social dimension or the Ukrainian national one? Can the Famine be considered genocide? Who is responsible for the death of millions of peasants – communism as a system and an ideology, or the Stalinist leadership in particular? What criteria are to determine the understanding of this tragedy: legal, moral, or political? Finally, what does the concept of the 'Ukrainian people' mean in this instance – an ethno-culture or a political community?

In the Ukrainian (post-)Soviet academic mainstream, the conceptualisation of the Famine as genocide has been institutionalised by the academic Research Center on the Genocide of the Ukrainian People, established in 2002. Stanislav Kulchytsky emphasises the territorial and political, not the ethno-cultural sense of 'Ukrainian people', using this concept to encompass all 'national, ethnic, and religious groups' living on Ukrainian territory.[28] Ukrainian nationalist historiography, by contrast, accents the ethno-cultural factors, resorting at times to openly anti-Semitic and xenophobic expressions. Contrary to this, the official Russian historiography denies that the Holodomor had an ethnic – in particular, a specifically Ukrainian – aspect and that it can be termed genocide at all. Modern Ukrainian historians prefer to focus on representations of the Famine in contemporary public and academic discourses.[29]

The world of the academic community of scholars is split in its attitude to this theme. Some Western historians (Andrea Graziosi, Bohdan Krawchenko, Taras Kuzio, Elizabeth Haigh) share the view, with certain reservations, that the Famine in Ukraine bore all (or at least the main) characteristics of genocide. Others acknowledge the man-made character and scale of the Famine but deny that it was the genocide of ethnic Ukrainians (Hiroaki Kuromiya, Mikhail Molchanov, David Marples, John-Paul Himka, Terry Martin). It seems that the topic of the Ukrainian Holodomor is capable of reanimating the old 'totalitarianists-revisionists' discussions in Western Russian/Soviet studies of the second half of the twentieth century.

The historiography of Ukraine in World War II is no less, or even more, replete with passion than that of the Holodomor.[30] It ties several competing national narratives into a tight knot: the Polish narrative, which emphasises the heroic struggle of the Home Army (Armia Krajowa) against two totalitarian regimes (Stalinist and Hitlerite), as well as the Ukrainian nationalists; the Jewish narrative, based on the paradigms of anti-Semitism and the Holocaust; the Ukrainian narrative, which resembles the Polish one in its depiction of Ukraine as the victim of Hitler and Stalin, while its heroic discourse is associated with the activity of the OUN-UPA; and, finally, the Russian/Soviet narrative, rooted in the mythology of the Great Patriotic War and the 'struggle of the whole Soviet people' against the external enemy.

With reference to the latter, it is worth noting that for some Western historians it is difficult to grasp the double nature (*Neslitnost' i nerazdel'nost'*) of the Soviet/Rus' phenomenon.[31] Sometimes in giving preference to the 'communist' component of the Soviet ideology over the Rus'-Orthodox one, even well-known specialists in the field turn out to be poor prophets. This was recently brought to mind by Sheila Fitzpatrick, who in 2004 predicted that the myth of the 'Great Patriotic War' would gradually lose influence in Russian society.[32] She based this on the disappearance of the Soviet nation and the Soviet superpower, for which the Great Patriotic War had been the principal legitimising myth. This prognosis turned out to be the exact opposite of what actually happened.

Not only did the mythology of the 'Great Patriotic War' fail to disappear, but it laid the main foundations for the Russian post-Soviet, neo-imperial ideology and policy, heavily seasoned with anti-Westernism and Orthodoxy along with an almost inevitable glorification or even sacralisation of Stalin.[33] Like the Jewish national narrative of the war, the Russian one has a religious basis and, as Lev Gudkov points out, it is undergoing intensive sacralisation that blocks all attempts to take a rational view of the past. Unlike the Jewish narrative, however, the Russian one is based on motifs of martial glory and victory, not tragedy and suffering. In this instance, the drumbeat drowns out motifs of remembrance, reconciliation and empathy. It should be noted that some Ukrainian historians share the contemporary Russian interpretation of the Great Patriotic War mythology in their political struggle with Ukrainian nationalism.

Ukrainian national historiography strives to represent Ukraine as a conquered nation that fought heroically against two totalitarianisms, Nazi and Soviet, at once.[34] The place occupied by the Home Army in the Polish national narrative is reserved in the Ukrainian narrative for the OUN-UPA, whose programme announced a struggle for Ukrainian national statehood against Nazis, Communists and Polish nationalists. But the attempt to include the OUN-UPA into Ukrainian historical narrative encounters insurmountable difficulties associated with evaluations of the ideology and the representative nature of these organisations.

Should the OUN and the UPA be regarded as nationalist or fascist organisations? Whom exactly did they represent: the western region, or the whole Ukrainian nation? These questions – raised by efforts to arrive at a rational assessment of the recent past – encounter competition on all sides, either from the tradition of a Manichean distinction between communism and fascism inherited from the times of the Second World War, or from resistance to the Ukrainian traditional, Russian, Jewish and Polish national narratives.[35] Ukrainian-Polish debates about the Volhynia massacre of 1943 have demonstrated the immanent incompatibility of the two respective national myths of WWII.

Ukrainian post-Soviet historians, unlike Russian ones, have resorted to an eclectic combination of the national and Soviet paradigms of the 'Second World War' and the 'Great Patriotic War'. David Marples has noted the contradictory coexistence in some Ukrainian history textbooks of assertions about Soviet 'slavery', 'Victory Day', and 'liberation from fascist slavery'.[36] The same historians, in his words, are capable of coming out simultaneously with opposing assessments of the role of the Red Army in battles on Ukrainian territory, depending on the genre of the publication and the prevailing political conjuncture. Consequently, the prospects of a Ukrainian 'nationalisation' of the Second World War look rather cloudy.

Post-Soviet Ukrainian historiography attempts to present Ukraine as an independent subject, not only an object of military operations, by stressing the fact of Soviet Ukrainian statehood. Naturally, this endows the Soviet version of the Great Patriotic War with a certain 'Ukrainocentrism', but only at the price of distorting historical perspective. It is also clear that this largely official interpretation of the problem looks particularly unconvincing against the background of Russian 'statist' historiography. The symbolic capital of Soviet Ukraine in the Stalin era is insufficient to provide either academic respectability or a competitive national mythology.

In general, most Ukrainian historians remain not only hostages of, but also active participants in the wars over nationalised historical memories and their respective mythologies.[37] However, the Ukrainian historical mythology of the Second World War in its nation state version yields substantially both to the Soviet/Russian and Polish national mythologies of military glory. Against this background it puts up a pessimistic tableau of suffering and defeat, but in this case the Ukrainian narrative is challenged openly by Jewish mythology and the Holocaust. To make matters worse, the Ukrainian national paradigm of the War not only entails a war of mythologies but has also provoked an open split within the professional historical community both in Ukraine and beyond.[38]

In recent years, Ukrainian historiography has seen growing efforts to go beyond the framework of a national paradigm. Yaroslav Hrytsak, for instance, does not relieve the UPA leadership of responsibility for unleashing mass terror against the Polish inhabitants of Ukrainian territory, but he acknowledges that in the suicidal struggle between two nationalisms, Ukrainian and Polish, 'neither side ... was either completely right or completely guilty'.[39] A new generation of Ukrainian scholars, rather than calculating who was good and who was bad, is turning to an anthropological perspective, focusing on Ukrainian ordinary people and dealing with oral history, historical memory, and replacing 'social reality' with the problems of representation.[40]

Generally speaking, the subjects of the Ukrainian Holodomor and Ukrainian War now seem so politicised that public discussions increasingly obscure not only the tragedies of particular individuals but also the strictly scholarly aspects of the problems. Under such circumstances, it is very hard to expect the attainment of a consensus in the academic community. The only viable intellectual alternative to the war of national mythologies, as Olexandr Zaitcev suggests, may be found in the gradual desacralisation and demythologisation of the history of the War[41] and, it should be added, of the whole recent history of Ukraine. However, this seems an unlikely scenario, at least for the near future.

All the main trends of Ukrainian post-Soviet historiography, in their own ways, vividly reveal the limits of the nation state paradigm in depicting the Brezhnev epoch of Ukrainian history. In the Ukrainian national narrative it is coloured darkly as the period of stagnation, economic decline and moral degradation, and is perceived in terms of dissidents' heroic struggle with a corrupt regime and Brezhnev's neo-Stalinist policy of persecuting Ukrainian culture and Russification. Political history traditionally dominates the Ukrainian historical narrative of the period, while the influence of the cultural anthropology or memory studies in the field are still insufficient to have a major impact.

Generally speaking, neither the national nor the post-Soviet schools of historiography in Ukraine have put forward new approaches or versions for the interpretation of recent Ukrainian history. The mythology of national suffering and heroic resistance that oppose the founding Soviet myths – those of the Great October Socialist Revolution and the Great Patriotic War – often do not stand up to criticism, since Ukrainians are to be found not only among the victims but also among the perpetrators as well.

The traditional nation state paradigm is unable to draw a clear line between imperial and modern nation state. That is why it sometimes describes imperial political and ideological phenomena as national, which is misleading, as the history of the Russian empire and Soviet Union suggests. The same could be said about another dichotomy – national and modern phenomena: all that is 'Ukrainian' is often depicted by Ukrainian historians as inherently 'modern', although in social reality the two sometimes were and are hardly compatible.

Employing dubious national terminology – the *Naród*/Nation dichotomy – is another original sin of Ukrainian historical writing, reflected in the Ukrainian language. The Slavic equivalent for 'nation', *naród*, coined by Polish intellectuals and borrowed by Russian and Ukrainian authors, has acquired a double meaning in the Ukrainian cultural context: it is social as well as national. Any English translation of the definition of '*naród*' seems inadequate. The *Naród*/Nation dichotomy has given rise to many controversies and mutual misunderstandings not only between socialism and nationalism but between Ukrainian and Russian interpretations of their recent history as well.

In the search for alternatives to both the Soviet and national paradigms of Ukrainian history, at least some Ukrainian intellectuals take into account that the Soviet regime would not have existed so long or left such deep traces in society unless it had enjoyed social support. In this connection, the observations of the prominent literary scholar and essayist, Ivan Dziuba, also deserve attention. I would like to emphasise the importance of this author, for he represents the 'lost' generation of the 1960s with its leftist, national-Marxist state of mind and its orientation toward social history. This trend in Ukrainian historiography was suppressed first by the bureaucratic academic discourse of the Brezhnev epoch and second by traditional national discourse, but it still holds intellectual, theoretical potential that could be useful under the current Ukrainian circumstances.

Another alternative to the nation state paradigm in the interpretation of Ukrainian recent history was offered recently by a group of modern historians under the leadership of Natalia Yakovenko.[42] Participants in the project of elaborating the new version of the Ukrainian history textbook

> renounced the previous view of Ukraine as a victim of the communist system.... On the contrary, an effort is being made to show that the Ukrainian SSR was a co-participant in the functioning of that system in both positive manifestations (education, industrialisation, and the like) and criminal ones—mass political repression, collectivisation, and the Holodomor.[43]

The new conception is oriented less toward a total condemnation and rejection of the Soviet system than toward 'a discussion of the advantages and drawbacks of the Soviet order in everyday human life'. In other words, the search for an alternative to the nation state paradigm of Ukrainian history is leading in the direction of cultural anthropology. Naturally, a project of this nature has already been subjected to sharp and uncompromising criticism by representatives of the national Ukrainian and Soviet traditionalists.

There are several other intellectual, scholarly alternatives that could be employed in the process of renovation and modernisation of Ukrainian historiography in its attempt to come to terms with the Soviet past. For example, cultural anthropology, memory studies, border studies and modernisation paradigm, to name just a few, offer viable approaches and interpretive frameworks that could be applied to recent Ukrainian history. The problem, however, is that the Ukrainian community of scholars is still half-closed, has no motivation to adopt intellectual innovations or is not yet ready to act on the principles of constructive dialog. At the same time, it must be said that Ukrainian studies reveal not only significant political and emotional implications but some theoretical limits of contemporary Western Soviet and Russian studies as well, especially those ones dealing with the phenomenon of nationalism.[44]

History as politics

Once again: who holds the keys to the Ukrainian past? Professional politicians, of course, or so they think. In what follows, the discussion includes the ways in which Ukrainian post-Soviet political elites are participating in the process of shaping, re-shaping and manipulating narratives of the Ukrainian Soviet past for political purposes, beginning with the first President, Leonid Kravchuk, and ending with the incumbent President, Viktor Yanukovych.[45]

President Kravchuk's politics of history were based on the concept of a Ukrainian national revival, developed by the founding father of Ukrainian national historiography, Mykhailo Hrushevsky, enhanced by the 'state' school of Ukrainian historical writing in the first half of the twentieth century and adopted by Ukrainian post-Soviet historiography. This formula combined an imagined '1000 years of Ukrainian state' with a European geopolitical identity that was conceptualised in opposition to the Russian imperial and Soviet/Russian official narratives.

The history of Ukraine, previously downplayed, became the main tool in a process of political legitimisation of the new political regime under

Kravchuk. Historians were promoted to high-ranked administrative positions in the state apparatus at all levels, much like those occupied earlier by professional party ideologists in the party bureaucratic hierarchy. For example, the position of Vice-Premier in charge of the Humanities during Kravchuk's and Kucham's presidencies was usually reserved for representatives of the respective academic institutes of Ukrainian Academy of Sciences.

During this period, Cossack mythology became an important component of the 'Ukrainisation' of the previously Soviet cultural landscape.[46] The history of the short-lived Ukrainian national state of 1917–1920 (Ukrains'ka Narodna Respublika [UNR] or Ukrainian People's Republic) became of no less political importance. President Leonid Kravchuk, a former leading Communist party ideologue, solemnly accepted the symbols of state authority of their predecessors – the Cossack hetman's mace along with the regalia of the UNR government. National symbols of the UNR – the 'trident' coat-of-arms and the yellow-blue flag – acquired official status in Ukraine.

During Kravchuk's presidency, the mythology of the Great October Socialist Revolution began to be replaced by the mythology of Ukrainian modern national statehood and its main representatives such as Mykhailo Hrushevsky, Pavlo Skoropadsky, Symon Petliura and other 'great statesmen'. Two national historical myths were inherited from this epoch by the new political regime. The first symbolised the idea of Ukrainian territorial and national unity, when the two parts of Ukraine – the Western Ukrainian People's Republic and the Ukrainian Peoples Republic – were proclaimed a one and 'indivisible' nation state in 1919. The second myth was an embodiment of national glorification and victimisation known as the Battle of Kruty of 1918, when several hundred Ukrainian students were killed by Bolshevik detachments approaching Kiev.

As to the Soviet mythology of the Great Patriotic War of 1941–1945, it began to be counterbalanced by the mythology of Stalinist crimes. The government opened the doors of the Communist Party and KGB archives to professional historians and sponsored several publishing projects aiming at revealing Soviet crimes during the Great Terror and the Great Famine of the 1930s. A special editorial board and institution, 'Rehabilitated by History', was created, with the academic historian Petro Tron'ko, a representative of the republican Soviet nomenclatura of the 1960s, at its head. It was followed by the newly established and officially sponsored periodical 'From the archives VUChK-GPU-NKVD-KGB', which published some of the documents of the Soviet secret police. In order to marginalise the mythology of the Great Patriotic War, an attempt was made to replace it with the more universal, more neutral and more Western-oriented term 'World War II'.

President Leonid Kravchuk was replaced in 1994 by the former Soviet manufacturing director from Dniepropetrovsk, Leonid Kuchma, whose professional background seemingly made him more suitable under the hard economic circumstances. The new political elite of his time in office had spent its formative years during Leonid Brezhnev's reign. No wonder the political regime established in Ukraine in 1994 turned out to be, according to Ilia Prizel, 'national by form and Brezhnevite in essence'.[47] President Kuchma began the ten-year period of his presidency with political maneuvering between nationalism and communism, using the rhetoric of 'national revival' in parallel with the familiar rhetoric of Soviet-era propaganda. The new political regime, as was expected, demonstratively rejected the 'national romantic' concept of Ukrainian nation state building, and began a cautious, selective rehabilitation of the Soviet/Russian historical legacy. At the same time, President Kuchma continued the policy of historical legitimisation of the independent Ukrainian nation state with its current borders.[48] The official politics of history underwent some important symbolic changes in terms of both time and space. In terms of chronology, the new political regime gradually re-oriented its historical preferences from the remote past to the modern epoch. A new generation of the political elite preferred to initiate the history of a Ukrainian independent state not with Kievan Prince Volodymyr the Saint, or Cossack hetman Bohdan Khmelnytsky, or even historian-politician Mykhailo Hrushevsky, but with themselves. Hence, the slogan of the 'young Ukrainian state' began to replace the previously popular slogan of the '1000-year' Ukrainian state; it became visible especially during the pompous official celebration of the tenth jubilee of Ukrainian independency in 2001. In Kharkiv, the new monument to Ukrainian independent statehood erected that year represented the image of a 10-year-old girl.[49]

President Kuchma also decided to restore the Soviet-era mythology of the Great Patriotic War, which was reinstated in the Ukrainian educational curriculum. The celebration of Victory Day on 9 May once again became one of the most important state rituals, as it had been in Brezhnev's epoch.[50] However, the Soviet version of the Great Patriotic War appeared to be incompatible with the Ukrainian national mythology of heroic military resistance to the Soviet army led by OUN-UPA.[51] Thus, the annual official celebration of the Great Patriotic War came to be marked by street clashes between Soviet veterans and their nationalist counterparts. The government, unable to reconcile these competing national mythologies, not unreasonably turned to the Ukrainian Academy of Sciences: a special commission of historians was established to investigate the political nature and activity of the OUN-UPA. Several monographs, articles and primary sources were published by this commission, but both sides of the struggle over this topic in history refused to recognise its findings.

In order to counterbalance the mythology of the Great Patriotic War, President Kuchma continued the policy of his predecessor of revealing the crimes of Stalin. So the state continued to support both the 'Rehabilitated by History' and the 'From the archives VUChK-GPU-NKVD-KGB' initiatives that were devoted to the theme of the Great Terror. In parallel with this, the Great Famine of 1932–3 was for the first time officially christened 'genocide of the Ukrainian people' by the Ukrainian Verkhovna Rada (parliament). However, the inconsistencies of Kuchma's politics of history were revealed as the government officially commemorated the seventieth year of the Great Famine while simultaneously celebrating achievements of Stalin's industrialisation such as the Dnieproges dam.

In contrast with the Great Patriotic War theme, the mythology and celebration of the Great October Socialist Revolution suffered further decline in Kuchma's Ukraine. This greatest of the Soviet state holidays was officially abolished in 2000 and replaced by the obscure Day of Social Workers. It is worth stressing that in Russia the Great October holiday was replaced by the pure nationalistic Day of National Unity, marked by the expulsion of 'unholy' Catholic Poles in 1612 from behind the 'sacred wall of the Kremlin'. At the same time, President Kuchma's government continued to exploit the mythology of Ukrainian National Re-unification of 1919 and the Battle of Kruty of 1918; Mykhailo Hrushevsky's cult was also preserved and widely popularised. This kind of policy met with comparatively weak resistance in Ukraine but came into collision with both the Polish mythology of national revival, and the Jewish mythology of national suffering on Ukrainian territory.[52]

President Kuchma's regime attempted to reconcile the conflicting memories of the most important epoch of Soviet history, namely the Brezhnev epoch, of which contemporary Ukraine is a direct product. The official commemoration of the former political dissident Viacheslav Chornovil, who died in an accident under suspicious circumstances in 1999, was followed by the official commemoration of the 85th anniversary of the head of the Ukrainian branch of the Communist Party of the Soviet Union, Vladimir Shcherbitsky. Needless to say, both camps – orthodox Communists and orthodox Nationalists – remained dissatisfied.

President Kuchma's 'Change of Signposts' in his politics of history resulted in even more contradictory consequences. He managed to achieve economic stability partly through concessions to regional post-Soviet elites who in turn won a significant opportunity to correct the historical policy of official Kiev. The cultural landscape of Ukraine during Kuchma's presidency began to absorb local historical symbols in growing quantity: Ukrainian ones in the Western part of Ukraine, along with Soviet and neo-Soviet ones in its eastern and southern regions. The President, visiting these various regions, addressed local groups of auditors with what each of them wanted to hear: in Lviv he expounded on the glories or sorrows of the national past, while in Donets'k, on the great achievements of Soviet power.

Kuchma's regime offered no ideological alternatives; instead, he simply canned mutually antagonistic communist and nationalist myths and stereotypes. This approach resulted in the further regional and political polarisation of Ukrainian society. Besides, the Brezhnev-style double-thinking was accompanied by widespread corruption, political criminality, and 'wild' privatisation; no wonder it had alienated a new, western-oriented generation of the middle class. In the end, Kuchma's regime, sharing some of its most basic features with those of Brezhnev's, shared also its political fortune. Kuchma lost all moral legitimacy and was swept away by the Orange Revolution of 2004.

The newly elected Ukrainian President, Victor Yushchenko, refused to pursue the tactics of political maneuvering between nationalism and communism that had been employed by his predecessor. Instead, President Yushchenko decided to activate the good old 'national revival' mythology with its theme of '1000 years of Ukrainian state'. The new political regime relied upon the nationally oriented segments of Ukrainian academia and society. However, for the first time since 1991, professionals from academia were not represented in the new government. It seemed that the new President was not happy with the Ukrainian Academy of Sciences. Maybe that's why he entrusted himself with the task of being the primary expert in Ukrainian history.

President Yushchenko was personally attracted to the mythic abyss of the Trypillia archaeological epoch and Ukrainian Cossackdom. However, political expediency forced him to pay most attention to recent, mainly Soviet, history. Thus, the new regime decided to rush into a frontal attack on both Soviet foundation myths simultaneously. The myth of the Great October Socialist Revolution was confronted by the traditional mythology of the National Re-Union and the Battle of Kruty. The mythology of the Great Patriotic War, the main target of the new politics of memory, was challenged by the Holodomor and OUN-UPA mythologies. These tactics were accompanied by a new wave of the war on Soviet symbols, the dismantling of monuments to Soviet leaders involved in Stalin's crimes, and the renaming of streets and other public spaces.

President Yushchenko made the reasonable decision to institutionalise his anti-Communist politics of history. He created the State Institute of National Memory, following Polish and Slovak models. The Institute began to collect and study all materials related to the mass repressions of Stalinism, especially the Famine of 1932–1933 and the anti-Soviet resistance movement of the OUN-UPA. At the same time, museums of Soviet occupation were created in Kiev and Lviv. However, none of these institutions, poorly equipped, with modest budgets and small staff, bore much resemblance to other similar institutions established in former socialist countries.[53] President Yushchenko entrusted the SBU (the Ukrainian secret service, former republican branch of the Soviet KGB) with the task of revealing Stalin's crimes, but the conviction of Stalin-era officials by the Kiev Court of Appeal, hastily prepared on the evidentiary basis of documents delivered by SBU on the eve of the next Presidential election of 2010, looked rather like political farce.[54]

The Great Famine (Holodomor) of 1932–1933 occupied the central place in the President's Yushchenko's politics of memory. Its commemoration became perhaps the greatest campaign in the official politics of history since 1991, resulting in large-scale publishing projects, monuments, public ceremonies, conferences, and films. At the same time, I would be cautious about accepting the conclusions of analysts who maintain that the affirmation of the Holodomor was an achievement of Viktor Yushchenko's politics of historical memory and that it served to consolidate Ukrainian society. In fact, it deepened political confrontation in Ukrainian society by exacerbating the regional polarisation in Ukraine on the one hand and contributing to a prolonged opposition between Ukraine and Russia in the realm of historical memory on the other.

While the national paradigm of Ukrainian history saw very little change during that time, the Soviet paradigm in neighbouring Russia underwent an active ideological transformation, combining the historical mythology of World War II with neo-imperial Orthodoxy. Consequently, the historical politics of Ukraine's President Yushchenko came to be subjected to increasing criticism in both Ukraine and Russia. Almost every step he took or action he made was confronted by vehement public protest and opposition from the Russian government. In fact, President Yushchenko's five-year term in office can be summarised as a Ukrainian-Russian war of national mythologies, which often turned into diplomatic and even economic wars.

Although little time has elapsed since Viktor Yanukovych came to power in 2010, the central tendencies of his politics of history have already manifested themselves clearly, especially given that in the southern and eastern parts of the country the now governing Party of Regions has been in power for quite some time. Yanukovych and his team perceived the Orange Revolution of 2004 in very much the same way the Russian political elites did. Both saw it through the lens of conspiracy theories and of belief in the subversive activities of Western secret services in post-Soviet space whose objective was to control local resources and fight against their post-Soviet rivals in the world market.[55] Thus the historical politics of the new regime have been mostly premised, at least so far, on denying the strategy of Yanukovych's predecessors rather than on working out a new course for national and state development aimed at national consolidation.

The humanities are manifestly excluded from priority in the policies of the Yanukovych post-Soviet technocratic government. They have, it seems, simply ceased to exist for the incumbent authorities. In fact, they are controlled and articulated by the Ministry of Education, Research, Youth and Sports, or more specifically, by its head, pro-Russian public intellectual, Dmytro Tabachnyk. The new regime initiated its attack on any historical institutions that demonstrated signs of having a national agenda. The government reshuffled the management of the Institute of National Memory and appointed as its new director Valery Soldatenko, a historian with an orthodox, Soviet-type reputation. Consequently, even by comparison with the post-Soviet Academy of Sciences, the Institute today resembles a typically Soviet ideological department. Its influence on the interpretation of the recent past is limited by the framework of Soviet historical discourse.

The new Ukrainian government doesn't complicate its existence by attempting to develop its own historical politics. Instead, it draws heavily on ready-made examples from official Russian sources. Therefore, the dimensions of contemporary historical policy in Ukraine are currently being shaped under the influence of neo-Soviet (Orthodox and Communist) ideology; hence the steps to partially rehabilitate Stalin and his policies. Today, the Ukrainian state archives and the Institute of Historical Memory are controlled by orthodox communists, who also erect monuments to Stalin in the south-eastern cities of Odesa and Zaporizhzhia. High-ranking politicians and administrators make public statements that seek at least partially to justify Stalin's repressions.[56]

One bizarre example of this new policy on historical memory comes from the Cabinet of Ministers of Ukraine decree of 11 August 2010 on the commemoration of the 75th anniversary of the Stakhanovite movement – the mass movement of shock workers during Stalin's industrialisation named after the Donbas coal miner Alexei Stakhanov. The movement was originally intended to raise the efficiency of the socialist economy and to create a model Soviet worker. Shortly before the decree was issued, Ukrainian mass media reported on a coal miner from the 'Novodzerzhynska' mine, Serhiy Shemuk, who, with the blessing of the Metropolitan of Mariupol of the Ukrainian Orthodox Church of the Moscow Patriarchate, beat Stakhanov's productivity record by producing 2023 per cent of the required daily output.[57]

The attempt to revive the official enthusiasm for Stalin's industrialisation in the oligarch-controlled and robbed post-Soviet country failed. President Yanukovych's regime has decided to focus instead on the symbols of World War II, referred to as the Great Patriotic War in the Soviet tradition. This focus, however, is framed not so much by the earlier Soviet discourse on 'the friendship of peoples' but rather by the contemporary Russian discourse with a strong emphasis on Orthodoxy. One testament to this comes from the large-scale celebrations of Victory Day (May 9) as well as an insistent public display of the corresponding symbolism.

It seems highly unlikely that President Yanukovych will be able to repeat President Kuchma's politics of maneuvering between national and Soviet historical discourses.[58] The room for political maneuvering is much more limited today, while Yanukovych's intellectual resources pale in comparison with those of his predecessors. On the other hand, following Kuchma's geopolitical approach to historical memory, which was basically 'tacking' between Russia and Europe, also appears problematic as Ukraine, which increasingly begins to resemble the notorious case of Belarus, finds itself gradually surrounded by a wall of international self-isolation.

Ivan Lysiak-Rudnytsky once noted that 'the regime which has become entangled in insoluble contradictions with the principles from which it derives its legitimacy cannot endure for very long'.[59] The only plausible way out of this situation for the new government is to engage in an open dialogue with civil society, which, however, is quite unlikely. Another, albeit theoretical, possibility could be a symbolic reorientation toward the historical legacy of Ukrainian national communism. But most contemporary Ukrainian communists have no affinity for this idea, and the number of genuine followers of this tradition, the generation of the 'sixties' is clearly declining.

Overall, the historical policies of previous Ukrainian governments were controversial and thus largely ineffective. The newly born political elites in Ukraine appeared to be unprepared to execute a national project at the theoretical level. They hardly anticipated that their task would be not so much to revive the Ukrainian nation with its political rather than ethnic culture, as essentially to create it. Ukrainian politicians, at least some of them, widely believed that it would suffice to 'enlighten' the masses and 'explain' to them 'the historical truths', and that as a result people would eagerly support the new political regime as they did during the 1991 independence referendum. Instead, Ukrainian society has witnessed political, social, national, cultural, linguistic and religious differentiation.

Neither were the Ukrainian political elites ready to implement the national project at the practical level as they relied primarily on old institutions and a cadre that compromised themselves by their closeness to or even affiliation with the Soviet Communist Party nomenclatura. However, they proved quite ready to divide and privatise the Soviet material – rather than symbolic – legacy. In fact, they completed the property and assets division so quickly and cynically that the trust of society, which was still naively governed by the concept of social justice, was completely lost. Consequently, other initiatives of the Ukrainian government in the realm of nation-building and historical policy could not but be morally discredited, especially after an economic collapse and the growing sentiment of protest in all spheres of social life.

The government does not possess many resources to implement its decisions, because of a catastrophically low level of state prestige, an absence of moral legitimacy and popular trust, widespread cynicism in an atomised society, miserable financial resources and the decrepit infrastructure of the cultural process. Since Ukraine regained its independence, it has even failed to revitalise 'the most popular art among the masses' – the national cinema. Ukrainian television is brimming with propagandistic Soviet and contemporary Russian nationalistic films that glorify militarism and the daily feats of the police and national security agencies.

None of the Ukrainian presidents has made any attempt to elaborate a new, more sophisticated politics of history. They have all borrowed *finished articles* from the past or from outside. One may speak of growing incompetence in managing those politics in Ukraine over the past several years. All of them have followed the Soviet pattern of implementing identity politics from above and avoiding an open public dialogue with Ukrainian civil society.

Naród/society

Ukrainian society still demonstrates its virtuosity in the culture of survival, but until now it has had nothing to contribute to the cultural model of development.[60] As Catherine Wanner has observed, the practice of adaptation and survival in such a society promotes the maintenance of the Soviet component of identity, finding support on the individual level.[61] According to a survey conducted by Kiev-based Razumkov Centre in 2005, more than 25 per cent of Ukrainian citizens would at that time have liked to return to the Soviet Union,[62] while in 2011 more than 54 per cent of them think that it would be better for the Soviet Union to have been preserved.[63] Soviet-like isolationism is also recognisable: suffice it to say that about 77 per cent of Ukrainians have never been abroad;[64] it is no wonder that 45 per cent of them maintain a negative attitude toward Western culture.[65]

The problem of (re)shaping collective as well as individual memories in (post-)communist societies under the new political circumstances has begun to attract more scholarly attention.[66] Taras Kuzio has pointed out that a 'black-and-white' picture of the recent past has proved too simple to find acceptance and support in Ukrainian society.[67] From the one side, the Soviet historical legacy was only partly in conflict with the national legacy and did not come down to the mere destruction of everything Ukrainian. From the other side, 'it is debatable whether Ukraine can be considered a complete nation' on the eve of the Communist revolution or even before 1991.[68] Much of the population does not accept a wholly negative representation of the Soviet past at the level of either the individual or the group. Traumatised by the collapse of the USSR, collective psychology has tended to reject the memory of even greater traumas and sufferings of the Soviet past or has sought to reformulate them in a more optimistic light.

To be sure, nostalgia for communist times is typical not only of Ukraine but also of the other post-communist countries, where on average more than half the population now holds a positive view of the communist past.[69] That indicator is even higher in Russia: in 2005 up to 60 per cent of young Russians with no personal experience of life in the USSR felt nostalgia for it.[70] It is only in Ukraine, however, that different attitudes to the recent past take on existential significance, as they are deeply associated with problems of collective identity and the very legitimacy of the post-Soviet 'Ukrainian project'.

Reactions to the 'nationalisation' of the recent past in Ukraine have been varied. Abandonment of the Soviet schema and conceptualisation of Ukrainian history in the Soviet period provoked an active resistance on the part of the communists and Rus'-Orthodox nationalists that grew into a full-scale war over the content of school textbooks. Ukrainian parliamentary commissions have considered the demands of communist deputies that the Great October Socialist Revolution be rein-stated in academic literature; that the enthusiastic labour and heroic achievements of the first Five-Year Plan be given due recognition; that the Great Patriotic War regain its previous status; that positive assess-ments of the OUN-UPA be eliminated, and so on. In the Crimea, there have been incidents involving the public burning of Ukrainian history textbooks.

For a society that finds itself in difficult circumstances, mythological consciousness promotes psychological adaptation and offers a refuge from traumatic historical experience.[71] Such a society becomes habitually dependent on myth; hence its collective consciousness remains open to new mythologies that relieve society itself of collective responsibility for the state of affairs. As a result, the mythology of the Soviet period gradu-ally has been transformed into the new myth about the Soviet Union. The Great October Socialist Revolution mythology no longer plays the same social role as it did in the 1980s: only about 10 per cent of Ukrainians consider the 7th of November – when the Russian Communist revolu-tion occurred – a major holiday, while for about half of them it's just one among many ordinary days.[72] Instead, the mythology of the Great Patriotic war is rising as a new manifestation of Russian neo-Soviet Orthodox nationalism.

The myth of the Great Patriotic War associated with Stalin appears to be at the heart of the new mythology about the Soviet Union as a whole. According to data collected by the Razumkov Center, 71.7 per cent of Ukrainian residents polled in 2003 considered Victory Day a major holiday; in 2010 their number grew up to 74.9 per cent.[73] In general, the collective historical memory of Ukrainian society shows a steady depend-ence on the politics of memory in Russia, dominated as it is by historical amnesia and the glorification of Stalinism.[74] The same may be said about the memory of Stalin himself. Thus, in 1991, if 27 per cent of Ukrainians agreed that Stalin was a 'great leader', while 44 per cent disagreed, by 2006 there were more in the first group (38 per cent) than in the second (37 per cent). Moreover, Stalin's popularity is increasing in every segment of Ukrainian society, especially among young people (by 10 per cent) and the middle-aged (also by 10 per cent).[75]

Clear manifestations of this influence are apparent to the naked eye: the St. George ribbon, symbolising the 'nationalised' Russian mythol-ogy of the Great Patriotic War, continues to wave from the antennas of many passenger cars in Ukraine, although several months have passed since the solemn celebration of Victory Day. It is perfectly obvious that the meaning of this symbol has gone beyond the bounds of a particular holiday and turned into a manifestation either of Russo-Slavic national identity or of support for the pro-Russian political orientation of the current government. In southern and eastern Ukraine at least, the new Russian orientation of (the victors of) the Great Patriotic War easily outweighs the historical mythology of the Holodomor and the OUN-UPA (the defeated).

Collective memory of the Brezhnev era of relative stability and more or less satisfactory material status has advanced to the forefront of historical priorities in post-Soviet Ukrainian society. It has become the main source of nostalgic moods, stimulated by means of well-known cultural symbols and rituals. Many people in Ukraine and Russia see it as a Golden Age rather than an epoch of stagnation and persecution. Characteristically enough, the Brezhnev era of Ukrainian-Soviet history remains one of the periods least studied and represented in academic historiography while being highly praised by political elites.

Widespread cynicism and indifference to the traumatic past in Ukrainian society, or efforts to reduce it to the level of a culture of ridicule and parody, may be regarded not only as one form of such collective escape but as a collective spiritual heritage of the Brezhnev epoch as well. Ukrainian (post)Soviet society has sunk into a state of deep depression brought about, on the one hand, by the inertia of the Soviet way of life and, on the other, by the openly cynical and incompetent policies of the Ukrainian elite. Ukrainian society is also afflicted by profound cynicism and the devaluation of many socio-cultural and professional values and norms. It is alienated from the ratification of important political decisions and from government institutions, which it treats more or less as it did Soviet institutions – with simultaneous fear and desire to deceive or bribe them.

Back in the late 1990s James Mace, the well-known American historian of the Holodomor, was already struck by the fact that the publicising of events previously covered up had not endowed them with national significance in Ukraine, and that a good many people completely denied what had actually happened.[76] Tanya Richardson, who studies the historical memory of current residents of Odessa, writes about young people's indifference to traumatic history.[77] Tatiana Zhurzhenko describes local 'memory wars' on the Holodomor issue in Kharkiv, on the Ukrainian-Russian borderland.[78] Liudmyla Hrynevych attests to the aggressive public reaction to the official politics of memory of the Holodomor during the presidency of Viktor Yushchenko all over Ukraine.

There has been a palpable decrease in the level of tolerance and a coarsening of the tone of discourse among groups representing different viewpoints. There is a general lack of public dialogue about the past;

of a common search for answers to difficult questions in which the process is regarded as more important than the result. Society has become used to truth 'with no right of appeal,' orienting itself on dogma, canon, and winners and losers. Given the relentless struggle of diametrically opposed mythologies – communist and nationalist – in Ukraine, people take one side or the other or, alternatively, seek a complete escape from history so as to relieve stress or avoid yet another dilemma of consciousness and responsibility.

In sum, the Ukrainian academic and political elites have not managed to effect any radical change in the traditional 'autonomist' or 'imperial' models for the representation of Ukrainian history in the imperial and Soviet eras. According to a poll conducted by the Razumkov Center in 2005, an average of almost 44 per cent of Ukrainian citizens still consider Ukrainian history 'an inalienable part of the history of the great East Slavic people, as is the history of Russia and Belarus'.[79] Those who consider Ukrainian history wholly autonomous and Ukraine the sole successor of Kyivan Rus' constitute about half that number – 25 per cent. In the third place are those who found it hard to respond to questions dealing with Ukrainian history at all. Thus, about half the Ukrainian people deny their state a national history of its own: in other words, they reject its political legitimacy.

Conclusions

It is sometimes said that Ukrainians are so obsessed with their past that they become prisoners of their imagined history. In this regard, Ukrainians are quite similar to other Eastern European peoples. Is it possible for them to get rid of history? Or at least to overcome the 'burden of history', to 'escape' from history somehow? I do not think so ... the Soviet past/present cannot be simply rejected, or ousted from contemporary Ukraine. The Soviet heritage is the only one that is commonly shared by all Ukrainian citizens. So the only possible way to come to terms with such a historical legacy is a historical revisionism – a complete reinterpretation of the communist past in a positive way, as an integral part of a new national narrative.[80]

It seems as if Ukrainian post-Soviet historians have erred in rejecting a nuanced approach to the whole Soviet era by uniting the Brezhnev, Stalin and Lenin epochs into a single unit defined by the totalitarian paradigm. An alternative approach that distinguishes nuances among the various political regimes of the Soviet era could serve better from the viewpoint of creating a Ukrainian 'usable past'. For example, it could be argued that there are two different kinds of Soviet history: that of the Communist-reformists (Lenin, Khrushchev and Gorbachev), and that of Communist-traditionalists, or, better, Russian national-Communists (Stalin and Brezhnev).[81] Soviet Leninists-Westernisers could base their political legitimacy on the mythology of the Great October Socialist Revolution, while the Stalinists-Russophiles emphasise the Great Patriotic War.[82]

Such an approach would at least make it possible to come to terms with the Leninist historical and cultural legacy in Ukrainian history, which was actively employed by Soviet reformers of the 1960s and the late 1980s but is rejected by the contemporary Russian political and intellectual elite. In this context, for example, Ivan Lysiak-Rudnytsky's and Roman Szporluk's observations about Lenin's understanding of the modern phenomenon of nationalism, and his constructive role in a positive communist solution of the 'Ukrainian question', deserve more scholarly and political attention.[83] The problem is that there is no social, political or intellectual gropes that could be a main carrier or promoter of such an ideology in Ukraine.

The post-Soviet Ukraine of today does not present a convincing alternative to the Ukrainian Soviet Socialist Republic. The official nation state paradigm that replaced the Soviet conception of the 'friendship of peoples' under the aegis of the 'more equal' Russian people is in many ways reminiscent of the Polish conception of an enslaved nation, subsequently liberated, which fought heroically against the totalitarian Russian and German regimes. In contrast to the Polish situation, however, the paradigm of Ukrainian national statehood did not become a consolidating factor in socio-political life or a worthy alternative to the Soviet Russian paradigm of the history of the 'short' twentieth century.

It would be worthwhile, however, to attempt to replace the traditional mythology of suffering and heroic struggle for salvation with a more optimistic and more secular historical mythology based on the concept of modernisation, in the broad sense of the word. The Soviet historical and cultural legacy, its reformist aspect first and foremost, also holds the potential to facilitate modernisation that a renewed Ukrainian national discourse could 'appropriate' and even turn to the advantage of its own democratic transformation. In the Ukrainian context, the modernisation paradigm could and should be employed not for the rehabilitation of Stalinism and its 'revolution from above,' nor for the aping of Russian contemporary neo-imperial historiography, but in order to reveal in the recent Ukrainian past basic characteristic features that defined its present. Those include the nature of relations between ecclesiastical and secular rule; institutions of private property; the interplay of law and morality; corporative and individual cultures; relations between elites, government and society; mechanisms of political and cultural domination; interaction of a centre and a periphery and so on. In this way the Ukrainian traditional political culture of survival could be supplemented with a culture of development or modernisation.

Condemning Soviet totalitarianism and Russian nationalism is not the same thing as being prepared to take responsibility for the Soviet past. Are Ukrainian historians prepared to discuss personally unpleasant aspects of authoritarian traditions of political culture; and to seek the roots of such widespread social phenomena as antidemocratic, antiliberal values, xenophobia and anti-Semitism, religious fundamentalism, conformism and lack of freedom? Are they prepared to overcome the mental traditions of conservatism that condemn Ukrainian society to chronic stagnation? Are they prepared to reform their own professional milieu according to the principles of an open society? For the time being, these questions remain open.

The creation of an alternative to the Soviet\Russian paradigm of a 'common history' requires a rethinking not only of its Ukrainian component but also the reformulation of the entire Soviet historic-cultural legacy that still weighs upon Ukrainian society. Russia and Ukraine now interpret their joint Soviet cultural legacy in different ways, according to the needs of their own national projects. Nevertheless, these interpretations are directly linked. Considering that Soviet, Russian and Ukrainian national discourses are intertwined in the Ukrainian historical legacy, it must be admitted that the simple rejection of any of them in favour of another seems problematic. Ukraine cannot rid itself of its Soviet/Russian legacy: it can only strive to reinterpret it. In other words, it is impossible to create a *national text* in Ukraine representing an alternative to the Soviet Russian one without transforming the *transnational context*.

A 'good' Ukrainian historical mythology can become 'workable' only if the political elite is able to integrate the broader population into the decision-making process and to share political responsibility with civil society; the intellectual elite, in its turn, must be able to reconcile 'Ukrainian' and 'modern', at least symbolically. However, this is unlikely to happen in the near future. Nascent Ukrainian politicians have in no way proved themselves different from those of the Soviet party *nomenklatura*. Ukrainian academia in general has not passed through a stage of institutional and methodological transformation, and continues to be more responsive to the volatile political conjuncture than motivated by the desire for intellectual innovation. Since neither political nor intellectual elites are ready to adopt the principles of an open society, Ukraine remains a battlefield of competing mythologies and identities as well as memories and histories.

Notes

1. T. Kuzio, 'Desiat "svidchen" toho, shcho Ukraïna—neoradians'ka derzhava', in *Ukraïns'ka pravda*, (25 March 2004) [online]. Available at: http://www.pravda.com.ua [Accessed 27 March 2005]; M. Karmazina, 'Ukraïna nasha – radians'ka?' *Dzerkalo tyzhnia*, [online] 23–29 October. Available at: http://gazeta.dt.ua/SOCIETY/ukrayina_nasha__radyanska.html [Accessed 23 August 2013]. B. Harasymiw, *Post-Communist* Ukraine (Edmonton and Toronto: Canadian Institute of Ukrainian Studies Press, 2002); I. Shapoval, 'Komunistychnyi totalitaryzm ta ioho obraz u suchasnykh pidruchnykakh v Ukraïni', in *Ukraïns'ka istorychna dydaktyka: Mizhnarodnyi dialoh (fakhivtsi riznykh kraïn pro suchasni ukraïns'ki pidruchnyky z istoriï)*, *Zbirnyk naukovykh statei* (Kyiv: Geneza, 2000), pp. 29–44.
2. S. Kotkin, *Armageddon Averted: The Soviet Collapse, 1970–2000* (NY: Oxford University Press, 2001), pp.1–2.
3. A. Wilson, 'Myths on National History in Belarus and Ukraine', in G. Hosking, G. Schopflin, (eds), *Myths and Nationhood* (London: University of London Press, 1997), pp.182–97; C. Wanner, *Burden of Dreams: History and Identity in Post-Soviet Ukraine* ([Philadelphia] University Park, PA: Pennsylvania State University Press, 1998); K. Wolczuk, 'History, Europe and the "National Idea": The "official" Narrative of National Identity in Ukraine', *Nationalities Papers* vol. 28, no. 4 (2000), p. 674; T. Kuzio, 'History, Memory and Nation Building in the Post-Soviet Colonial Space', *Nationalities Papers* vol. 30, no. 2 (2002), pp. 241–64; G. Kasianov, 'Rewriting and Rethinking: Contemporary Historiography and Nation Building in Ukraine', in T. Kuzio and P. D'Anieri (eds), *Dilemmas of State-Led Nation Building in Ukraine* (Westrort, Conn: Preager, 2002), pp. 29–46.
4. B. Crawford and A. Lijphart (eds), *Liberalization and Leninist Legacies: Comparative Perspectives on Democratic Transitions* (Berkeley: The Regents of the University of California, 1997), pp. 1–39; K. Jowitt, *New World Disorder: The Leninist Distinction* (Berkeley: University of California Press, 1992), pp. 284–305; M.M. Howard, 'The Leninist Legacy Revisited', in V. Tismaneanu, M.M. Howard, and R. Sil (eds.), *World Order After Leninism* (Seattle and London: University of Washington Press, 2006), pp. 34–46; M. Minkenberg, 'Leninist Beneficiaries? Pre-1989 Legacies and the Radical Right in Post-1989 Central and Eastern Europe. Some Introductory Observations', *Communist and Post-Communist Studies* vol. 42, no. 4 (2009), pp. 445–58; V. Tismaneanu, 'Is East-Central Europe Backsliding? Leninist Legacies, Pluralist Dilemmas', *Journal of Democracy* vol. 18, no. 4 (2007), pp. 33–39; V. Tismaneanu, M.M. Howard, and R. Sil (eds), *World Order After Leninism* (Seattle and London: University of Washington Press, 2006).
5. Y. Hrytsak, 'On Sails and Gails, and Ships Sailing in Various Directions: Post-Soviet Ukraine', *Ab Imperio* vol. 1, (2004), pp. 229–54.

6. A.I. Miller, 'Tema Tcentralnoi Evropy: istoria, sovremennye discursy i mesto v nikh Rossii', *Novoe Literaturnoe Obozrenie*, (2001) [online]. Available at: http://magazines.russ.ru/nlo/2001/52/mill.html [Accessed 30 May 2012].
7. J.-H. Meyer-Sahling, 'Varieties of Legacies: A Critical Review of Legacy Explanations of Public Administration Reform in East Central Europe', *International Review of Administrative Sciences* vol. 75, no. 3 (2009), p. 509; G. Pop-Eleches, 'Historical Legacies and Post-Communist Regime Change', *The Journal of Politics* vol. 69, no. 4 (2007), pp. 908–26; M. Minkenberg and T. Timm Beichelt (eds), *Cultural Legacies in Post-Socialist Europe: The Role of the Various Pasts in the Current Transformation Process* (Frankfurt/Oder: Frankfurt Institute for Transformation, 2003).
8. Kuzio, 'History, Memory and Nation Building in the Post-Soviet Colonial Space', p. 249.
9. As Andrew Wilson has put it, 'the existence of this middle ground is key to the very understanding of Ukrainian society, but its very essence makes it difficult to define'. A. Wilson, 'Elements of a Theory of Ukrainian Ethno-National Identities', *Nations and Nationalism* vol. 8, no. 1, (2002), pp. 31–54.
10. M. Riabczuk, 'Has the Second Rzecz Pospolita Expanded to the Borders of the First RP in the Contemporary Ukraine?' *Nationalities Affairs = Sprawy Narodowoś ciowe* no. 31 (2007), 35; V. Shlapentokh, *Contemporary Russia as a Feudal Society. A New Perspective on the Post-Soviet Era* (NY: Palgrave Macmillan, 2007); A.J. Motyl, 'The New Political Regime in Ukraine—Toward Sultanism Yanukovych-Style?' *Cicero Foundation Great Debate Paper* no. 10/06 (2010), pp. 1–8, http://www.cicerofoundation.org/lectures/Alexander_J_Motyl_THE_NEW_POLITICAL_REGIME_IN_UKRAINE.pdf [Accessed 23 August 2013].
11. Robert Tucker, for example, emphasised that Soviet political history progressed in distinctive stages under different leaderships (R. C. Tucker, Political Culture and Leadership in Soviet Russia: From Lenin to Gorbachev [New York: Norton, 1987]).
12. See: Edwin Bacon, 'Reconsidering Brezhnev', in E. Bacon and M. Sandle (eds), *Brezhnev reconsidered* (New York: Palgrave Macmillan, 2002), pp. 1–21.
13. In this article the definition of 'recent past' is used as an equivalent to Ukrainian Soviet past, beginning with 1917.
14. The paper is based on my essay 'Ponevolennia istorieju' [Enslaved by history: Soviet Ukraine in contemporary historiography] published in the collection of articles: V. Kravchenko, *Ukraïna, imperiíā, Ros iíā: vybrani statti z modernoï istoriï ta istoriohrafiï* [Ukraine, Empire, Russia: Selected Articles on Modern History and Historiography; in Ukrainian] (Kyiv: Krytyka, 2011), pp. 455–528.
15. O. Subtelny, 'The Current State of Ukrainian Historiography,' *Journal of Ukrainian Studies* vol. 18, no. 1–2 (1993), pp. 34–54; M. von Hagen, 'Does Ukraine Have a History?' *Slavic Review* vol. 54, no. 3 (1995), pp. 658–73; Y. Hrytsak, 'Ukrainskaya istoriografiya: 1991–2001. Desyatiletie peremen', *Ab imperio*, (2003) [online]. Available at: http://abimperio.net.ezp-prod1. hul.harvard.edu/cgi-bin/aishow.pl?state=showa&idart=734&idlang=2&Code= [Accessed 30 May 2012]; G. Kasianov, 'Sovremennoe sostoyanie ukrainskoi istoriografii: metodologicheskie i institutsionalnye aspekty', in L. Zashkilniak (ed.), *Ukrains'ka istoriohrafiya na zlami XX I XXI stolit: zdobutky i problemy. Kolektyvna monohrafiya* (Lviv: Lviv National University Press, 2004); T. Stryjek,

Jakiej przeszłości potrzebuje przyszłość? Interpretacje dziejów narodowych w historiografii i debacie publicznej na Ukrainie, 1991–2004 (Warszawa: Instytut Studiów Politycznych PAN and Oficyna Wydawnicza Rytm, and others, 2007).

16. V.A. Smolii (ed.), *Ukraina kriz' viky*, tt. 1–15 (Kyiv: Al'ternatyvy, 1998).
17. It is represented, among others, by the Institute of Ukrainian Studies affiliated with Taras Shevchenko Kyiv National University, the Ivan Krypiakevych Institute of Ukrainian Studies in Lviv, and the Mychailo Hrushevsky Institute of Ukrainian Archaeography and Source Studies of the National Academy of Science in Kyiv, not to mention numerous NGOs of national-patriotic orientation.
18. Regarding Ivan Lysiak-Rudnytsky, see: O. Pritsak, 'Ivan Lysiak-Rudnytsky, Scholar and "Communicator" ', in P.L. Rudnytsky (ed.), *Essays in Modern Ukrainian History* (Edmonton: CIUS Press, 1987), pp. XV–XXII.
19. Such as 'Ukraina Moderna' (Lviv) or 'Krytyka' (Kiev), or 'Ukrainian Humanities Review' (Kiev).
20. Y. Hrytsak, 'Chorni knyhy chervonogo teroru', *Krytyka* vol. 31, no. 5 (2000) pp. 4–6.
21. Z.E. Kohut, *History as a Battleground: Russian-Ukrainian Relations and Historical Consciousness in Contemporary Ukraine* (Saskatoon: Heritage Press, 2001), p. 36.
22. V. Holubko and L. Zashkilniak (eds), *Ukrains'ka istoriohrafiya na zlami XX I XXI stolit: zdobutky i problemy. Kolektyvna monohrafiya* (Lviv: Lviv National University Press, 2004) p. 184.
23. V. Verstiuk (ed.), *Problemy vyvtchennia istorii Ukrains'koi revolutcii 1917–1921 rr.* (Kiev: Instytut istorii Ukrainy NAN Ukrainy, 2002); O. Pavlyshyn and L. Zashkilniak (eds.), *Ukrains'ka istoriohrafiya na zlami XX I XXI stolit: zdobutky i problemy. Kolektyvna monohrafiya* (Lviv: Lviv National University Press, 2004), p.168–83; S. Velychenko, 'Ukrainians Rethink Their Revolutions', *Ab Imperio* no. 4 (2004), 1–16; C. Ford, 'Reconsidering the Ukrainian Revolution 1917–1921: The Dialectics of National Liberation and Social Emancipation', *Debatte: Journal of Contemporary Central and Eastern Europe* vol. 15, no. 3 (2007), 279–306; V.F. Soldatenko, *Ukrains'ka Revolutcia: kontceptsia ta istoriohrafia (1918–1920 rr.)* (Kiev: Knyha Pamiati Ukrainy, 1999).
24. V. Buldakov, 'Attempts at the "Nationalisation" of Russian and Soviet History in the Newly Independent Slavic States, The Construction and Deconstruction of National Histories in Slavic Eurasia', in H. Tadayuki (ed.), *The Construction and Deconstruction of National Histories in Slavic Eurasia, Proceedings of the July 2002 International Symposium at the SRC* (Sapporo: SRC, 2003), pp. 3–34.
25. Polit.ru. Rossia-Ukraina: kak pishetsia istoria. Beseda Alexeia Millera i Georgia Kasianova. Tchast' 5. Pervaja mirovaja, (2009) [online]. Available at: http://www.polit.ru/analytics/2009/07/02/worldwar.html [Accessed 30 May 2012].
26. Y. Hrytsak, *Strasti za natcionalizmom. Istorytchni esei* (Kyiv: Krytyka, 2004), p. 84.
27. L. Grynevych, 'The Present State of Ukrainian Historiography on the Holodomor and Prospects for its Development,' *The Harriman Review* vol. 16, no. 2 (2008), 10–20.
28. G. Kasianov, 'Revisiting the Great Famine of 1932–1933. Politics of Memory and Public Consciousness (Ukraine after 1991)', in M. Kopecek (ed.), *Past in the Making: Historical Revisionism in Central Europe After 1989* (Budapest-New York: Central European University Press, 2008), p. 215.

116   *Mass Dictatorship and Memory as Ever Present Past*

29. G. Kasianov, *Dance Macabre: holod 1932–1933 rokiv u polinytci, masovij svi-domosti ta istoriohrafii (1980—potchatok 2000)* (Kyiv: Nash Tchas, 2010); Millera i Kasianova (2009); Kasianov, 'Revisiting the Great Famine of 1932–1933. Politics of Memory and Public Consciousness (Ukraine after 1991)', pp. 197–220; J. Dietsch, *Making Sense of Suffering: Holocaust and Holodomor in Ukrainian Historical Culture* (Lund: Lunds universitet, 2006); F.E. Sysyn, 'The Famine of 1932–1933 in the Discussion of Russian-Ukrainian Relations', *The Harriman Review* vol. 15, no. 2/3 (2005), 77–82 and so on.
30. O. Lysenko, '"Druha svitova vijna jak predmet naukovykh doslidzhen" ta fenomen istorytchnoi pamiati', *Ukrains'kyj istorytchnyj zhurnal* no 4 (2004), 3–16; Idem. 'Ukrains'ka istoriohrafia Druhoi svitovoi vijny: mizh zakonomirnistiu i paradoksom,' in V.F. Verstiuk (ed.), *Ukraina-Rosia: dialoh istoriohrafij. Materialy mizhnarodnoi naukovoi konferentcii* (Kyiv-Chernihiv: Desnians'ka Pravda, 2007), pp. 143–57; V. Hrynevych, 'Istoria Druhoi svi-tovoi vijny u sutchasnij istoriohrafii ta politytchnij borot'bi', *Ukrains'kyj Humanitarnyj Ohliad* vol. 11, (2005), 9–29.
31. See, for example: J. Brunstedt, 'Building a Pan-Soviet Past: The Soviet War Cult and the Turn Away from Ethnic Particularism', *The Soviet and Post-Soviet Review* vol. 38, no. 2 (2011), 149–71.
32. Sh. Fitzpatrick, 'Introduction: Soviet Union in Retrospect—Ten Years after 1991', in W. Slater and A. Wilson (eds.), *The Legacy of the Soviet Union* (Basingstoke: Palgrave Macmillan, 2004), p. 9.
33. L. Gudkov, ' "Pamiat" pro vijnu ta masova identytchnist" Rosijan', *Krytyka* vol. 91, no. 5 (2005); T.J. Uldricks, 'War, Politics and Memory. Russian Historians Reevaluate the Origins of World War II', *History & Memory* vol. 21, no. 2 (2009), 60–82.
34. J.-P. Himka, 'Victim Cinema. Between Hitler and Stalin: Ukraine in World War II—The Untold Story,' in G.Kasjanov and Ph. Terr (eds.), *A Laboratory of Transnational History* (Florence, Italy: European University Institute, 2009), pp. 211–24.
35. M. Kuczerepa, 'Stosunki ukraińsko-polskie w II Rzeczypospolitej we współczesnej historiografii ukraińskiej,' in P. Kosiewski and P. Motyka (eds.), *Historycy Polscy i Ukraińscy wobec problemów XX wieku* (Kraków: Universitas, 2000), pp. 146–65; D.R. Marples, *Heroes and Villains: Creating National History in Contemporary Ukraine* (Budapest [u.a.]: CEU Press, 2007), pp. 203–38; G. Kasianov, 'The Burden of the Past', *Innovation: The European Journal of Social Science Research*, vol. 19, no. 3–4 (2006), 247–59.
36. Marples, *Heroes and Villains*, p. 244.
37. O. Zaitcev, 'Vijna mitiv pro vijnu v sutchasnii Ukraini', *Krytyka* no. 3–4 (2010), 149–50; V. Hrynevych, 'Mit vijny ta vijna mitiv', *Krytyka*, no. 5 (2005) .
38. 'Ukrainisty ta Bandera: rozbizhni pohliady', editorial, *Krytyka* no. 3–4 (2010), pp. 149–50.
39. Y. Hrytsak, *Narys istorii Ukrainy. Formuvannia modernoi Ukrains'koi natcii XIX–XX stolit'* (Kyiv: Heneza, 1996), p. 254.
40. G. Grinchenko, *Ukrains'ki ostarbaitery v systemi prymusovoi pratci Tretioho. Raichu: problemy istorytchnoi pamiati. Dysertatcia na zdobuttia naukovoho stupenia doctora istorytchnykh nauk* (Rukopys. Kharkiv, 2011); V. Hrynevych, *Suspil'no-politytchni nastri naselennia Ukrainy v roky Druhoi svitovoi vijny (1939–1945 rr.)* (Kyiv: NAN Ukrainy, 2007).

41. O. Zaitcev, 'Vijna mitiv pro vijnu v sutchasnii Ukraini', *Krytyka* no. 3–4 (2010), 149–50.
42. N. Yakovenko (ed.), *Shkil'na istoria otchyma istorykiv-naukovtciv*. Materialy *robotchoi narady z monitoring shkil'nykh pidrutchnykiv istorii Ukrainy* (Kyiv: Olena Teliha Press, 2008).
43. N. Yakovenko, 'Kontceptcia novoho utchebnika Ukrainskoj istorii', Polit.UA, (17 March 2010) [online]. Available at: http://www.polit.ua/lectures/2010/03/17/yakovenko.html [Accessed 30 May 2012].
44. Y. Hrytsak, 'On the Relevance and Irrelevance of Nationalism in Contemporary Ukraine,' in Georgiy Kasjanov and Philipp Ther (eds.), *A Laboratory of Transnational History*. (Italy Florence: European University Institute, 2009), pp. 225–48.
45. See: O. Ohorchak, *Role of Memory Policy in Constructing National Identity*. Case Study: Ukraine (Master of Arts Thesis, Georg-August Universität Göttingen, Germany and Palacky University in Olomouc, Czech Republic. Göttingen, Germany, 2011) http://theses.cz/id/d6v4ad/MA_Thesis_Ohorchak.pdf; V. Ishchenko, 'Fighting Fences vs Fighting Monuments: Politics of Memory and Protest Mobilisation in Ukraine', *Debatte: Journal of Contemporary Central and Eastern Europe* vol. 19, no. 1–2 (2011), 369–95; A. Portnov, 'Historical Legacies and Politics of History in Ukraine. Introductory Remarks', in H. Best and A. Wenninger (eds), *Landmark 1989: Central and Eastern European Societies Twenty Years After the System Change* (Berlin: LIT Verlag Münster, 2010), pp. 54–59; A. Kappeler, 'The Politics of History in Contemporary Ukraine: Russia, Poland, Austria, and Europe,' in J. Besters-Dilger (ed.), *Ukraine on its Way to Europe: Interim Results of the Orange Revolution* (Frankfurt am Main; Berlin; Bern: Peter Lang, 2009), pp. 217–32; Kasianov, 'Revisiting the Great Famine of 1932–1933. Politics of Memory and Public Consciousness (Ukraine after 1991)', pp. 197–220, and others.
46. F.E. Sysyn, 'The Reemergence of the Ukrainian Nation and Cossack Mythology', *Social Research* vol. 58, no. 4 (1991), 845–59.
47. Harasymiw, *Post-Communist Ukraine*, p. 428.
48. V. Sereda, 'Osoblyvosti reprezentatcii natcional'no-istorytchnykh identytchnostej v ofitcijnomu dyskursi presydentiv Ukrainy I Rosii', *Sotciolohia: teoria, metody, marketynh* no.3 (2006), 191–212.
49. V.V. Kravchenko, *Kharkiv/Khar'kov: stolitca pogranich'ia [Kharkiv/Kharkov: A Frontier Capital; in Russian]* (Vilnius: EHU Press, 2010).
50. K. Wolczuk, 'History, Europe, and the "national idea": The Official Narrative of National Identity in Ukraine', *Nationalities Papers* vol. 28, no. 4 (2000), 682.
51. L. Hrynevych, (ed.), *Protystoiannia. Zernennia, zajavy, lysty hromads'kykh orhanizatcij, politytchnyx partij, hromadian Ukrainy do komisii z vyvtchennia dial'nosti OUN-UPA, 1996–1998 rr* (Kyiv: Instytut istorii Ukrainy, 1999).
52. http://www.ji-magazine.lviv.ua/dyskusija/orlata-arhiv.htm
53. Kasianov, 'Revisiting the Great Famine of 1932–1933. Politics of Memory and Public Consciousness (Ukraine after 1991)', pp. 197–220.
54. T. Snyder, 'Ukraine's Past on Trial', *The New York Review of Books*, (3 February 2010) [online]. Available at: http://www.nybooks.com/blogs/nyrblog/2010/feb/03/ukraines-past-on-trial/ [Accessed 30 May 2012].
55. T. Kuzio, 'Soviet Conspiracy Theories and Political Culture in Ukraine: Understanding Viktor Yanukovych and the Party of Regions', *Communist and*

Post-Communist Studies vol. 44, no. 3 (2011), 221–32. I've found it difficult to agree with Taras Kuzio who explains the conspiracy-driven worldview of Yanukovych's team in terms of the political culture of the Brezhnev era. Such an explanation would be more relevant in the cases of Kravchuk and Kuchma, whereas Yanukovych and his team could be considered outsiders and marginals by Brezhnevite standards. Thus, their political culture is not a culture of the Communist Party *nomenclatura* but rather a culture of the notorious Homo Sovieticus, raised on the stereotypes of struggle with both internal and external enemies. From that perspective, the Party of Regions along with its political ally, the Communist Party of Ukraine, represents perhaps the most anti-intellectual power of post-Soviet Ukraine with a corresponding electorate.

56. Glavnoe: Internet-obozrenie iz Kharkova. *Regional Chechetov: Stalin—nie prestupnik, a spasitel*, (2010) [online]. Available at: http://glavnoe.ua/news/ n52734 [Accessed 31 May 2012].
57. Ura-inform. Donbass. *Na Donetchine pobili record Stakhanova*, (2010) [online]. Available at: http://ura.dn.ua/10.08.2010/99210.html [Accessed 31 May 2012]. It is not accidental then that the monument to the glory of a coal miner (1967), the visit card of the industrial eastern-Ukrainian city of Donetsk, is now presented against the background of a newly erected Russian Orthodox church.
58. Andriy Portnov reached a similar conclusion in his 2011 talk on Viktor Yanukovych's policy on historical memory (http://polit.ua/print/articles/ 2010/11/11/history.html)
59. I.L. Rudnytsky, 'Soviet Ukraine in Historical Perspective', in P.L. Rudnytsky (ed.), *Essays in Modern Ukrainian History* (Edmonton: CIUS Press, 1987), p. 472.
60. R. Inglehart and G. Welzel, *Modernization, Cultural Change and Democracy: The Human Development Sequence* (New York: Cambridge University Press, 2005).
61. C. Wanner, *Burden of Dreams*; V. Kulyk, 'Tiahar sproshchen', *Ukraïns'kyi humanitarnyi ohliad* vol. 3, (2000), 168–69.
62. Razumkov Centre. *Tchy prahnete Vy vidnovlennia Radians'koho Sojuzu ta sotcialistytchnoi systemy?* (2005) [online]. Available at: http://www.razumkov. org.ua/ukr/poll.php?poll_id=288 [Accessed 31 May 2012].
63. Glavnoe: Internet-obozrenie iz Kharkova. *Dve treti Ukraintcev ne schitajut 20-letie nezavisimosti znatchimoi datoi*, Opros (2011) [online]. Available at: http:// glavnoe.ua/news/n71413 [Accessed 31 May 2012].
64. Glavnoe: Internet-obozrenie iz Kharkova. *Tri tchetverti Ukraintcev nikogda nie byli za granitcej*, (2012) [online]. Available at: http://glavnoe.ua/news/ n101934 [Accessed 31 May 2012].
65. Razumkov Centre. *15 let spustia: strana ta zhe, liudi te zhe, vot tol'ko...* (2006) [online]. Available at: http://www.razumkov.org.ua/ukr/article.php?news_ id=459 [Accessed 31 May 2012].
66. M. James, *The Unfinished Revolution: Making Sense of the Communist Past in Central-Eastern Europe* (New Haven: Yale University Press, 2011).
67. T. Kuzio, 'Ukraine: Coming to Terms with the Soviet Legacy', *Journal of Communist Studies and Transition Politics* vol. 14, no. 4 (1998), 6–9.
68. Rudnytsky, *Essays in Modern Ukrainian History*, p.46; Kasianov, G. *Teorii natcii ta natcionalismu* (Kyiv: Lybid', 1999), pp. 296–97.
69. M. Velikonia, 'Lost in Transition: Nostalgia for Socialism in Post-socialist Countries', *East European Politics&Societies* vol. 23, no. 4 (2009), 544–45.

70. M. Laruelle, *In the Name of the Nation: Nationalism and Politics in Contemporary Russia* (London: Palgrave Macmillan, 2009), p. 155.
71. M. Riabchuk, *Dvi Ukraïny* (Kyiv: Krytyka, 2003), p. 35.
72. Razumkov Centre. *Sociological Survey on the Day of 7 November (formerly the Anniversary of the Great October Socialist Revolution)*, (2009) [online]. Available at: http://razumkov.org,ua/ukr/poll.php?poll_id-505 [Accessed 31 May 2012].
73. Razumkov Centre. *Sociological survey on the Victory Day of 9 May*, (2009) [online]. Available at: http://www.razumkov.org.ua/ukr/poll.php?poll_id=78 [Accessed 31 May 2012].
74. D. Khapaeva, 'Historical Memory in Post-Soviet Gothic Society', *Social Research: An International Quarterly Issue* vol. 76, no. 1 (2009), pp. 359–66.
75. Razumkov Centre. *15 let spustia: strana ta zhe, liudi te zhe, vot tol'ko...* (2006) [online]. Available at: http://www.razumkov.org.ua/ukr/article.php?news_id=459 [Accessed 31 May 2012].
76. Cited in M. Riabchuk, *Vid Malorosiï do Ukraïny: paradoksy zapizniloho natsiotvorennia* (Kyiv: Krytyka, 2000), pp. 181–82.
77. T. Richardson, *Kaleidoscopic Odessa: History and Place in Contemporary Ukraine* (Toronto, Buffalo, and London: University of Toronto Press, 2008), p. 73.
78. T. Zhurzhenko, '"Capital of Despair": Holodomor Memory and Political Conflicts in Kharkiv after the Orange Revolution', *East European Politics and Societies* vol. 25, no. 3 (2011), pp. 597–639.
79. Razumkov Centre. *Sociological survey on Ukrainian history*, (2005) [online]. Available at: http://razumkov.org,ua/ukr/poll.php?poll_id-285 [Accessed 31 May 2012].
80. M. Velikonia, 'Lost in Translation', p. 537.
81. The myth of 'good' Lenin and 'bad' Stalin was invented and employed both politically and academically in the second half of the twentieth century in order to corroborate the idea of a transformation of Communist regimes into 'socialism with a human face'. Chronologically this type of mythology was rooted in the two-fold process of de-Stalinisation and technological advance in Soviet Union, on the one hand, and the new leftist turn in the West after the WWII on the other. Here I'm considering the possibility of using the same mythology in the process of Ukrainian post-Communist transition.
82. Within specific Soviet/Russian intellectual and ideological framework, the two intellectual legacies could be connected to, respectively, 'Westernisers' and 'Slavophiles', two mainstreams of the Russia's pre-Communist geopolitical and national identification, well known to the students in the field.
83. R. Szporluk, 'Lenin, "Great Russia", and Ukraine', *Harvard Ukrainian Studies* vol. 28, no. 1/4 (2006), pp. 611–26.

6
History and Responsibility: On the Debates on the *Shōwa History*

Naoki Sakai

I asked myself: How many times do I have to explain that it is not *kokka shakai-shugi* (Socialism of the State) but *kokumin shakai-shugi* (Socialism of the Nation) that is the proper and more appropriate rendering of National Socialism?

It was more than two decades ago, and the *Asahi Journal*, a left-oriented weekly periodical published by the *Asahi Shinbun*, one of the largest national papers in Japan, still existed, and weekly copies of the journal were readily available in virtually every bookstore in Japan as well as at kiosks at railway stations. Recalling the political climate of the 1980s and 1990s, some aging baby-boomers may well portray that time as the 'good old days' not without a certain nostalgia.

I was requested to contribute an essay to this journal, so I submitted my manuscript, but the editorial office of the journal returned my manuscript and told me to work on it. First, I did not understand what was wrong with my essay, but after a few exchanges, I learnt that everything hinged upon one small detail. I translated National Socialism into *kokumin shakai-shugi*. Obviously the editor was enraged and politely but emphatically delivered his verdict that this was a gross mistake and totally unacceptable. He was determined to ask me to use the commonly accepted and more respectable term *kokka shakai-shugi* (State Socialism).

In English and other modern European languages, the word 'nation' is far from being singularly definable. Neither is it easily classified in East Asian languages. It means different things according to varying contexts – historical, disciplinary, semantic, geopolitical and so forth. To understand the concept of 'nation', therefore, is to appreciate the indexical instability of this word and its polysemic variability according to the context in which it is discussed.

In modern Japanese, the English word 'nation' has been rendered into such terms as *kokumin* (nation), *minzoku* (ethnic nation), *buzoku* (tribe), and not frequently but occasionally *kokka* (state). These different renderings are the results of Japanese scholars' endeavours to respond to the European conceptions of the nation as well as their theorisation of how the concept of nation could be actualised and concretised in the Japanese modernisation projects of nation-building. Taking into account the distinctly modern character of what the nation connotes – national community, national governance, peoplehood and so on – one may as well presume it safe to say that there was no equivalent in common parlance to 'nation' in Japan before the Meiji Restoration (1868). Both *kokumin* and *minzoku* were neologisms invented to translate the English word 'nation'.

Until the era of the Fifteen Year War (1931–1945), *kokumin* and *minzoku* were sometimes used interchangeably, but the international trends of the 1920s and 1930s alerted many Japanese intellectuals and urged them to differentiate *kokumin* (political nation) from *minzoku* (ethnic nation), under the international climate of fascism. Let us not forget that the Japanese Government remained hostile not only to *minzoku-shugi* (ethnic nationalism) but also to the idea of *minzoku* until the collapse of the Japanese Empire. To manifestly demonstrate that the primary education was designed for the manufacture of *kokumin* (political nation), for instance, the Konoe Fumimaro administration issued the imperial ordinance of changing the name of *shōgakkō* (primary schools) to that of *kokumin gakkō* (national schools) in 1941. As far as state-imposed nationalism was concerned, Japanese nationalists insisted on the principal distinction of the nation of Japan as a political community from the conception of a nation as an ethnic community. As a political community whose principle of integration could be sought in the ideal – a nationalist may well say 'we are together and form one nation as long as we dream together and share the same vision of the future we strive to in common'[1] – Japan could have been able to accommodate as many ethnicities as the situation allows her to.

As soon as the war in Asia and the Pacific was over and the multi-ethnic empire of Japan disintegrated in 1945, however, *kokumin* and *minzoku* began to be used almost synonymously among the Japanese as far as Japanese nationality was concerned. In reference to their own nationality and ethnic identity, the Japanese ceased to differentiate the nation of Japan as a political community from the nation as an ethnic one. This stands in sharp contrast to pre-war nationalism, indeed. And from the 1950s up to the 1990s and even in the present, many in Japan are totally indifferent to what was at stake in distinguishing the political nation (*kokumin*) from the ethnic nation (*minzoku*), and why it was necessary to do so before the loss of their empire. Indeed, historically, there have been many versions of national socialism. What I talked about in my essay for the *Asahi Journal* was nothing but *Nationalsozialismus* or National Socialism, usually abbreviated as Nazism. So I had to clearly indicate that the sort of national socialism I was talking about was not a socialist polity imposed upon people by the state authority or bureaucracy, but one that supposedly rose out of the people, supported by the grass-root movement against state bureaucracy.

I do not believe that the type of modern community called 'nation' has ever been constituted without the mediation of the state. In this respect, every nation derives from state policies, and every nationalism of an existent nation is a state-imposed nationalism. What was at issue in my exchanges with the editor was not the historical genesis of nationality, but rather, my concern with how a nationalism justifies its own genesis, and how it puts forth the logic of its own legitimacy. From this perspective, there was no doubt, as I saw it both then and now, that Nazism was hostile to the idea of the nation created by the state. It was an anti-state ideology to such an extent that it denounced the state endeavour to impose a common language to create a nation.

For the Nazis, the nation ought to be something *natural*; a human being was not cultivated into it, but the nation was a matter of whether one was born into it or not. Accordingly, the socialism that the Nazis advocated was not a state-imposed type of socialism. In that sense, it was definitely not *kokka shakai-shugi* (Socialism of the State). As a matter of fact, National Socialists themselves emphatically insisted that their political legitimacy did not derive from the state but from the nation.

In *Mein Kampf*, Adolf Hitler argues that what allows for the existence of a superior humanity is not the state but the nation possessing the necessary ability to produce higher culture and that, for the socialism he promotes, the state is neither an end nor a cause for the existence of the nation:

> The state is a means to an end. Its end lies in the preservation and advancement of a community of physically and psychically homogeneous creatures. This preservation itself comprises first of all existence as a race and permits the free development of all the forces dormant in this race. Of them a part will always primarily serve the preservation of physical life, and only the remaining part

the promotion of a further spiritual development. Actually the one always creates the precondition for the other.[2]

Cultural accomplishments may appear to be achieved by exceptional individuals, Hitler argues, but these are always rooted in the 'community of physically and psychically homogeneous creatures'. They serve the development of spiritual forces in the same race, while the others may work for the subsistence of the whole community. Nonetheless, no cultural genius is independent of the national substratum shaped by the underlying integrity of physical and psychic homogeneity, for the community is organically formed. Insofar as this community is assumed to be culturally homogeneous, it should be conceptually best described by *minzoku* (ethnic nation). But, in the sense that it is supposed to consist in a community of physically homogeneous creatures, it is no doubt a race. An ethnic nation is no different from a race when its identity is characterised in terms of the 'community of physically and psychically homogeneous creatures'.

In the Hitlerian apprehension of nationalism, the conceptual distinctions among the three terms – nation (*kokumin*), ethnicity (*minzoku*) and race – were gradually annihilated. Nation slides into ethnicity; ethnic nation slides into race. He would adamantly reject both that the nation derives from the state and that the state creates a specific cultural level. The state exists only to preserve the ethnic nation that conditions this level.

By now it should be obvious that a conceptual configuration similar to Hitler's was at work in the mind of the editor of the *Asahi Journal* when he demanded that I adopt *kokka shakai-shugi* (Socialism of the State) rather than *kokumin shakai-shugi* (Socialism of the Nation), even though it would probably be incorrect to claim that he was in fact a national socialist. The editor believed that fascism was something to abhor and that he would never support knowingly any kind of fascism, not to mention Nazism.

Soon after the end of the Asia Pacific War, the Japanese could not remain insulated from the news of the atrocities, the genocide and the acts of extraordinary cruelty committed by the Nazis. Neither could the Japanese public stay totally ignorant of the crimes and atrocities committed by Japanese nationals because the International Military Tribunal for the Far East – commonly known as the Tokyo War Crime Tribunal – was held in Tokyo from 1946 to 1948; in it some atrocities committed by the Japanese military were interrogated and a comparatively small number of war criminals prosecuted. The proceedings of the tribunal were widely propagated through mass media in Japan even though news releases were strictly censored by the offices of the Supreme Commander of the Allied Powers in charge of the occupation of regions in East Asia. In addition, the Tokyo War Crime Tribunal was often compared with the Nuremberg Trials held in Germany earlier in 1945 and 1946, in which the Nazi war criminals were interrogated and prosecuted under the categories of crimes including 'crimes against humanity'.

The Tokyo War Crime Tribunal had a different organisation from the Nuremberg Trials under different historical conditions and for different strategic considerations. For instance, the category of 'crimes against humanity' was never applied to Japanese war criminals inside Japan.[3] One must not forget about one historical context particular to postwar Japan: it was the strategic decision by the United States of America that the Emperor Hirohito of Japan was deliberately immunised from all charges of crimes, atrocities, violations of international law and other criminal actions committed in his name and under his command by the Japanese Government and the Japanese military.[4] At the same time the pardoning of Emperor Hirohito in due course implied that every subject working for the Japanese state under the jurisdiction of the Meiji Constitution (The Constitution of the Empire of Japan was in force until it was replaced by the Constitution of Japan in May 1947) was relieved of legal responsibility, for, at least in theory, every Japanese Government and military act of aggression was ordained by the Emperor. This was a decision taken by the United States Government to discharge Hirohito from legal liability for the sake of American postwar strategy in the Far East.

War criminals were prosecuted and executed in the name of the United Nations by the Allied Powers. But within the legal system of the Japanese state, no legal procedure has been defined whereby to arrest, interrogate, persecute or punish those who committed racist, colonial or genocidal crimes during or prior to the war.

Yet, one can hardly evade the comparative framework between Germany and Japan in post-war academic and journalistic discussions on fascism. Some may well argue that it is inappropriate to attribute the name 'fascism' to the kind of oppressive regime that developed in Japan in the 1930s. The regime was undeniably anti-parliamentarian, jingoistic, anti-Marxist yet manifesting certain socialistic orientations, so that calling it fascism does not seem totally off the mark. But, as Maruyama Masao pointed out in his famous articles on Japanese fascism,[5] the system that developed to promote totalitarian policies was hostile toward grass roots ethnic nationalism. In pre-war Japan (~1945), *minzoku-shugi* (ethnic nationalism) was commonly denounced by the government, and its followers were often regarded as something like pariahs in Japan's annexed territories. It is hard and actually impossible to demonstrate that an anti-state nationalism took over the state apparatuses in the 1930s in Japan. As a matter of fact, some historians have attempted to portray this oppressive regime in terms of the system of total war in consideration of the absence of the *Völkisch* tendency in it.[6] Nonetheless, from the late 1940s until the 1990s, the characteristic of Japanese fascism continued to be drawn up in reference to German National Socialism (or less frequently to Italian Fascism or other Clerical Fascism in Austria, Spain, Croatia and so forth). One would therefore naturally assume that the Nazi's emphasis on the national or *Völkisch* feature of National Socialism was fairly well-known in post-war Japan.

Surprisingly, however, very few Japanese intellectuals were aware – the general public even less so – in the 1980s that Nazism was a sort of *minzoku-shugi* (ethnic nationalism) abhorring the state-centred rationalisation and favouring the idealised image of people's communality. Precisely because the post-war image of the Third Reich emphasised the *rationalistic* character of the Nazi policies – the precision of planning with which Germany's re-militarisation was executed, the cold-blooded reasonableness that guided the management of the concentration camps and the idealisation of scientific and technological knowledge, and so forth – it was widely assumed that National Socialism was somewhat organised and directed by the scientific and technocratic spirit of state bureaucracy. Perhaps it was somewhat believed that the Japanese 'people' were less 'modern' than the Germans, and that the Japanese people were indisputably less 'rational'.[7] Some romantic fantasy prevailed among the Japanese public that the 'people' are incapable of embodying rationality, and that any sign of rational conduct in everyday life should mean coercion by the state bureaucracy against their tendency toward their innate irrationality.[8] The editor of the *Asahi Journal* was no exception to this thinking.

What are the historical conditions and prevailing images of the evil called 'fascism' that helped sustain this misrecognition of the ethnic nationalist character of Nazism for so long in post-war Japan? Why did the Japanese immediately assume that the oppressive nature of fascism had to be attributed or immediately equated to the oppressive coercion of the state? How could they manage to take for granted that national people (*minzoku*) were always passive and, therefore, incapable of victimising while the state was an agent of active oppression or a victimiser that imposed rules and commands on passive people against their will?

In order to address these questions in historically relevant contexts, let us switch to a different set of problems that were volatile in Japan after the loss of the empire. These are the problems of war and colonial responsibility that haunted the production of knowledge in the humanities and social sciences there, since they could set off a new and precarious process of decolonisation in which the Japanese would fashion themselves differently from before, even to such an extent that they would cease to adhere to their nationality. Post-war decolonisation could have forced the Japanese to reflect upon and call into question what they used to believe themselves to be.

I do not think that the decolonisation of the mind in the sense of radical self-doubt and self-refashioning of the peoplehood had ever taken place in Japan since the loss of the Japanese Empire. But I do not believe that the potentiality of decolonisation was non-existent either. What prevented the Japanese public from submitting themselves to the thorough process of decolonisation?

There are many aspects of decolonisation, but to the extent that decolonisation occurs as a historical process of transformation and is concerned with a person's or people's relationship to the past, it is not completely off the mark to say that decolonisation is first of all a matter of historicity. Of course, whether we approach the question of historicity from the standpoint of a single person or people is of crucial importance, but let me tentatively postulate the problem in terms of collective history. By historicity I mean the calling into question of collectivity's present in relation to the past and the future. On the one hand, our historicity is very much informed by the awareness that the present state of affairs, upon which our continuing lives are based, owes to what happened in the past in such decisive ways that we cannot change the present state of our being without fundamentally altering our relationship to the past. We do not choose the modality of our being – what and how we are in the present – and we are confined to the present by our historical conditions. On the other hand, our historicity implies that our present is conceivable only in relation to our future, which is essentially indeterminate. Thus, we are at a juncture in the projectile of historical time, which is at the same time open to the future and delimited by the past.

In August 1945, the Japanese Empire was defeated and subsequently collapsed, and this drastic change of state sovereignty gave rise to a wide spectrum of alternatives all of a sudden. As the annexed territories were liberated from the jurisdiction of the Japanese state, more than 30 per cent of the subject population was removed from the national population. That portion of the population, who used to be Japanese, ceased to fashion themselves as Japanese and began to identify with the different nationalities: Korean, Chinese and so forth. As a result, the multi-ethnic nation of Japan was now open to alternative modes of identification. Now let me focus on the other portion of the population that continued to identify themselves with the Japanese nation. In order for them to grasp this moment of opening to the future, it was necessary to examine the Japanese relationship to the past and to find an alternate way of belonging to the community. With respect to how the Japanese ought to redefine their relationship to the past, the remaining Japanese were not monolithic at all.

I understand that the problem of historicity in post-war Japan was most explicitly addressed in the discussions of war responsibility even though, among the populace continuing to retain Japanese nationality, there were many who rejected the topic of war responsibility outright. Even among those who entertained such discussions, a variety of positions existed: one might refer to that of Maruyama Masao and Yoshimoto Takaaki, perhaps two of the most famous discussants of war responsibility, for whom at issue was war responsibility of the leadership to the Japanese nation or of intellectuals to ordinary people for not preventing the war from starting and continuing, and for inflicting subsequent disasters upon the nation and ordinary folks.[9]

It is important to keep in mind that, for Maruyama and Yoshimoto, the war responsibility of the Japanese nation to the portion of the Japanese nation who ceased to be Japanese after the war, or to peoples beyond Japanese sovereignty was entirely outside their scope. The *Shōwa History* was another attempt by Marxists historians to address the issues of war responsibility by analysing how Japanese capitalism paved the way for the Japanese state through its ultimate defeat, and how imperialist policies were necessarily prompted by contradictions inherent in Japanese society and international politics.[10] It was a historiographic attempt to examine the Japanese relationship to the past, the historicity of which could be summarily addressed as that of war responsibility.

Yet, soon after the publication of the *Shōwa History*, a protest was launched by those who regarded Marxist historiography as 'too inhuman'.[11] The ensuing disputes were later called the debates on the *Shōwa History* (*Shōwa-shi ronsō*), and in these debates some of the problems concerning *kokumin shakaishugi* (Socialism of the Nation) that I mentioned above were unveiled.

In order to pursue the problem of historicity in war responsibility, it is essential to discern two types of responsibility: legal responsibility and political or historical responsibility.

In talking about legal responsibility, it may appear unavoidable to assume the persistent existence of the subject who is to respond to the charge of guilt or to be held culpable for it. In disputes over legal matters, it is supposed that the one who committed a crime must be the same as the one who is suspected culpable of the crime or who is held responsible for what was initially violated. In order to justifiably demand responsibility, therefore, there must be the assumption of a persistent and continual existence between the agent of a guilty action and the subject who is accused of that action. In modern jurisprudence, the identification of the agent of a crime with the indicted is an absolute requirement, and accusation by association is entirely rejected. A family member of a murderer, for instance, cannot be held culpable for the murder unless his or her involvement in the criminal action is proven. Neither can a member of the nation whose troops committed a genocide be punished for that atrocity simply because they share national membership with guilty troops. As long as the validity of legal responsibility is built on the individual identity of the perpetrator and the accused, legal responsibility vanishes when the indicted dies, and it cannot be transferred from one generation to another generation. Of course, the indicted can be an organisation such as a national state or corporation. In such cases, the legal responsibility persists until the state or other kind of organisation that has been indicted for a crime ceases to exist. The case of the Japanese state's responsibility for the system of the Comfort Stations (*jūgun ian-sho*) or the case of the Union Carbide for the Bhopal gas tragedy is a typical case of legal responsibility. It goes without saying that the responsibility of an individual, a nation or a corporation is not exhaustively legal, and that it can also constitute a case of political or historical responsibility.

When it comes to the problem of historical responsibility pertaining to past injustices of racism, sexism, military violence or colonialism, however, one cannot necessarily proceed with the same set of assumptions as legal responsibility. Perhaps it is still fruitful to appeal to Hannah Arendt's distinction of legal responsibility and political responsibility. It is important to keep in mind, that there are some that clearly fall within the purview of legal responsibility among the crimes of racism, sexism, war and colonialism, but what is at stake, particularly in view of what is often referred to as Japan's post-war responsibility, cannot be either exhaustively or adequately attended to according to the protocols of legal responsibility, even though it is true that many of those who occupied the authoritative positions – of political leadership, commanders in military hierarchies, administrative officers in the decision-making of governments, corporations and other institutions, and so forth – have neither been prosecuted nor interrogated.

In this respect, the preliminary stage in the question of Japan's post-war responsibility has been far from adequately addressed, even up to the present moment.

For one thing, the subject of historical responsibility is not necessarily an individual; there are many cases in which the national state or the nation as a whole must be regarded as the ultimate agent of a criminal act. Hence, it is not irrelevant to say, for example, 'the Japanese are responsible for the crimes committed by some individuals under colonial regimes'. Similarly one may argue that the West is responsible for racist violence in many places in the world. In these instances, the subject is not specified as individuals. Yet, the subject of historical responsibility is not merely collective. It is also a matter of responsibility that manifests itself in a dialogic situation involving individuals. Here, responsibility is primordial in its gist: it is responsiveness, that is, an obligation to respond to the charge of past crimes and is concerned with the fact that an individual who identifies with the Japanese nation ought to respond to another individual or individuals, Japanese or non-Japanese. We now have to confront a paradox.

It is beyond doubt that the nation, such as the Japanese nation, is accidentally and almost arbitrarily constituted. It is impossible to presume the persistence, substance or trans-historical identity of the Japanese ethnos or nation. No nation is based on any continuing ethnic basis; the collective identity projected in nationalist mythology is nothing but a case of fictive ethnicity. The history of modern Japan is one of the best illustrations of the arbitrary and inconsistent constitution of the nation. In the process of colonisation and through the policies of multi-ethnic integration, the Japanese state attempted to create a nation involving the population of the Japanese archipelago, Taiwan, the Korean peninsula and other Pacific islands. However, as noted earlier, about a third of the population lost Japanese nationality as soon as the Japanese Empire collapsed. Furthermore, among the 'people' supposedly Japanese, various discriminations have existed, and consequently since the beginning of the Meiji period – not to mention the periods prior to the establishment of the modern nation-state – there have been a number of groups who could not feel a belonging to the nation.

Nevertheless, the persistent existence of the Japanese nation must be assumed in order for us – let me note that 'us' in this instance does not unavoidably designate those who regard themselves as Japanese – to engage in historical responsibility or responsiveness. One who was born after the collapse of the Japanese Empire cannot be held culpable, for instance, for Japan's colonial or war crimes in the legal sense, but the same individual is not free from the historical responsibility of the Japanese nation. Even though those who committed colonial, racist or sexist crimes in the Japanese Empire have all passed away, the Japanese nation as a collective is not exempt from historical responsibility. Strange though it may appear, every individual is vulnerable to culpability by association in terms of nation, race, ethnicity or religious faith in the case of historical responsibility, while legally nobody can be held responsible by association.

Please keep in mind, however, that I am not saying that those who are historically responsible are invariably guilty of Japan's past. As has been pointed out by many, historical responsibility must be clearly distinguished from historical guilt, for the concept of responsibility assumes the acceptance of one's obligation to respond when one is called upon. The concept of responsibility is built on a structured situation where one is addressed by somebody else about an event that one has executed.[12] Therefore, just as with legal responsibility, the concept of historical responsibility requires four constituent moments: an addresser who asks about an addressee's responsibility, an addressee who is obliged to respond to the addresser, an event about which the addresser calls upon the addresser, and finally a witness who observes the transaction between the addresser and the addressee. The witness who occupies the position of the third person may well be absent in many cases of historical responsibility.

When the addresser and the addressee are of the same nationality, it is not necessary to consider the nation in our inquiry into historical responsibility. Of course, there are many cases – such as the history of slavery in the United States – in which the issue of historical responsibility can never be overlooked even though both parties may belong to the same nation. Only when the addresser and the addressee are of different nationalities, however, does the nation emerge as the indispensable moment. The nation is problematised when the addresser calls upon the addressee from outside the presumed closure of the national community. Japanese national subjectivity is at stake, therefore, only when someone who does not identify with the Japanese nation, a non-Japanese (*hikokumin*), problematises some event that the Japanese committed in connection with the non-Japanese or the Japanese who would cease to be Japanese. Thus, my query is about how Japanese historians could sustain this opening to the outside of Japanese nationality in order to keep the problem of historical responsibility viable. In other words, how did they articulate their historiography to the problem of historicity?

To elucidate the problem of historical responsibility, let us examine the debate on the *Shōwa History*, the intellectual debate about Japan's war responsibility and the writing of history that drew in many historians and literary critics in the 1950s.

Shōwa-shi (the Shōwa History), published in 1955, was written by leading Marxist historians of the time, Tōyama Shigeki, Imai Sei'ichi and Fujiwara Akira.[13] The book analysed the transformations of Japanese society and the emergence of Japanese Fascism from the first two decades of the Shōwa period until the end of the Asia Pacific War (1925–1945). It was an extensive analysis of Japanese imperialism and capitalism, and established the standard historiography of the early Shōwa period among the progressive readership in post-war Japan. What prompted the debates on the *Shōwa History* was the article 'A question to today's historians (*Gendaishi eno gimon*)' by Kamei Katsuichirō, a well-known literary critic who was once a Marxist in the 1920s and later converted to Japanese Romanticism (*Nihon Romanha*) in the 1930s.

In this article, Kamei poses the question as to why people want to know about history, arguing that when we want to study history, we are invariably possessed by 'a desire to confirm the origins of our life in our own ethnicity and the trends of times'.[14] Underlying this desire is a question about 'who the Japanese are'. Let me note in passing that the conceptual specificity of the Japanese is deliberately left undetermined. Perhaps, for Kamei, it is so self-evident that he need not bother to discuss it. Yet we cannot overlook that this tactic of his narrative performance gives rise to a certain rhetorical force.

Kamei also introduces another unspecified term 'man or men (*ningen*)'. Since historiography's mission is 'to describe men', and 'history is men's history', Kamei claims that the task of a historian is to present an alluring (*miryokuteki ni*) portrayal of men. Man lives in his own times to the best of his ability and then dies. 'Can the historian be judgmental without trying to re-live the conditions and the environment of the past era?'[15] The tropes of man, human, humanity, humaneness and humanism proliferate. Here, it is necessary to underline that Kamei does not differentiate 'man' and 'the Japanese', and that the Japanese is equated to Japanese nationality without any qualification. So his notion of the Japanese moves freely and almost at random from the broad generality of 'man' to the historically limited particularity of 'the Japanese nationality'. I must note that the rhetorical force of his argumentation derives largely from his demonstrative but deliberate oversight about what constitutes 'the Japanese'. We cannot but consider the political consequences of his laxity toward 'the Japanese'.

Kamei continues: the historian must be in sympathy with the Japanese of the past since his task is to re-live the 'man' of the past. It follows, he insists, that the historian must be endowed with literary talent. And this literary talent is the faculty of imagination to re-present or remember the experience of the past that he never actually lived as if he had experienced it for himself. Interpreting Kamei's argument philosophically, I think this faculty is a faculty to narrate a myth rather than the faculty of re-presentation in order to represent the past event as it happened. What is at issue is not historical objectivity, but a literary imagination by means of which to produce the sense of togetherness as a national community, as an ethnic nation of the Japanese. According to him, the task of the historian is, above all else, to fabricate a fictive ethnicity.

Kamei Katsuichirō feels that the authors of the *Shōwa History* are lacking in this literary talent, the faculty of imagination to represent the past as it was lived by the nation. It is no more than 'a history where the human being, that is, the nation, cannot be found'.[16] 'I called this feature [of the *Shōwa History*] an absence of "the nation" or of the human being'.[17]

What is glaringly obvious by now is this: Kamei deliberately confused the three distinct categories of humanity (*ningen*), Japanese ethnos (*nihon minzoku*), and Japanese nation (*nihon kokumin*) with one another. Therefore, implicitly in his argumentative demonstration but overtly in his performance, he repressed the conceivably logical possibility that could have crushed his reasoning right away: anybody could have asked, 'Are you saying that the non-Japanese are not humans?' It is a matter of course that he was implying that the non-Japanese are not humans. What was being asserted unambiguously by Kamei is the prototype of national humanism according to which humanity is primordially defined as nationality. Yet, he managed to prevent this unambiguous national humanism from manifesting itself in his argumentation by only addressing to 'us, Japanese', to the restricted audience who would presumably never ask such an upsetting question. This article was actually published in one of the leading Japanese monthly journals, *Bungei Shunjū*, and it was likely that, among the readers of this article, there were many people who did not identify with the Japanese nation since there were millions of *former* Japanese who were educated in Japanese all over East Asia including the Japanese Archipelago. Kamei preliminarily excluded from his putative audience those who would not consent to such a conformism. By setting the stage for his narrative address, he deliberately and decisively ignored those readers who would challenge his assertion about his national humanism.

If this is not a case of blatant racial discrimination, where else can we possibly find a more obvious instance? Is forming an exclusive group by putting up a sign 'For non-Japanese, off-limits' not an obvious case of racial favouritism? When, for the reason of his or her ethnicity, you feel entitled to ignore somebody who is asking a question in front of you, does this sense of entitlement constitute an instance of racial discrimination? Is the formation of an exclusive club of humanity whose membership is only granted to the Japanese not a case of blatant racism?

What we have so far recognised in the performativity of Kamei's argument is a version of national humanism that we have cursorily surveyed in the Hitlerian rhetoric concerning cultural genius. National humanism consists of a series of category confusions that are not merely oversights but also deliberate in the sense that this confusionism – humanity = nationality = race – constitutes a declaration or imperative: 'I adhere to my conviction that the non-Japanese are not human'; 'I would not engage in any dialogue with those who do not belong to the Japanese nation'. And let us not fail to notice the communalistic aspect of national humanism. This is a call for communal solidarity, an evocation of camaraderie. It is due to this alluring communalism that many were attracted to what is known as fascism in the interwar period.

Without inhibition, Kamei Katsuichirō resurrected the rhetorical strategy of national humanism ten years after the loss of the Japanese Empire. This urges us to confront once again the problem concerning the extraordinary popularity of fascism – not only National Socialism but also Italian Fascism and clerical fascisms – in Europe and elsewhere, but this time, the context is postwar Japan.

Now, let us see how the authors of the *Shōwa History* responded to the accusation launched by Kamei. Before receiving Kamei's criticism, they had touched on the question of history and responsibility in the preface of the book. The three authors said they wanted to describe the history of the Shōwa period up to the moment of Japan's defeat as 'representatives of the Japanese nation (*watashitachi kokumin*)'. In the 1955 edition, the subject of responsibility as the accused was identified as the Japanese nation, whereas the accusers were also the Japanese as a nation. Their initial question went as follows: 'Why were we, the nation, involved in the war, carried down, and helpless in preventing the war from continuing?' Even though the accused and the accusers are identical, the form of inquiry postulates a conflict or split between one portion of the nation and another. When the opposition between the accusers and the accused is obscured, however, the question of war responsibility would vanish. The issue of war responsibility can persist only as long as the subject who demands an answer and the subject who responds are differentiated from one another. It is important to recognise that the authors of the *Shōwa History*, at least, evaded such a conception of the nation as a homogeneous and integrated community by focusing on the element of class struggle.

Nevertheless, the historical responsibility of the nation as a whole was never clearly articulated in the *Shōwa History*. This was one of the weak links which did not escape Kamei's scrutiny. Kamei asks:

> Why was invasion into Manchukuo and China undertaken? The problem would be simple if 'the ruling class' alone were guilty. Moreover, we must take into account our contempt towards the Orientals that grew step by step among our nation ever since the first Sino-Japanese war. There must have been a great number of soldiers who literally believed in the Holy War and died uttering 'Long live the Emperor.' There must have been military officers who sincerely loved the country and died for it. Are these dead all idiots who were manipulated by the ruling class?[18]

Instead of yielding to Kamei's simplistic rhetoric, it is worth noting the semantics implied in the concept of the nation here. The laxity of Kamei's use of 'the Japanese as a nation' can be partly blamed for the polysemy of the very concept of the nation. The nation is a principle by which to create the bonds of fantastic communality among the residents of a state territory, despite the disparities and conflicts of economic, ethnic, class, gender, tribal, religious, or geographic nature. Depending upon relative positions within kinship networks, the configurations of social ranks and other societal elements, each individual is endowed with particular privileges, obligations, and ethical norms. Yet, as a member of the nation, an individual is encouraged to transcend these differences. While an individual is identified in terms of relative positions within kinship, the configuration of social ranks and so forth, every individual is entitled to be treated as equal in the nation. An individual belongs to the community of the nation just as an animal belongs to its own species in the classification of zoology. While it is impossible to uphold the principle of equality in human relations regulated by kinship, the nation is a community that, at least in theory, consists of equal individuals. Through the commitment to the principle of formal equality, therefore, the nation legitimates itself no matter how disparate, fragmented and discriminatory the actuality of the national society might be. The modern community we call 'the nation' has to be built on the premise of equality and the fantasy of homogeneity. This is the reason why formal equality was hardly recognised as a social norm before the formation of the nation-state in East Asia and elsewhere. Yet, as soon as the Meiji Restoration destroyed the feudal rank system of the Tokugawa Shogunate, the Japanese state declared that no member of the Japanese nation was born either above or below other members, at least in theory. The national community of the Japanese was built on the premise that every member of the Japanese nation was equal under the gaze of one emperor.

It may appear that Kamei tried to remind his readership of the historical responsibility that not only the ruling class, but also the ruled classes ought to hold. Let us recall, however, that the voice of the non-Japanese was excluded from the outset by emphasising sympathy among the nation while completely neglecting the plausibility of someone speaking from outside it. As a matter of fact, he foreclosed the possibility of addressing not only the legal but also the historical responsibility for war crimes by thus excluding the non-Japanese and addressing the problem of Japanese responsibility.

However, what is astonishing about the debates on the *Shōwa History* does not lie only with Kamei's presentation. Given the historical circumstances of the time, it is retrospectively apprehensible that he invoked anti-Marxist rhetoric and called for national sympathy rather than the ethics of class struggle.

What I found very difficult to appreciate is the fact that the authors of the *Shōwa History* completely failed to draw attention to the laxity of Kamei's use of the concept of nation. They too were entirely oblivious to the fact that there could be readers outside the Japanese nation who could have been listening to their debates. In the Japanese Empire, the state promoted education in the medium of the standard Japanese language even in the annexed territories in the last years of colonial rule. How many of these former Japanese subjects could have become incapable of reading Japanese in the ten years that had elapsed since the end of Japanese colonial rule? Despite Kamei's overt exclusion of the non-Japanese from the forum of these debates, there must have been a large number of educated people who could easily read the debates on the *Shōwa History* in the 1950s outside as well as inside the shrunken Japanese territory. It seems to me that Tōyama, Imai, and Fujiwara too acquiesced to national humanism.

In his review article on the *Shōwa History*, Matsuzawa Hiroaki drew attention to the very dichotomy of the nation (*kokumin*) and the non-nation (*hi-kokumin*) that continued to serve as an important tool of political justification throughout the Asia-Pacific war (1931–1945) and thereafter.[19] The term *hi-kokumin*—also rendered as 'non-national' or 'anti-national'—carried a very strong emotive connotation, just like pejorative terms like 'communists' and 'red'. Those who wanted to justify their political agenda often appealed to this dichotomy and labelled their opponents *hi-kokumin*; they tried to characterise them as spies or infiltrators into the nation. By layering this dichotomy onto the distinction of the ruled people and the ruling class, the authors of the *Shōwa History* attempted to exorcise the ruling class from the interior of the nation, thereby postulating the configuration of the accusers and the accused. This is to say that the nation was assigned to the position of the accusers and the ruling class to that of the accused. For Tōyama, Imai and Fujiwara too, the Japanese nation was not an agent whose historical responsibility must be addressed by the non-Japanese. Not surprisingly, Matsuzawa observed, 'the [Shōwa History] authors' use of the basic terms suggest that the nation consists of the people, who share the objective features of shared ethnicity in common, minus the ruling class'.[20] By ostracising the ruling class by calling them *hi-kokumin* (non-Japanese), they succeeded in reserving the position of the accusers for the nation. But Matsuzawa expressed his doubt in due course: 'Was the subjective responsibility of the nation somewhat obscured in the *Shōwa History*?'[21]

Just like Kamei Katsuichirō, the authors of the *Shōwa History* foreclosed the plausibility of someone asking about the nation's historical responsibility. As far as the historicity of the Japanese national is concerned, Tōyama Shigeki, Imai Seiichi and Fujiwara Akira were accomplices of Kamei, rather than serious interrogators.

This explains why Kamei's narrative strategy of national humanism was so effective. This is to say that, already in 1955, the régime of ethnic foreclosure that would later be called the myth of the mono-ethnic nation had been fully institutionalised. Captured in this régime were not only romantic racists like Kamei Katsuichirō, but Marxists such as the authors of the *Shōwa History* too could not escape the allure of national humanism. After all, they could be no other than Marxist nationalists.

It is commonly accepted that fascism was one of the most popular topics of academic discussion in the humanities and social sciences in post-war Japan. A huge number of monographs and articles were produced about war responsibility, the presence or absence of resistance in Japan, the conversion of intellectuals from Marxism to Ultra-nationalism, and Emperorist Fascism (*tennōsei fashizumu*). Yet, facing such a blatant indifference to the problem of how fascism was so attractive to many intellectuals and ordinary folks, one wonders whether the question of fascism has ever been discussed on a serious level in Japan. Have Japanese intellectuals ever critically confronted the problem of fascism in post-World War II history? Do they continue to absolve the nationality of the Japanese for the oppressive and coercive nature of the modern state? Will they not return to the idolisation of national camaraderie as the only remedy for their current helplessness? Will they ever be able to commit themselves to a strategy of community other than national humanism? Will they continue to blame *kokka shakai-shugi* (Socialism of the State) rather than *kokumin shakai-shugi* (Socialism of the Nation)?

It goes without saying that today this situation is not particular to Japan, but the utter absence of a critique of racism in Japan makes me distraught. It is clear that the affinity of nationalism with racism is not the monopoly of the German people.

Notes

1. This is exactly what Takata Yasuma, perhaps the most important sociologist of modern Japan, advocated in his publications in the 1930s and early 1940s. He talked about 'the integration in the future (*shōrai ni okeru tōgō*)' and an 'integral nation (*kōminzoku*)' and sought to find social scientific knowledge to design multi-ethnic nationality and construct the ideological justification for the oppression of anti-colonial ethnic nationalisms. Precisely because his sociology anticipated the agenda of post-war American social sciences, he was purged as a collaborator of the total war regime of Japan.
2. Adolf Hitler, *Mein Kampf*, Ralph Manheim trans. (New York: The Houghton Mifflin Company, 1999), p. 393.
3. At the Tokyo War Crime Trial, the category 'crimes against humanity' was not applied. This does not mean that no war criminal was prosecuted under this category at war criminal courts held in Asia. There are a great number of publications on the Tokyo War Crime Trial. One of the most reliable and concise books on this topic is: Hayashi Hiroshi, *BC kyū Senpan Saiban* (War Crime Trials for Class B and Class C war criminals) (Tokyo: Iwanami Shoten, 2005).
4. It is in this context that the verdict reached at the Women's International War Crimes Tribunal on Japan's Military Sexual Slavery (8–12 December 2000) is particularly significant. Emperor Hirohito was found guilty for the Japanese Government's crimes against humanity. It was an absolutely necessary correction to the Tokyo War Crime Trial.
5. Maruyama Masao's analysis of Japanese Fascism can be found in *Gendai seiji no shisō to kōdō* (Tokyo: Mirai-sha, 1964); *Thought and Behaviour in Modern Japanese Politics* (London: Oxford University Press, 1966).

6. Such an attempt can be found in Yasushi Yamanouchi, J. Victor Koschmann and Ryūichi Narita (eds), *Total War and 'Modernisation'* (Ithaca: Cornell East Asia Program, 1998).

7. This optimistic celebration of rationality and modernisation was not particular to Maruyama Masao and the followers of Modernisation Theory. It is an inherent investment in social sciences in general. An important critique of social scientific knowledge can be found in Zygmunt Bauman, *Modernity and the Holocaust* (Ithaca: Cornell University Press, 1989).

8. In this respect, Maruyama was explicit. He argued that Japanese fascist leaders manifested Japan's pre-modernity and lack of rationality, while Nazism indicated the modern political consciousness. Underlying Maruyama's assessment is the scheme that, in Japan, modernisation is imposed upon people by the state bureaucracy while, in Western Europe, which represents a social formation innately 'modern', rationality is internalised by people. (Masao Maruyama, *Gendai Seiji no Shisō to Kōdō, op cit.*, pp. 11–28, 29–87, 88–130)

9. Cf. Masao Maruyama, *Gendai Seiji no Shisō to Kōdō, op cit.*, Takaaki Yoshimoto, *Gisei no Shūen* (Tokyo: Gendai Shichōsha, 1962); Takaaki Yoshomoto, *Jojō no Ronri* (Tokyo: Miraisha, 1976).

10. Tōyama Shigeki, Imai Seiichi and Fujiwara Akira, *Shōwa-shi* (Tokyo: Iwanami Shoten, 1955).

11. Kamei Katsuichirō, *'Gendai Reshika eno Gimon'* (A question to present-day historians) in the monthly journal, *Bungei Shunjū* (March 1956). Reprinted in Kamei Katsuichirō, *Gendai-shi no Kadai*, (Problems in the History of the Present), Tokyo, Chuō Kōron-sha, 1957: 11.

12. This can be rephrased as follows: we are addressed by somebody else about an event that we have executed. Even if the first person singular is replaced by the first person plural, the problem of responsibility may still be valid, precisely because at issue is *historical* responsibility.

13. *Shōwa-shi* (Tokyo: Iwanami Shoten, 1955).

14. *Ibid.*, p. 58

15. *Ibid.*, p. 61

16. *'Gendai Reshika eno Gimon'* (A question to present-day historians) *op cit.*, p. 22

17. *Ibid.*, p. 24

18. *Ibid.*, pp. 25–26

19. Matsuzawa Hiroaki, 'Book Review: the new edition of the Shōwa History (*shohyō: shōwa-shi shinpan)'* in *Shiso* (October 1959), 109.

20. *Ibid.*

21. *Ibid.*, p. 110.

7
Widukind or Karl der Große? Perspectives on Historical Culture and Memory in the Third Reich and Post-War West Germany

Peter Lambert

Heritage sites in lower saxony: A travelogue, June 2010

In Verden an der Aller, a small town in Lower Saxony, there is a stone henge. Publicly accessible, but half-concealed among trees, it comprises nearly 4500 standing stones. They are variously arranged: in stone circles, in an ensemble typical of neolithic long barrows and above all in long, winding tree-lined avenues. These help form a roughly oblong enclosure, so large that one might drop several football pitches into it. A number of the smaller groupings of stones look ancient. Many of the individual stones themselves do, too. In more than a few cases, the latter appearances are not deceptive. Though several now have Christian crosses chiselled into them, there are dolmens and megaliths among them, taken from genuine prehistoric sties in a region once strikingly rich in such monuments. Some allegedly bear traces of prehistoric decoration (though – try as I might – I could find no such evidence myself). Some may even have originated on the site itself – vestiges of a ritual site predating the present one by millennia, and largely destroyed by it.

The henge does betray its own modernity – even to the untrained eye. Not a few of the stones look like (and almost certainly are) mere pieces of rubble brought from building sites or ruined modern buildings. A fair few were self-evidently shaped by machine-tooling. For whole stretches of the main avenues, the generally impressive lines of substantial boulders, well over head-high, give way to rows of quite pathetically insignificant, jagged and misshapen stones dragged along in desperation for completeness' sake but otherwise regardless of the aesthetic of the totality.

I went to the tourist office in Verden to inquire whether it had a published guide to or other kind of literature on the site. With a show of regret, the staff told me, no. I also asked at the local museum, where the same answer was accompanied with an explanation: '*Es gibt keine Belege* (there is no evidence)'. My protestations of disbelief were met with repeated denial. Perhaps this was a mantra, masking discomfort with the site itself on the part of the local community. Perhaps the henge attracts unwelcome attention. Certainly, there is next to no effort made to exploit its tourist potential.

This henge was constructed in 1934–1935 on the instructions of *Reichsführer-SS* Heinrich Himmler and with the active encouragement of *Reichsleiter* Alfred Rosenberg, second only to Hitler as an ideologue of Nazism. Each standing stone was intended to commemorate a Saxon allegedly 'slaughtered' in 782 AD on the orders of 'Charles the Frank' – Charlemagne. The henge was called the *Sachsenhain* (Saxon Grove). It was intended more broadly to honour the Saxon resistance to Charlemagne and Duke Widukind, its 'heroic' leader, and perhaps also to encourage vilification of Charlemagne, the *Sachsenschlächter* ('Butcher of Saxons'). Certainly, its pagan appearance was intended as a homage to the paganism of the Saxon tribesmen allegedly executed there. From the outset, it was meant to combine two functions: first, it was designed to serve as a venue for ritual performance; second, as a heritage tourist attraction. Part of it was a designated site for the *Thingspiel* – the failed Nazi experiment in mass open-air theatrical performances whose name evoked the gatherings of Germanic tribesmen. With the failure of the *Thing*-movement, this particular use of the henge of course became redundant. A second plan had entailed the construction of an open-air museum within the remainder of the enclosure. This was to be composed of half-timbered buildings characteristic of the region and reassembled on-site. The Nazis promoted mass tourism and encouraged tourists to approach 'their ancestral heritage' with due reverence. In the event, only one such *Fachwerkhaus* was reconstructed at Verden – just beyond the perimeter of the henge. The concentration-camp prisoners also erected a handful of new buildings in the *Heimatschutzstil* – a German equivalent to English 'mock-Tudor', but imbued with racialist ideology. The relatively modest final use of the site in the Third Reich was as a Hitler Youth and SS training establishment.

For years after 1945, tourists continued to visit the *Sachsenhain* in substantial numbers. They appear to have associated it with *Heimat*, the comfort zone of twee, homely local patriotism, in what was arguably a depoliticised echo of habits developed in the period of Nazi rule. Today, the site is owned by a Protestant youth hostel-*cum*-school. Giving the lie to the line peddled by the member of the Verden museum staff who had spoken to me that there is no evidence relating to the origins and early use of the henge, the Church has laid out a series of informative (and self-evidently in some sense researched) explanatory boards that stand at intervals along the stone-lined avenues. Every now and again, however, neo-Nazis congregate there – to celebrate in the spirit of Himmler (vintage 1934, as we shall see) and to 'reclaim' the henge from usurpation by the Church.[1]

I also visited Enger, a still smaller community further west in Lower Saxony, where Duke Widukind himself is said to lie buried in the local church. Enger feels more remote and rural than Verden. Just beyond the graveyard, an impressive half-timbered building houses the Widukind Museum. Its origins go back to 1939, when it was opened – not indeed as a museum per se, but as a *Weihestätte*, a shrine, dedicated to Widukind by the SS. In striking contrast to Verden, Enger appears neither to pass over its ninth-century past nor to be disposed to clam up about its Nazi heritage. On the contrary, there has been a longstanding concern to maximise the tourist potential of Enger's association with Widukind.[2] In 2008, the Christian Democrat mayoral candidate made this a central platform of his campaign for election to office.[3] The museum itself makes no bones about its own Nazi past. In recent years, it has returned (albeit in a very different spirit) to one of the themes its Nazi precursor had pursued: the representations of Widukind through the centuries. That exhibition nears its end with an informative display dedicated to the museum's own origins, and to the Widukind cult in Enger during the Third Reich.

Contested reputations: Widukind and Charlemagne in the Third Reich

While a wealth of literature has addressed Germans' 'coming to terms with' the Nazi past, and an increasing number of recent micro-studies have been devoted to historical culture within the Third Reich, there have been few attempts at exploring the relationship between them. This argues that memory-work and commemorative practices conducted between 1933 and 1945 played a part in shaping Germans' social memories in the post-war period. Examining both continuities and elements of change, it considers the place of the eighth and ninth centuries in the historical culture of the twentieth.

The defamation of the emperor Charlemagne and the concomitant cultic embrace of Widukind were pivotal to Alfred Rosenberg's attempt at fundamentally revising the form and content of German historical culture in the early years of the Third Reich. They might even be described as the flagship policy of his programme, dedicated to a rethinking of German history ambitious enough to have incorporated an intention to accomplish a substantial population transfer between the national pantheon of heroes and a conventional rogues' gallery of anti-national villains. This chapter begins by exploring Rosenberg's and his allies' reasons for denigrating Charlemagne and hero-worshipping Widukind. Setting them in the context of Nazi uses of the Germanic tribal as well as of the more recent past, it then considers the interplay of religious and secular motifs both in their own campaign and in a range of increasingly hostile responses to it. On both sides, there was a striking emotional investment in the events of the eighth and early ninth centuries. They were discussed in ways that collapsed chronologies, making the struggle between Widukind and Charlemagne appear to belong to an immediate, tangible past. Medieval*ism* and myths of origin were of course common tropes in European nationalism.[4] Here, they not only came together, but did so at a moment when a still-young regime depicted itself as the facilitator of a national rebirth. The convergence helps explain the passions that were then aroused. Many prominent Nazis – including Hitler himself, Goebbels and Himmler – distanced themselves from Rosenberg, even appearing to side with his Christian and conservative critics. The latter ranged from Cardinal Michael von Faulhaber through to a number of academic historians who were all Lutheran Protestants. What had, in 1934 and 1935, been an open and hard-fought contest became eerily indirect. It ended only when, in 1942, the Nazi regime performed a remarkable u-turn. In one of its last grand commemorative performances, and to the evident satisfaction of a German public, it rehabilitated Charlemagne.[5]

The charges Rosenberg laid against Charlemagne revolved around what he revealingly called 'Germany's first Thirty Years' War', namely the struggle Charlemagne had waged to subjugate the Saxon tribes. Under Widukind's leadership, the latter 'had arisen in defence of Blood and Soil'.[6] 'Blood', of course, was the stuff of which Rosenberg had made his 'Myth of the Twentieth Century'; German 'soil' on which that 'blood' had been spilled by Germans in defence of Germany became 'holy'. More specifically, Widukind was the first in a line of 'great rebels against the universal monarchy of the Holy Roman Empire'. Widukind's defeat had resulted in a millennium in which 'great' Germans had necessarily been forced into the position of 'rebellion'. Only now, in the wake of the Nazis' coming to power, had 'the page turned' so that 'rebels' could be seen in their proper light: as forerunners of a national 'rebirth'.[7] From Widukind, Rosenberg and his allies drew lines of continuity in both directions, 'so that *three* decisive figures of the German past and present rise up before our eyes'.[8]

Backward, the view led to Hermann the Cheruskan. In the ninth century, the Saxons had 'faced exactly the same fateful struggle as the Germanic princes had done when the Roman legions had flooded across western Germania at the beginning of the Christian era', and 'just as Hermann had stood opposed to Varus 800 years earlier, so did ... Widukind later stand against King Karl'. Though products of a 'once great culture', Varus and his legions had brought with them 'an alien idea of the State' and 'the spirit of an already corroded epoch ... poisoning the German territory.' Charlemagne and his Frankish following, similarly 'built by Germanic-Frankish might' had 'become alienated from their customs', adopting those of the Romanised Gauls they had defeated. Returning eastward, they had then 'flooded back in order to subjugate brother-tribes in their erstwhile homeland'. A Roman victory in the Teutoburger Wald in 9 AD would have 'eaten into the heartlands of Germany and put the birth of a culture true to its people's real nature in question for a thousand years'. That Hermann should instead have 'emerged as the victor against the Roman legions' had had an equally enduring impact. For more than 700 years, his victory had secured conditions permitting the 'unhindered growth and vigorous strengthening of the Germanic peoples, radiant with life'.

Forward, the gaze fell on Hitler who had emerged '1000 years later as the immediate continuer of the work of Hermann the Cheruskan and of Duke Widukind'. The Nazis' triumph was, in the long run, a triumph over Charlemagne and all his works, and so a sort of delayed victory for the Saxon resistance. The Nazi Party press did not herald Widukind simply as a sort of fore-runner of Nazism, however; nor did it depict Hitler merely as having achieved a bleated kind of revenge for the Saxon Duke. The relationship between them was depicted as being far more intimate still: 'Duke Widukind was defeated in the ninth century; in the twentieth, he has triumphed in the person of Adolf Hitler'.[9] The claim surely went beyond mere metaphor. It is suggestive rather of reincarnation.

It followed that in the Third Reich, 'not only the present, but also the past' must 'appear in another light. Different judgments thus come into force'. It was 'not only the victors in their triumphs' who were revered by the German people. Quite rightly, the *Volk* 'loved the tragic figures of its history still more.' These were men who had 'fought in loneliness, and had not always been victors'. Rosenberg further insisted that Nazism concerns itself not only with re-evaluating German history but that it approaches the past with a new sensibility. Thus, what mattered most was that the 'shock of those far-off days' when, in 478 AD, 4500 Saxons had been 'murdered' at Verden on the river Aller was 'felt by us again *today*, and from now on we National Socialists will not forget' the day of the massacre. 'German history is not so much written in ink' he continued; 'far rather it must *live* in the hearts and in the consciousness of the nation, which is living through the struggles of those decisive days of German history and drawing the power to create the State from the experience'.[10]

Not least among the cruelties inflicted on them were those perpetrated by 'the King of the Franks' and 'slaughterer of Saxons': the destruction of the Irminsul (the principal shared object of Saxon tribal veneration) and the prohibition, on pain of death, of pagan worship. Pointedly, Rosenberg quoted Charlemagne as having declared that the 'war is to be waged on the faithless *Volk* of the Saxons until they are either defeated and converted to Christianity or completely eradicated (*ausgerottet*)'. Even those committing the act of cremation, integral to pagan Saxon funerary rites, risked incurring the death penalty. On the other hand, 'whoever had committed a crime that did warrant the death penalty could flee to the priest, and be spared on his good word after and confession and penance' [sic]. Once he had put an end to all remnants of Saxon resistance, and having denuded Lower Saxony of all defensive capacity and of the bulk of its population, Charlemagne had imposed tributes on all who remained. Then, 'the Church demanded still more payments from the subdued'. Jewish petty traders and middlemen had followed in the wake of the Carolingian army, much as they had once followed in the steps of the Roman legions. Altogether Charlemagne had, Rosenberg alleged, distorted German history by imposing a Roman and cosmopolitan version of Christianity essentially alien to the Germans.

From the outset, there was a measure of defensiveness alongside the aggression in Rosenberg's campaign. First, his campaign had in fact been preceded by a vehement statement of a Christian and pro-Carolingian reading of Germany's origins enunciated by Cardinal Michael von Faulhaber. Second, Rosenberg was obliged to tread carefully and to guard against the danger of finding his views lumped in with the eccentricities of neo-paganism common in *völkisch* circles in Germany because, even if he himself was not, then many of the Nazi regime's other leading lights most certainly *were* concerned lest they unnecessarily offend Christian sensibilities.

The first prominent public response to Nazi neo-paganism and the celebration of the Germanic tribal past in the Third Reich came from the Roman Catholic Church. This is hardly surprising. What was at stake for them was simultaneously their religion, its position and reputation in Germany, and their understanding of German national history and identity. Cardinal Faulhaber's 1933 New Year's Eve sermon, 'Christentum und Germanentum', was published as a pamphlet, selling some 200,000 copies in and beyond Germany. Though Faulhaber was emphatically not an anti-Nazi, his sermon aroused the ire of many Nazi propagandists. The latter seized on Faulhaber's themes and programmatic statements – notably his declaration that a 'return to the old heathen *Germanentum* would be the greatest of follies', but also on his assertion that 'German *Volk* will either be Christian or it will not exist at all. A falling away from Christianity, a falling back on heathendom, would be the beginning of the end of the German *Volk*', He was no less outraged at Faulhaber's remarks on Charlemagne. 'Kaiser Karl der Große', Faulhaber had stated.

> linked the conversion of the Saxons to their political defeat, in part with violent pressure, because he knew that the political unity of these tribes of peoples was impossible to achieve without religious unification. Today, people direct blind hatred toward Karl der Große because he wanted to put paid to heathendom among the German people.

Leers contended that something close to the opposite was true: the Saxons had never been 'barbarians or dreadful heathens'; Charlemagne had 'broken a living *Volk* "at its root"' and had added the obstacle of struggles over faith to the other hindrances to a process of the 'unification of the German tribes', which was in fact already underway, and had 'planted mutual opposition deep into the soul of the people'. Not unreasonably, he dated the beginning of German history not to Charlemagne's Reich, but to its dismemberment.[11]

'When we are accused of wanting to build Woden-Halls next to gothic towers', he declared.

> then we reply: we have not fought in order to build heathen temples, but in order to unify the German *Volk* for all eternity. … Just as we do not build temples against the Christian churches, so we do not want to build a Valhalla as an ersatz for the Christian heaven.

It was, he added, only the divisive effect of Christian confessionalism on the Germans that Nazism sought to counter. Von Leers, who described his own religiosity as 'Nordic' and 'Germanic', was likewise careful to assert that

> of the millions of people who support or are close to the Nordic Movement in Germany today, there are certainly not even ten who

intend to worship Thor and Woden again, to sacrifice white horses on mountain tops or even to pick up the threads from the point at which Christianisation had torn them off – as if nothing had happened. Nowhere is there an issue of a 'return to the old heathen *Germanentum'*.

He dismissed any 'attempt artificially to revive that which has died' as 'childish'. But then he denied that such madcap designs were being entertained in any case.[12] Yet, in the very same texts, much of what he and Rosenberg both described and the language in which they described it smacked distinctly of the neo-pagan traits they disowned. If the Christian cross would retain its proper place within church buildings in the Third Reich, then Rosenberg demanded that the 'swastika should reign supreme on the *Thingplatz'*. But the praxis of the Nazis persistently blurred and contravened the clear delineations Rosenberg indicated.

At the 'Thingsteads', whose very name evoked a mythicised Germanic world, Nazi rituals had a pronounced tendency to fade into cultic practices. Yet even there the Nazis *did* at first sometimes accommodate Christian ritual. That was true of one of the most successful events in the Nazi ritual calendar, namely the Reich Harvest Thanksgiving Festival. It was held at the Bückeberg, where ditches had been dug and ramparts built for a *Thing*-site resembling nothing so much as an Iron Age enclosure. When the role of the church within the ceremony performed there declined, so did the popular appeal of the occasion.[13] And, on the field of Verden, close to the place at which 4500 Saxons had (allegedly) been executed by Charlemagne, the Nazis built the *Sachsenhain*, the grove each of whose 4500 standing stones was to represent one of the victims of the 'blood bath'. For this was also 'holy soil'. The 'Thirty Years' War' in which they had fallen was not to be construed as a *civil* war, and the Saxons had not fought merely for their tribal independence. Theirs had been the 'blood sacrifice of the best defenders of Germany'; 'in the decisive hour' they had 'fought with their last strength for the freedom and honour of *Germania'*. But, in the course of an intensive weekend's commemoration of Widukind in late June 1934, churches and their graveyards were bound in to what might otherwise have appeared a straightforward celebration of paganism. In Enger, at the opening ceremony, a Hitler Youth guard of honour stood in the old church, at the crypt in which Widukind was buried. Rosenberg, together with regional and local Nazi bosses, visited the grave and laid on it a hedge-rose wreath bearing the legend, 'To the German Duke'. On the following day, when Rosenberg's road-show had moved on to Brunswick, it was not only the town streets that were 'festively decorated': above, 'high up from the towers of the Cathedral of St. Blasien wave the vast banners of the Revolution'.

Nazi festive and commemorative practices, then, tended to confuse and conflate Christianity and neo-paganism both in the sites they selected and in ritual performances. If they denied that their position was reducible to one of pagan revivalism, Nazi ideologues kept formulations of their own religious beliefs vague – whether deliberately, to allow them to avoid ridicule or simply because they were inchoate. Von Leers saw himself as a representative of the 'very many' contemporary Germans 'who believe in God (*die gottgläubig sind*), but can find no spiritual home in Christianity and therefore return or stride forward – call it what one may – to the religious basic values conveyed in the tradition of their own *Volk*'. Their concern was 'everywhere with a religious quest aimed at accentuating the particular values of one's own religiosity'.[14] The Nazis thus picked and mixed among religious forms and traditions, added a seasoning of neo-paganism and created a hybrid of their own. In Quedlinburg, for example, they purloined the cathedral and turned it into a mock-up of a Germanic hall and simultaneously into an SS shrine dedicated to Henry the Fowler. They were able to do so by degrees: at first with the willing collaboration of the local (Protestant) Church official. Even after the full scale of their ambition to de-Christianise the cathedral had been revealed, they had curiously little opposition to face from a local Church community in which the pro-Nazi German Christians were relatively strong and their opponents in the Confessing Church movement weak. The local population seems to have enjoyed the public festivities and appreciated the trade they brought to the town.

Elsewhere, the semi- and neo-pagan cult did not have so smooth a path. During the first years of Nazi rule, the Propaganda Ministry found itself under a bombardment of requests for permission to perform a myriad of newly penned Widukind-dramas. In the Rhineland town of Hagen, tempers flared over the performance of one of these – a piece written by the future SS heritage custodian Edmund Kiß. For Hagen had a substantial and organised Roman Catholic minority within its population that felt itself insulted and perhaps threatened by the play. The play's first night occasioned formal protests to the Propaganda Ministry from Catholic dignitaries; at the second, matters got wholly out of hand. A monarchist publication was one among several to publish a police report on what ensued:

> After Principal Director Hoffmann had made an announcement to the effect that the play was being performed not only with the

permission, but with the express approval of the Reichsminister for Popular Enlightenment and Propaganda, things calmed down at first. But the attempts at disruption were repeated in the second Act, and took on even stronger forms in the third Act. Such calls as 'No falsification of history!' were to be heard, and were countered with loud answers from the stalls. The police and SA cleared the gallery seats, whereupon the performance was brought to its end without further disturbance. It has been established that the disturbers of the peace were youths coming from Roman Catholic circles. [...] The play premièred in Hagen [...] presents us with as crass and regrettable a denigration of the national and religious convictions of the German *Volk* as can well be imagined. The German press has carried the protest of the Christian visitors to the Hagen theatre further and to considerable effect. This pseudo-artistic drama *à thèse* encountered energetic rejection not only in the [Roman Catholic newspaper] *Germania*, but also among countless other newspapers and periodicals [...][15]

One consequence was that Kiß's play did not enjoy a long run. It was performed in public only for a third night, and thereafter was performed exclusively in front of invited Nazi audiences on some 30 occasions.[16] Undeterred, its author went on to embellish on his themes in a novel published later that year:[17] The scenes that had so outraged elements of the theatre audience were just as evident here. The neo-pagan Widukind-cult had always struggled to integrate into their narrative what might be called an anomaly, namely the fact that, while localised Saxon resistance had continued into the first years of the ninth century, Widukind had surrendered in 875 and, according to the sparse surviving sources, had converted to Christianity. Charlemagne may himself have acted as godfather at the baptism in Attigny. Rosenberg, of course, had simply circumvented the issue by dint of misdating Widukind's defeat to the *ninth* century. Kiß, by contrast, confronted it head-on. So, in 785 Charlemagne's priestly Anglo-Saxon envoy, Alcuin, Rector of York, was depicted by Kiß negotiating peace terms with Widukind. He faced an uphill struggle, since his task was to persuade Widukind to surrender in spite of the Saxon's track record of military successes and the clear indication that these would continue. At first, Widukind contemptuously dismissed Alcuin's repeated insistence that the Saxons *could not win*, even when Alcuin explained to him that, in continuing to fight, he was jeopardising the survival 'of the entire German people'. A spiritually tormented Alcuin – whose healthy racial instincts were permanently in conflict with his alien religion and with his service to an utterly unscrupulous monarch – was left with no other option than to reveal his full hand:

'You choose not to understand me, Lord Duke', the Rector said with haughty decision. Now he had to show his real colours, and express the shameful truth. 'That is why I will now speak plainly. As you know, on the Rhine, in Cologne, in Mainz, and also in Trier and Aachen, there lie the punishment camps of the Frankish army. There, the dregs of the whole world are gathered: the murderers and thieves, the polluted of all the lands, the Jews and the Syrians, the Arabs and Moors, the deserters and the desecrators of dead bodies and necrophiles. They live in great lagers, crammed together behind walls of stakes in dirty huts of wood and stone. And the breath of the plague billows out of these lagers. Lord Widukind! My King, Carolus, has commanded that the [60,000] German girls and women who were taken are to be housed in these camps. The scum of the earth will not first have been removed from them. Rather, the cankers will move closer together to make room for the German women. And Lord Karl has ordered that no fence, no wall, is to be erected between the convicts and the Saxon women. No victory of Duke Widukind will be able to make good what will have transpired in the course of a single winter. One or another of your German women will not wish to endure the shame, and will take her own life. But do not forget that the long road through the hard winter will break resistance and pride, that hunger and sickness will wear down the poorest. Yes, Widukind: you will fetch your women back. Your sword will ring victorious over the Franks; your axe will drive Karl's armies before you. Yet no victory of arms will be able to heal what the winter in the punishment camps on the Rhine will have destroyed for ever. You will bring only sick, cheerless women back into your homeland. And, in a very few years' time, as you ride through the Phalian land you will look upon alien, dark children with sickly eyes. Then the wellspring will have been lost, and there will never again be a Widukind to open his gates. For the well will have been fouled. Between the Rhine and the Weser, the German people will be no more'.[18]

Now, to preserve his race, Widukind necessarily had to surrender – and so of course also to give up his religious faith. It hardly needs saying that all this was indeed 'falsification of history' – and on a grand scale. There is of course not a shred of evidence to support any one of Kiß's grotesque assertions. But Kiß had an explanation for the absence of such evidence. For, in his narrative, a final sacrifice was demanded of his hero. Almost overcome by his own rising sense of shame, Alcuin went on to insist that Widukind and his allies Helga and Albion never make reference to the terms on which he had been brought to give up their struggle. They must let it appear that they had been bought by Charlemagne, relinquishing all personal honour in return for land and position. The Frankish King's chroniclers would see to the rest, and no trace would remain of Charlemagne's own dishonourable threats. Widukind, meanwhile, made the ultimate heroic sacrifice, accepting the destruction of his treasured personal reputation since that was the price demanded of him to secure the life of the German *Volk*.[19]

A remarkable feature of the mixed reception Kiß's play received was that the public polarisation spilled over into the Nazi Party itself. The President of the Aachen City Government, Eggert Reeder, noted in a report that 'on the one hand the National Socialist mayor of Hagen continues to support [the play's] performance', while 'on the other hand the Essen Gau press [...] refutes it in the sharpest tones, devastatingly describing it as a sordid piece.' Thanks to the widespread press coverage, the performance in Hagen had been 'very critically discussed' among the citizens of nearby Aachen. It was not just that Aachen's population was around 95 per cent Roman Catholic: given Charlemagne's historical associations with the city, attempts to defame 'our Karl' were bound to encounter the wrath of local patriots. The campaign of defamation nevertheless spread into the city itself days after the debacle in Hagen. Many uniformed members of the Nazi Party had, Reeder's report continued, taken part in the traditional commemoration of Charlemagne held in the Cathedral on the first Sunday of February, and the procession of the Karl's Archers' Guild had been led by the Aachen SA choir. A performance of Bruckner's Mass was among the highlights of the event. It was disrupted when the Hitler Youth arrived outside the minster to create rough music 'with drums and trumpets'. The following day, the German Faith Movement followed up with a public lecture. Reeder's discomfort was plain. The lecture, provocatively entitled 'Karl, the Great Butcher of the Saxons', became the focus of a degree of 'public attention, including among Catholic Party members, which was in no sense justified by the significance of the speaker'. The lecture had left a part of the population 'greatly embittered'. Roman Catholic dignitaries had complained that, while they were prohibited from holding meetings except in the churches themselves, the German Faith Movement had an office in the headquarters of the local Labour Front. The Aachen Nazi newspapers – which had themselves vociferously condemned Charlemagne – responded with a deafening silence, leaving the views of the offended Roman Catholic majority to be articulated only in the Catholic press. Small wonder, then, that the latter steadily outsold the former.[20]

An as yet incomplete censorship regime combined with disunity in the Nazis' ranks and the emotional investments of so many Germans in the years 1935–1936 to give rise to an openly and vigorously conducted public debate. Here, Germans were still relatively free to express their views and not reliant on rumour: they could hold a fairly free conversation informed by the media and the disparate versions of the past presented by regime propagandists, by theologians (including members of the Confessing Church and their German Christian opponents as well as Roman Catholics) and, perhaps not least, by academic historians.[21] This was a circumstance that had few parallels – if any – in the Third Reich. And, of course, it was intolerable to the regime. It is surely testimony to the importance the Nazi hierarchy attached to the issue that Hitler's response should have arrived in his closing speech at the Nuremberg Rally of September 1935. He asserted that the use of force had been necessary to transform Germanic tribes into a German *Volk*, and that its simultaneous Christianisation had a positive impact on the medieval development of the nation's character. While Hitler did not refer to Charlemagne by name, a ritual gesture made earlier at the same rally confirms that he was nevertheless at the heart of the message.[22] Hitler had ceremoniously received a copy of Charlemagne's sword from the hands of Nuremberg's Mayor, Wilhelm Liebel.[23]

At that moment, the pendulum began to swing back in the direction of the defenders of Charlemagne's reputation. Rosenberg immediately recognised himself as a target of Hitler's polemic.[24] He and some of his allies moderated their tones; Himmler wobbled, caught between a residual fondness of Widukind and the temptation to seize opportunities to embarrass his rival, Rosenberg; among senior Nazis, only R. Walther Darré carried on quite regardless of Hitler's intervention. The Widukind cult did continue, but its celebrants were now comparatively modest in their ambitions and muted in their tones. When the Widukind museum-*cum*-cultic site in Enger opened in 1939, it was with SS financial support. An SS guard of honour and local and regional dignitaries were present.[25] Himmler stayed away. Indeed, no nationally significant representative of the regime was present. Hitler had succeeded in what was no doubt his primary intention, namely to close down the public debate. Had he entertained a secondary motive and wished also to inaugurate a cult of Charlemagne; he would presumably have gone further.

In any event, no new cult of Charlemagne materialised. In Aachen, the old, Roman Catholic one was at least permitted to rumble on in the absence of further disruption. Much to the relief of the city's authorities, the 1936 *Karlsfeier* in the Cathedral passed off without incident.[26] And, in the later 1930s, a variety of writers found that they could now praise Charlemagne without fear of contradiction, or at any rate of denunciation by what were or appeared to be authoritative spokesmen of the regime. Academic historians who had so recently found it necessary to mount concerted efforts to redeem Charlemagne for German nationalism in the face of the loud chorus of denunciation[27] began to feel confident enough simply to ignore such further harping criticisms of Charlemagne as were occasionally ventured. Their 'labor of enlightenment' had paid off.[28] With the beginning of the war, instances of the instrumentalisation of Charlemagne for the purposes of Nazi expansionism gathered in frequency and stridency. Yet the individual hymns of praise to Charlemagne fell far short of adding up to a new Nazi-sponsored cult. In Matthias Pape's view, Charlemagne was simply too contentious a figure to permit his full-blown, nationwide cultic embrace by the regime. Pape's view has much to recommend it. An awfully large number of senior Nazis would have had to forget their previous commitments to the programmatic denigration of Charlemagne. Nevertheless, in 1942, on the occasion of the 1200th anniversary of Charlemagne's birth, that is exactly what they were asked to do.

'The Reich honours Karl der Große', the banner-headline of the western German Nazi regional newspaper announced: 'Gauleiter State Councillor Grohé pays tribute to the work of the great Carolingian on behalf of the German nation'. The occasion was a grandiloquent celebration in the very place – the minster in Aachen – where the Church's *Karlsfest* had been disrupted by the Hitler Youth just seven years earlier. It was to be the last grandly conceived and lavishly conducted historicist commemoration organised by the regime. One of its premises was that, while Germans would 'remember' the eighth and ninth centuries, their memories would fade when it came to the years 1934 and 1935. For Grohé reminded his audience that Rosenberg had 'called Karl's government a "historic decision for a millennium"'.[29] It was an unintentionally revealing statement. Grohé took Rosenberg's phrase of 1934 entirely out of context, making it mean the precise opposite of what Rosenberg had explicitly intended. The 'millennium' at issue had been ushered in, of course, precisely by Charlemagne's subjugation of the Saxons. Charlemagne's rule had indeed determined the course of German history for a 1000 years, but these had been a 1000 years of 'tragedy'. Increasingly 'nationally conscious'

Germans had revolted 'in defense of blood and soil' against the 'alien oppression', the Christianisation and the miscegenation that had been the means by which Charlemagne's 'First Reich' had been created and had proved to be its lasting legacy. The Third Reich emphatically did *not* stand in continuity with the First, but with the 'rebels' who had struggled against its 'yoke'.[30] All this was now most conveniently 'forgotten'. For, in 1942, the Third Reich remade the imagined line of continuity with the First that so many of its own propagandists had been anxious to break or to deny. Grohé not only echoed the arguments Charlemagne's modern German protagonists had long advanced but added reflections that resonated with the ambitions and triumphalism of the Third Reich at the peak of its territorial power. As I have suggested, in the infancy of the Third Reich it had been commonplace to insist that a new epoch demanded a new vision of history – one that sank Charlemagne and raised Widukind in Germans' estimation. In 1942, the same notion of revising historical interpretations in the light of new understandings generated by the present was invoked in order to raise Charlemagne's reputation to new heights. Grohé declared that

> In our epoch, which is determining Europe's fate anew, our view is also clearer than the view of those who, in decades and in centuries gone by, had neither a feel nor a measure for world-historical achievements because they pursued confessional, separatist or dynastic political interests. It is therefore with a profound open-mindedness that our *Volk* views its great past.

A crucial aspect of Charlemagne's empire had been that it had created 'a secure bulwark against Slavification':

> Thus, what we see in Karl der Große is not only the towering individual, the value of whose rare personality we admire; beyond that we see the enforcer of German unity and the founder of our First Reich. He brought the Germanic tribes of the Franks, the Allemans, Bavarians, Langobards, Thuringians and Saxons together, and from them he forged a mighty Reich. Through the subjugation of the Huns' relatives, the Avars, in the year 796, space was created for the Bavarian settlement of Lower Austria and the Alpine territories. After the resistance of the Saxons had been overcome, Karl forced through recognition by the Slavic border-peoples in the East to whom he gave order, *just as order is being created in the service of Europe by the outcome of the present war* [my emphasis].

Unmistakably, the First Reich could enjoy a new vogue because it could be held up as a model for the Nazis' 'New Order in Europe', and a 'European' Charlemagne could be reconciled with a 'German' Karl der Große. Here was the ideological basis on which it became possible, two years later, to name the *French* SS contingent the 'Charlemagne Legion'.[31] If Charlemagne had, by creating the Reich, 'eternal proof of the force of German creativity', then that creativity was displayed above all in the pursuit of a European mission:

> Just as it was then, so the goal of German policy today is directed toward a happy Europe. And if in our own age the attempt to determine the fate of Europe has been and is being made from beyond the ocean, then Europe rejects this presumption not only with reference to the right to determine its own fate, but also in a spirit of contempt for those who have no respect for our great and proud past because they have no such past themselves.

The pre-Carolingian 'horizon' of the Germanic tribes had, by contrast, been 'very narrow'. As he sang the praises of its inauguration, the journalist who reported on Grohé's speech lamented the 'decay' of the First Reich under Charlemagne successors; its *foundation*, however, was no longer deemed in the least problematic. By implication, of course, the horizons of Charlemagne's detractors had, in the mid-1930s, also been narrow; their concerns, from the perspective of 1942, had been petty and provincial. Re-enforcing the view Hitler had first promulgated in 1935, Grohé depicted Christianisation as integral to national unification and dismissed caveats concerning Charlemagne's methods as a sheer irrelevancy. It was therefore now essential that Germans

> appreciate the work of Karl der Große while recognising that, in Christianity, he gave the antique idea of the state of a bygone age the spiritual platform which facilitated commonality in people's thought, and overcame tribal egotism in the interests of the greater community [*Gemeinschaft*]. The methods used to achieve that outcome are irrelevant to an historical judgment of the work itself. ... What does matter is that a Reich came into being ... . And this was the most important precondition for all that we proudly venerate in the deeds of subsequent great Kaiser.

The charge of wilful neglect of Charlemagne's legacy was laid at the door of nineteenth- and earlier twentieth-century German regimes that had 'increasingly consigned to oblivion' even Aachen itself. The implication was clear: the third Reich had steadily committed itself to the heroisation of Charlemagne.[32]

Perhaps, then, it was not so much the manifest disagreements over, and contradictions and abrupt shifts in Nazi uses of the past that militated against the creation of a Charlemagne cult as the fact that the Nazis had no time left in which to develop it. In the heady atmosphere of 1942, it had seemed appropriate to the regime and was widely welcomed by the public.[33] But a Charlemagne cult was imaginable only in that fleeting moment – when Charlemagne's *Reich* could be served up as a precursor to the Third Reich and an inspiration for limitless conquest. In 1944 and until the moment the Nazi war-effort and regime collapsed in 1945, other models were needed for other purposes. They veered between success stories of desperate defence against overwhelming force and 'heroic' death or suicidal martyrdom.[34] There was, of course, no room here for Widukind. Unlike Hitler and Goebbels, he had, after all, preferred surrender to the destruction of his *Volk*.

Remembering and forgetting: Widukind and Charlemagne after the Third Reich

Widukind was never again to occupy the position of national significance in which Rosenberg had sought to place him. In Lower Saxony, however, he has remained a regional hero. Both the Free Democratic Party and the Christian Democratic Union frequently end their regional party meetings and congresses by singing an anthem, the *Sachsenlied*, which identifies Widukind as a sort of father-figure for the *Land*. The town of Enger, described on its official website as '*Widukind-Stadt*' and in whose church Widukind was reputedly buried, holds an annual festival (the *Timpkenfest*) commemorating the Duke. *Heimat* culture has continued to venerate him, and even to encourage an uncritical touristic view of cultic sites created by the Nazis to commemorate the Saxon resistance to Charlemagne.

Neo-Nazis have been able to latch on to such elements of continuity between the historical culture of the Third Reich and the (no doubt largely naive) efforts of post-war West Germans to preserve some of its features. Thus, in a volume celebrating the *Sachsenhain*, Patrick Agte suggests that the Widukind Museum in Enger testifies to a continuing and in essence unaltered local appreciation of the 'Saxon Duke'.[35] As far as Enger's historical culture in the immediate post-war period is concerned, he may not be far wrong. Town pageants continued to commemorate Widukind much in the way they had done in the Third Reich. The process of transforming Enger's Widukind-*Weihestätte* from an SS-sponsored cultic 'sacred site' into a conventional museum proved to be a long-drawn-out affair, testifying at first to a process of 'de-Nazification' so ludicrously superficial as to have entailed, for example, leaving a Hitler-quotation on the wall of the museum's foyer while painting over the attribution to its author. It was only under pressure exerted on Enger from the outside in the 1970s – pressure which included interventions of foreign historians – that the exhibition was genuinely and radically altered, so that it finally ceased to be a 'relic of the National Socialist period'. The change, culminating in a re-opening ceremony held on 23 April 1983, took place in the absence of local participation.[36]

Agte also notes that, just three days after Germany's capitulation, concerned citizens met in Verden's town hall to prevent a putative demolition of the henge.

> For them, the *Sachsenhain* constituted 'a worthy memorial to our Lower Saxon ancestors ... [who] stood and fought faithfully for their *Heimat* ...'. Here, the oft-cited faithfulness of the Lower Saxons to their history, to their *Volk*, to *Boden* and *Haimat* was once again displayed. For that, no ideology of any kind whatever was required.[37]

On the far Right, there have been sporadic outbursts of enthusiasm for Widukind and expressions of loathing for Charlemagne and all his works.[38] These appear to have increased in vehemence and frequency in recent years. National Democratic Party (NPD) neo-Nazis held a rally at the *Sachsenhain* in 2008.[39] They frequently employ pagan imagery – and are reviled by other neo-pagans for merely instrumentalising pagan symbols.[40]

The tones in which neo-Nazis propagandists have addressed the hoary old question 'Charlemagne or Widukind?' eerily echo those Rosenberg and his allies had adopted in 1934 and 1935. Agte describes Charlemagne's conduct in his campaigns against the Saxons thus: 'With methods of terror, through murder, fire and expulsion, Karl forces Christianity onto the Saxons. It is alien to their nature.' Agte angrily takes issue with mid-1930s deniers of the 'bloodbath of Verden' (and represents Nazi Concentration Camps as harmless – comfort zones whose inmates had maximised their chances of surviving the Second World War). In turn, he denies the reliability of the evidence of Widukind's conversion. Agte does, as an afterthought, add that Himmler (the real hero of his story, who is praised above all for his outstanding contribution to German heritage, conservation and preservation!), eventually came round to acknowledging Charlemagne's contribution to German nation-building. But it is nevertheless striking that neo-Nazism has in general drawn a veil of silence over everything – from Hitler's closing speech at the 1935 Nuremberg rally through the commemoration of 1942 – that had tended toward Nazism's cultic embrace of Charlemagne.

Neo-Nazi circles appear to have restored the enthusiasms of Rosenberg and of the first years of the Third Reich and seem almost entirely oblivious of the u-turn the Nazi regime subsequently performed, and of Hitler's own predilections. Nevertheless, there is at any rate one deeply anti-Christian and anti-Semitic Widukind-admirer to whom neo-Nazis are unlikely to return. In contemporary German far-right circles, anti-Islamism vies with anti-Semitism in a ranking order of prejudices. Johann von Leers, however, had declared in 1934 that, were it ever to prove impossible for a man who 'had for long years been in the vanguard of the struggle for the German re-awakening' to follow his own religiosity in Germany, and were his children to be pressed into Christianity, he might just as well 'go over to Islam and wait to see whether a devout Muslim would be subjected to harassment'.[41] In 1942, he celebrated the 'world-historical' accomplishment of Islam in having blocked the expansion of Christianity.[42] Having fled first to Italy in 1945, then followed so many unrepentant old Nazis by moving on to Argentina in 1950, von Leers resurfaced in Nasser's Egypt in 1956, was hired as a regime propagandist, recycled his old anti-Semitism under the guise of anti-Zionism ... and converted to Islam, changing his name to Omar Amin.[43]

Karl der Große, by contrast, has not only endured since 1945 as a local hero in Aachen but has persistently if patchily been upheld as a national hero in the Federal Republic of Germany; increasingly, he has been revered also as a transnational one. Work by Matthias Pape has shown that the cult of Karl had a legitimising function in the early years of the Federal Republic of Germany.[44] Among Christian Democrats in particular, Karl der Große remains a frequent and positive point of reference. In some respects, the Nazi celebrations of Karl, by dint of portraying his achievements as a kind of model for their expansionist aims in Europe prefigured the subsequent recycling of his Reich as a model for contemporary European integration. After all, the characterisation of Charlemagne as the 'Father of Europe' itself has a Third Reich provenance (among others).[45] Not only because the territorial expansion of the European Union into east-central Europe has diminished its geographical resemblance to Charlemagne's empire and introduced populations for whom Charlemagne has little or no cultural historical relevance, whether he has prospects of a significant afterlife as a site of European memory must be open to doubt. German academic historians, whose interpretations had converged with and served to legitimise those of the Nazi regime during the Second World War, have latterly been more concerned to explore the construction of myths surrounding Charlemagne than to contribute to or to instrumentalise them for political purposes. They tend also to be sceptical as to the continuing appeal of those myths.[46]

In Aachen, the tradition of the *Karlsfeier* in the Cathedral was revived after the war, and continues to the present. The same city has, since 1950, awarded an annual *Karlspreis*. In principle, the prize recognises outstanding contributions toward European integration, but in fact its recipients have very largely been identifiable with the European Right. In 2008, it was shared by the then French President Nicolas Sarkozy and the German Chancellor Angela Merkel. Hotly contested between French and German nationalists for more than a century, Charlemagne/Karl der Große could symbolically stand, it seemed, for a post-nationalist Franco-German collaboration in the 'leadership' of Europe.[47] Four years later, however, at the time of writing, Sarkozy has lost the Presidency and, in his absence, Merkel has begun to appear increasingly isolated in European Union politics. The austerity measures the two have espoused seem to many commentators to have brought the EU to the brink of collapse. The proposition that 'Merkozy' had made a real and lasting contribution to European unity looks as dubious as the notion that the Reich of Charlemagne/Karl der Große will ever serve as a convenient and popular myth of origin for that cause.

In Köln, another 'Karls-Prize' is awarded. But, in what is perhaps a sideswipe at Aachen's pomposities and is certainly an affront to the most basic rules of German grammar and syntax, it is awarded in honour of *'Karl den Marx'*.

Notes

1. For rumours of pagan celebrations and neo-Nazi marriage ceremonies conducted there, see Patrick Agde, *Der Sachsenhain bei Verden. Naturdenkmal für 4500 durch Karl den Großen getötete Sachsen* (Pluwig: Mumin Verlag, 2001), p. 111.
2. Wolfgang Krogel, 'Widukind—ein historischer Mythos und Chance für die Stadtentwicklung', in Stefan Brakensieck (ed.), *Widukind: Forschungen zu einem Mythos* (Bielefeld: Verla für Regionalgeschichte, 1997), pp. 21–31.
3. URL:http://www.cdu-herford.de/cdu.../enger/400-karsten-glie...
4. See e.g. R. J. W. Evans and Guy P. Marchal (eds), *The Uses of the Middle Ages in Modern European States: History, Nationhood and the Search for Origins* (Basingstoke: Palgrave Macmillan, 2010).
5. There is as yet no full-scale study of the evolution of the controversy, but a considerable number of shorter general accounts on the one hand, and

explorations of its individual aspects on the other have accumulated. As well as the references in the notes below, see Rolf Kühn, 'Kirchenfeindliche und antichristliche Mittelalter-Rezeption im völkisch-nationalsozialistischen Geschichtsbild', in Peter Wapnewski (ed.), *Mittelalter-Rezeption. Ein Symposium* (Stuttgart: Metzler, 1986), pp. 581–609; Gordon Wolnik, *Mittelalter und NS-Propaganda. Mittelalterbilder in den Print-, Ton- und Bildmedien des Dritten Reiches.* Doctoral thesis. Universität, Frankfurt am Main. (Münster: Lit, 2003); Sabine Kuhlmann, *Der Streit um Karl den Großen, Widukind und den 'Tag von Verden' in der NS-Zeit.* Thesis (Stade: Landschaftverb. der Ehemaligen Herzogtümer Bremen und Verden, 2010).

6. Kurt Teserich, 'Herzog Widukind unterlag im IX. Jahrhundert. Im XX. hat er in Adolf Hitler gesiegt. Alfred Rosenberg auf dem Niedersachsentag in Enger, Verden, Wildeshausen und Braunschweig', *Völkischer Beobachter* (hereafter *VB*), 26 June 1934.
7. *Ibid.*
8. *VB*, 24/25 June 1934, p. 2.
9. *VB*, 26 June 1934: 'Herzog Widukind unterlag im IX. Jahrhundert, im XX. hat er in Adolf Hitler gesiegt'—which was simultaneously the text of the article's headline.
10. *VB*, 24/25 June 1934.
11. Kardinal Faulhaber, *Judentum. Christentum Germanentum. Adventsprädigten gehalten in St. Michael zu München 1933* (Munich: A. Huber, 1934), pp. 103, 112; Cf. Johann von Leers, *Der Kardinal und die Germanen* (Hamburg: Hanseatische Verlagsanstalt, 1934), quotations pp. 10, 49, 52, 51.
12. Von Leers, *op. cit.*, pp. 10–11.
13. Bernhard Gelderblom, *Die Reichserntedankfeste auf dem Bückeberg 1933–1937* (Hameln: Niemeyer, 1998), pp. 15, 52.
14. Von Leers, *op. cit.*, pp. 10–11.
15. Anonymous, 'In Sachen Widukind', *Weiße Blätter* (February 1935), pp. 53–57, p. 53.
16. See Glen W. Gadberry, 'An "Ancient German Rediscovered". The Nazi Wdiukind Plays of Forster and Kiß', in Hellmut Hal Rennert (ed.), *Essays on Twentieth-Century German Drama and Theater* (New York: P. Lang, 2004), pp. 155–75; Gerwin Strobl, *The Swastika and the Stage. German Theatre and Society, 1933–1945* (Cambridge: CUP, 2007), pp. 143–47.
17. Edmund Kiß, *Wittekind der Große* (Landsberg/Wathe: Pfeiffer & Co., 1935).
18. *Ibid.*, pp. 291–93.
19. *Ibid.*, pp. 294–302.
20. Bernhard Vollmer (ed.), *Volksopposition im Polizeistaat. Gestapo und Regierungsberichte 1934–1936* (Stuttgart: Deutsche Verlags-Anstalt, 1957), pp. 167–69 (report of 7 February 1935).
21. Among contributions from Confessing Churchmen, see e.g. Karl Mensing, *Karl und Widukind und die Bekehrung der Deutschen* (Dresden: A. 1 Bekenntnisgemeinschaft d. Ev.-luth. Kirche in Sachsen, 1934) and Karl Koch, *Widukind. Heide und Heiliger* (Cologne: Bachem, 1935); for the failed attempt by the artist Ida Ströver to create a memorial to Widukind in German Christian style (i.e., by celebrating his ultimate conversion as well as his long resistance to Charlemagne, and so harmonising *völkisch* and Christian motifs), see Heinrich Rüthing, *Der Wittekindsberg bei Minden als 'Heilige Stätte'*.

1000 bis 2000 (Bielfeld: Verlage für Regionalgeschichte, 2008); most promi-
nent among historians' contributions to the defence of Charlemagne was
Karl Hampe et al., *Karl der Große oder Charlemagne? Acht Antworten deutscher
Geschichtsforscher* (Berlin: E.S. Mittler, 1935). On academic historians' con-
tribuiton in general, see Karl Ferdninand Werner, *Das NS-Geschichtsbild und
die deutsche Geschichtswissenschaft* (Stuttgart: Pp. 123, 1967); Idem, *Karl der
Große oder Widukind? Von der Aktualität einer überholten Fragestellung* (Munich:
Verlag der Bayerischen Akademie der Wissenschaften: In Kommission der C.H.
Beck'schen Verlagsbuchh, 1995); Walter Zöllner, *Karl oder Widukind? Martin
Lintzel und die NS-'Geschichtsdeutung' in den Anfangsjahren der faschistischen
Diktatur* (Halle: Martin-Luther-Universität, 1975).

22. Adolf Hitler, *Die Reden Hitlers am Parteitag der Freiheit 1935* (Munich: Eher,
1935), speech of 16 September 1935.

23. Max Domarus (ed.), *Hitler. Speeches and Proclamations 1932–1945* vol. 2
(London: Tauris, 1992), p. 691.

24. Reinhard Bollmus, *Das Amt Rosenberg und seine Gegener. Studien zum Machtkampf
im nationalsozialistischen Herrschaftssytem* (1969; 2nd ed. Munich: Oldenbourg,
2006), pp. 195–96.

25. Martin Griepentrog, 'Die Widukind-Gedächtnisstätte von 1939—Außenseiter
oder Prototyp der nationalsozialistischen Museumsentwicklung?', *Stadft
Enger—Beiträge zure Stadtgeschichte* vol. 7, (1991), 119–40.

26. Vollmer (ed.), *Volksopposition*, p. 357; unsigned report of 15 February 1936.

27. Zöllner, *Karl oder Widukind?*, pp. 21–34.

28. See Friedrich Schneider, *Die neueren Anschauungen der deutschen Historiker über
die Kaiserpolitik des Mittelalters* (Weimar: H. Böhlaus nachf., 1942), pp. 26–27,
p. 178, note 28.

29. P. Sch., 'Das Reich ehrt Karl den Großen. Gauleiter Staatsrat Grohé würdigt
für die deutsche Nation das Werk des großen Karolingers', *Westdeutscher
Beobachter. Amtliches Organ der NSDAP und sämtlicher Behördeen Köln-Stadt*
(3 April 1942).

30. Kurt Teserich, 'Herzog Widukind unterlag im IX. Jahrhundert. Im XX. Hat
er in Adlof Hitler gesiegt. Alfred Rosenberg auf dem Niedersachsentag in
Enger, Verden, Wildeshasuen und Braunschweig', *VB* 26 June 1934. See
also Carl Cranz, 'Der Kampf um die Weltanschauung. Alfred Rosenberg an
Deutschland und an die Welt', *VB* 23 February 1934; 'Widukind für immer
das Symbol des hlednhaften Widertandes. Reichsleiter Alfred Rosenberg
weiht den Ehrenhain am Leutfeld an der Aller', *VB* 24/25 June 1934.

31. George Stein, *The Waffen-SS: Hitler's Elite Guard at War 1939–1945* (Ithaca,
NY: Cornell University Press, 1966), pp. 163–64.

32. P. Sch., 'Das Reich ehrt Karl den Großen.'

33. For the reception of the Aachen celebration, see Peter Lambert, 'Heroisation
and Demonisation in the Third Reich: The Consensus-building Value of
a Nazi Pantheon of Heroes', *Totalitarian Movements and Political Religions*
vol. 8, no. 3–4 (200), 523–46; here, 537–8.

34. For examples, see Christian Goeshcel, *Suicide in Nazi Germany* (Oxford:
Oxford University Press, 2009), pp. 154–55.

35. Agte, *Der Sachsenhain*, p. 108.

36. Griepentrog, 'Die Widukiind Gedächtnisstätte', p. 126; Ute Specht-Kreusel,
'Widukind: Rezeptionsgeschichtliche Denkansätze zu einer historischen

und unhistorischen Gestalt', in Specht-Kreusel and Olaf Schirmeister (ed.), *Widukind und Enger: Rezaeptionsgeschichte und Bibliographie* (Bielefeld: Verlag für Regionalgeschichte, 1992), pp. 6–19, quotation p. 19. On the conceptual underpinnings of the revamped exhibition, see Hartmu John, 'Die Neukonzeption des Widukind-Museums in Enger', *Stadt-Enger —Beitrüge zure Stadtgeschichte* vol. 2 (1983), 9–16.

37. Agte, *Der Sachsenhain*, pp. 107–08.
38. See the essay by the late regional NPD leader and neo-pagan Jürgen Rieger, *Sachsenmord und Sachsenhain in Verden* (2nd ed. Hamburg, 2002).
39. Cf. URL:http:// antifa-aktionen.blogspot.com/.../npd-umtrunk-im. [Last accessed 19 May 2012].
40. Cf. bloggers' comments on 'NPD und "Odin statt Jesus?" ', URL:http://www.paganforum.de › ... › Das Heidentum-. [Last accessed 19 May 2012].
41. Von Leers, *op. cit.*, p. 57.
42. Von Leers, 'Judentum und Islam als Gegensätze', *Die Judenfrage* vol. 6, no. 24 (15 December 1942), 275–8; translated as 'Judaism and Islam as Opposites' in Andrew G. Bostom (ed.), *The Legacy of Islamic Antisemitism: From Sacred Texts to Solemn History* (Amherst, NY: Prometheus Books, 2008), pp. 619–25. See also Jeffrey Herf, *The Jewish Enemy: Nazi Propaganda during World War II and the Holocaust* (Cambridge: Belknap Press of Harvard University Press, 2006), pp. 180–81.
43. For Leers' career in Egypt, see Jeffrey Herf, *Nazi Propaganda for the Arab World* (New Haven: Yale University Press, 2009), p. 260, p. 309, notes 78 and 79.
44. Matthias Pape, 'Der Karlskult an den Wendepunkten der neueren deutschen Geschichte', *Historisches Jahrbuch* vol. 120, (2000), 138–81; Idem, 'Franke? Deutscher? oder Europäer?', *Jahrbuch für europäische Geschichte* vol. 4, (2003), 243–54.
45. Rudoph Wahl, *Karl der Große. Eine Historie* (Berlin: S. Fischer, 1934), p. 17.
46. As well as Pape's work (cf. note 39), see Max Kerner, *Karl der Große. Entschleierung eines Mythos* (Köln: Böhlau, 2001), esp. pp. 273–77 (Ausblick: Hat Karl der Große eine Zukunft'); Bianca Dost, *Karl der Große—ein deutscher Erinnerungsort? Die Bedeutung des Frankenkaisers für die deutsche Erinnerungskultur* (Saarbrücken: DVM Verlag, 2010).
47. For their acceptance speeches, see URL:http:// www.karlspreis.de. While Merkel made no reference whatever to Charlemagne, Sarkozy remarked that 'to see Karl as the first founder of Europe would be an exaggeration', but that 'his Reich was not only the common matrix from which what was to become Germany and France eventually emerged'; Karl himself was 'also and above all an especially inspiring example for unity in our so deeply divided continent'.

Part III
Pluralizing Memories: Fragmented, Contested, Resisted

8
The Suppression and Recall of Colonial Memory: Manchukuo and the Cold War in the Two Koreas

Suk-Jung Han

Introduction

After liberation in 1945, a number of candidates in the general or gubernatorial elections in South Korea solemnly wrote on their election posters that they had spent their whole lives fighting for the liberation movement in Manchuria (the region which the PRC now calls 'Northeast', *Dongbei*) during the colonial period. Politicians in the 1950s and 1960s would claim they were exiled anti-Japanese fighters in Manchuria, just as those in the 1970s and 1980s posed as ex-ringleaders of the April 19 student movement that toppled the Syngman Rhee regime in 1960.

Until the 1960s, it was not rare to hear about the existence of those in South Korean neighbourhoods who had returned from Manchuria, whoever they might have claimed to be. Manchuria was a mythic land or a clean sheet of paper on which some Koreans could freely draw their own pasts, as the region belonged to a socialist country during the Cold War era and was therefore completely disconnected from South Korean memory. At the same time, 'the liberation movement in Manchuria' was valorised as the main theme in the historiography on the contemporary Korea. In North Korea, the memory of Manchuria suppressed all other narratives, where the armed guerrilla activities of the deceased North Korean leader Kim Il Sung in Manchuria monopolised official historiography of colonial history.

The memory of Manchuria was unconsciously recalled by the fierce rival regimes of North and South during the Cold War. It would be meaningful to ask how this memory was conversely restrained and exploited, and by whom on the Korean peninsula, one of the last remnants of the Cold War. This paper suggests that contemporary Manchuria is not only the nodal point of the state-formation connecting the old and new states in East Asia but also the root of the Cold War strategy formulated by the opposing leaders of the two Koreas who had spent the early stages of their careers there – either as independence fighters or as collaborators – and who came to imitate their former colonisers later.

The suppression of the Manchurian memory

After 1945, the contemporary history of Manchuria was largely ignored by all of East Asia. Manchuria belonged nowhere in the academic community, compartmentalised as academia was along nation state boundaries. It was a periphery in the fields of Chinese, Japanese or Korean studies and was, in fact, severely marginalised in the Chinese nationalist discourse whose main target was Japanese colonialism. Chinese nationalism, therefore, did not allow for a historically complex Manchuria.

Manchuria was the home of the Manchus, who founded the Qing dynasty (1644–1911) of China. To preserve their sacrosanct land, the Manchu rulers instituted a long-term ban on the migration of Han Chinese from the mainland. It was not until the late eighteenth century that the Qing court permitted the migration of Han Chinese to Manchuria, only to have the region become heavily Sinicised. The influx of immigrants from North China rose to nearly 5 million in the 1920s alone. From 1890 to 1942, half a million people arrived annually in Manchuria from the mainland, one of the largest world-scale migrations in modern history.[1] 'Racial Harmony', the official ideology of the Japanese puppet state Manchukuo (1932–1945), reflected the historical hybridity of Manchuria.[2] It was a land of multiple ethnic groups including Manchus, Han-Chinese, Koreans, Russians, Mongols, Oroqens and Goldies. In Harbin, the 'Paris of the East' built by Russians during the construction of the Chinese Eastern Railway, there were about 50 different ethnic groups with as many as 45 languages spoken there during the Manchukuo period.[3] However, the history of non-Han Chinese in Manchuria is seldom recognised in official the Chinese historiography. Plans to hold an international conference in Harbin to commemorate its centennial in 1998 were blocked by the Chinese government, for example. As far as Chinese nationalist discourse is concerned, Harbin is a Chinese city built by the Chinese.

The suppression of the memory of Manchuria is deeply related to the state of Manchukuo, which was established by the Kwantung Army (the garrison army stationed in Manchuria since Japan's victory in the Russo-Japanese War) after initiating a war (the so-called Manchurian Incident) against the warlord regime in 1931 without receiving orders from Tokyo. In fact, Chinese nationalist discourse has exaggerated the heroic resistance of the Chinese and suppressed any other accounts since the incident occurred.[4] Manchukuo is depicted as a nightmare, and the Chinese have religiously attached the prefix, '*wei* (false)' to any mention of it. Some Japanese, by contrast, have tried to recall only the idealism of the state-building, while the Japanese government itself has been silent about its relationship with Manchukuo. In a sense, the memory of Manchukuo was intentionally suppressed by the international community.[5]

In Korea, the suppression of the memory of Manchuria came in two varieties: in North Korea, the memory of Manchuria actually shaped much of the country's post-liberation politics. Kim Il Sung and his guerrilla group became the nucleus of the new regime and his armed resistance against Japanese imperialism in Manchuria monopolised the narrative of colonial history.[6] According to the official historiography, he single-handedly led the liberation movement, and his cooperation with Chinese communists as a member of the Northeast Anti-Japanese Allied Army (*Dongbeikangrilianjun*) (1934–1940) and membership in the Chinese Communist Party were elided from the official histories of the period. Instead, his 'independent resistance activity' became the core of the official discourse. It was not until the 1990s that the armed resistance in Manchuria was somewhat diluted after the regime claimed to have discovered the tomb of Tan'gun, the mythical ancestor of the Koreans, and emphasised 'Taedong river culture' (this essentially amounts to a re-interpretation that places Pyongyang at the center of ancient Korean history).[7]

In South Korea, by contrast, Manchuria became a forbidden space largely due to ex-president Park Chung Hee's career as an officer in the Manchukuo Army. Manchuria was conveniently forgotten as it became communised during the Cold War era. Some people touted themselves as ex-nationalist fighters during this blank period, but it was not until the 1970s that Manchuria appeared in history textbooks in South Korea when the government launched its official management of the memory of Manchuria based on the liberation movement there. This can be seen as a reaction to the monopolisation of the resistance narrative by the North Korean leaders. However, most texts have only delivered an image of Manchuria as the space of the resistance, never proffering the historical reality of the nearly 2 million Koreans who were there in 1945. For several decades, the purpose of contemporary historiography was heavily skewed to the sole theme of resistance. However, there was a wide spectrum of experiences in Manchuria between brutal fascist rule and heroic nationalist resistance.

The real lives of Koreans in Manchukuo

Contrary to the claims of a number of South Korean politicians since liberation, resistance in the Manchukuo period was almost impossible. The number of anti-Japanese forces that the Manchukuo government loosely designated 'bandits' dramatically decreased from 200,000 or 300,000 at the establishment of Manchukuo to a few hundred in the late 1930s. The Northeast Anti-Japanese Allied Army, the last resistance force made up of Korean and Chinese fighters was hunted down to its final stand at the Korea-Manchukuo border in the winter of 1939 when it was finally quashed, with some survivors including Kim Il Sung crossing over the Russia–Manchukuo border to seek shelter in Russia in 1941.[8] The Japanese rulers persistently and brutally quelled resistance forces over the 14 years of the Manchukuo period.[9]

In the 1920s, Koreans were a means of infiltration for Japanese imperialism in Manchuria. Japanese imperialism in Manchuria was a kind of 'osmotic expansion' using Korean farmers as proxy settlers.[10] They were in turn persecuted by the Chinese warlord in Manchuria Zhang Xueliang, who considered them vanguards of Japanese imperialism. The Wanbaoshan Incident (a minor conflict between Korean and Chinese farmers near Changchun that triggered the killing of over 100 Chinese people in Korea on the eve of the Manchurian Incident) and the subsequent attack on Koreans by Chinese bandits and the remnants of the warlord army during the Manchurian Incident occurred within the framework of ethnic conflict between Koreans and Chinese set up by Japanese imperialism.

After Manchukuo was founded, however, the status of Koreans changed significantly: strict regulations previously enforced by the warlords (limitations on land ownership, for instance) were lifted, and some were even provided with subsidies for migration. Following a succession of natural disasters, the Korean colonial government and the Manchukuo government promoted the migration of Koreans to Manchuria on a large scale, leading to the so-called 'Manchuria boom', or 'Manchuria fever' and exodus of Koreans to the area beginning in the mid-1930s. The total number of immigrants reached 700,000 in the 1930s alone, and the number of Koreans rose to nearly 2 million (compared to 1.6 million Japanese) in 1945.[11] Of these transplants, about 800,000 Koreans returned to Korea after 1945.

Koreans occupied a marginal status in Manchukuo. The rumour (heard by the Chinese) and expectation (of the Koreans) that Koreans were 'second-class citizens' (occupying a middle position between the Japanese rulers and Chinese farmers), or that Koreans and Chinese received unequal wages, grain rations and so forth, spread throughout the Japanese empire (and is still even supported by most contemporary South Korean historians), but the aggregate statistics do not actually support this assumption. Although there was some difference in the wage scale in the cities, there was no difference in grain rationing between the Korean and Chinese in the area.[12] The two groups experienced an equal amount of hardship, however, particularly in the final stages of Manchukuo.

The majority of Koreans in Manchuria were in the primary sector of the economy, and their numbers in business, factory work, government and professional work was meagre. There was no Korean capital to speak of, nor any political power. Their only comparative advantage was in the government sector in the late Manchukuo period, when there were about 13,000 Korean officials albeit in low-ranking positions. The number of professionals was also rising in the late period. Over 2000 Koreans were engaged in medicine, for instance.[13]

The Korean population in Manchuria was diverse, and included those who worked for the Manchukuo government, army and police. There were also vagabonds, opium dealers and pimps. Just prior to the founding of Manchukuo, it was estimated that 10–20 per cent of the Koreans in Changchun, Andong and Fengtian and 90 per cent of those in Harbin were opium dealers,[14] and it is questionable whether this tendency changed radically in the Manchukuo period. In the ethnic hierarchy of Manchukuo in which Japanese settlers occupied the top position, Koreans were objectively denied second-class citizen status. However, there were episodes where Koreans who subjectively perceived their status as such sometimes harassed other powerless ethnics like Russians in the big cities.[15] The memory of the Koreans in Manchukuo engaged in ignoble occupations or simply unrelated to the nationalist liberation movement was somewhat known in Korea immediately following liberation,[16] but this memory was soon silenced by the narrative of heroic resistance in Manchuria.

The eruption of the Manchurian memory

Although Manchukuo fell with the Japanese empire, it refuses to perish. To label Manchukuo a mere puppet state would overlook its complex history and potential as a model. Manchukuo, once a periphery in East Asian studies, is now becoming illuminated as a place of paradox from the viewpoint of post-structuralism, which emphasises the deconstruction of privileged concepts and boundaries. It appears to be a place where it becomes 'difficult to disentangle imperialism from nationalism, modernity from tradition, frontier from heartland'.[17] Above all, it is a kind of black box for contemporary East Asian history that also gestures toward the Janus-faced nature of the authoritarian developmental states in East Asia after 1945 that not only ardently pursued economic development but also severely disciplined their subjects.

Manchuria provides a clue to the Japanese economic miracle in the 1930s. Japan built a grand economic autarky after occupying abundant natural resources there and eventually confronted the West. When Manchukuo collapsed, it left a tremendous legacy to the Chinese economy.[18]

For Koreans, Manchukuo became a land of opportunity. Over 10,000 Koreans worked for the Manchukuo government in the late period. Also, Kyŏngbang, which has long been hailed as the 'first Korean nationalist capital', actually established a branch in Manchukuo with the assistance of the Korean colonial government.[19] Manchuria absorbed not only Koreans, but also millions of Chinese and Japanese. Japanese imperialism in Manchuria truly opened a transnational stage in East Asia. A number of Korean and Japanese intellectuals including the literary luminaries Yom Sang-sŏp and Natsume Soseki travelled to (or lived in) Manchuria and left behind numerous works about it. There was even a 'Manchurian romance' genre, and hundreds of songs about Manchuria were made in Korea and Japan. The express trains *Nozomi*, *Hikari*, and *Dairiku* ran like 'bullets' from Pusan, the so-called 'gate of East Asia' to the big cities of Manchukuo and Beijing. The starting point of the express was extended to the port for Japanese passengers who crossed the strait between Pusan and Shimonoseki. Gigantic ferryboats carried 2000 daily, and 2 million passengers yearly in the late 1930s.[20] The rhythm of the Japanese settlers' lives in Pusan was set to Manchuria through various fields involving trade, travel, and war mobilisation.[21]

Although the much touted 'ethnic harmony' of the Manchukuo regime failed in its claim, it was a pioneering project reminiscent of the official discourse of the current governments in the globalisation era. The films with the theme of Japanese Orientalism made by the Manchurian Film Association (*Man'ei*) and starring the prodigious actress Li Koran swept through all of East Asia. Even after 1945, an extremely popular theme song, 'the nights of China' (*sina no yoru*) flowed to American soldiers in the Korean War. Those inhabitants in Harbin who later dispersed to Australia, Canada and Israel cannot forget the city, a breathing space of multi-culture in the colonial period.[22]

The transnational character of Manchuria went beyond East Asia. Manchuria before 1931 was a space of collective imperialism not only for Japan but also for the Western powers, including the United States.[23]

Manchukuo maintained this transnational aspect through its fascist alliance with Japan and Germany, exchanging ideas of social mobilisation and a control economy.

In terms of state-formation, Manchukuo is a proto-type of the so-called 'client states' or 'stooges' during the Cold War era. Japanese leaders were prodigious in inventing puppet states in Manchuria and mainland China, an excellent mode of imperialist rule through the sovereign state form, which in turn influenced the super powers after WWII. Also, the Manchukuo regime was a pioneer for the new authoritarian developmental states in East Asia. The Manchukuo regime crushed many different forms of resistance and mobilised tremendous human and material resources for the Sino-Japanese War and the Pacific War. The regime deeply penetrated and transformed the lives of the civilians in the region. At the same time, it constructed modern cities, including impressive industrial complexes, railways and sanitation systems. For instance, Xinjing, the capital of Manchukuo, was the cutting edge of modern cities in city planning, running water, sewage, and flush toilet systems. By contrast, it was not until after the 1960s that the modern toilet system was introduced in the cities of Japan.[24]

While Manchukuo was largely an experimental ground for Japanese modernity (even for its architects, city planners, and museum managers), it was even more so a training ground for bureaucrats in their management of a new state. State-building is a lengthy process that involves not only building a bureaucracy and a standing army, but also imprinting the will of the state on its subjects through various means. It is a 'great arch' that took centuries in the British case.[25] However, the Manchukuo State was established at record-breaking speed due to Japan's experience with its own state building during the Meiji Restoration, and with the establishment of the Taiwanese and Korean colonial states.[26] Manchukuo was also key to the formation of the postwar Japanese state; the heir of the so-called 'Manchurian clique', became a pillar of the ruling Liberal Democratic Party, for example.[27] In this way, Manchukuo can also be seen as the link between the Meiji state and the post-war Japanese state.

Manchukuo was also the space of gestation for the future leadership of both North and South Korea. The guerrilla group led by Kim Il Sung, which survived the last hunt-down of the Manchukuo expeditionary troops, later became the nucleus of the new North Korean regime. Likewise, the Korean members of the Manchukuo Army became a powerful faction in the new South Korean Army, and eventually came to the fore along with Park Chung Hee in the military coup of 1961.

Through these opposing groups, Manchukuo left indelible impression on the formation of the two Korean states in areas including the planned economies, development, dogged social mobilisation and disciplining. Manchukuo was thus a sort of laboratory for state formation linking the Meiji state and the later Korean regimes, in particular.

The 'Manchurians' as architects of new regimes

After liberation, close to 800,000 Koreans returned to Korea from Manchukuo. Among them were the architects of two Korean states. As mentioned earlier, Kim Il Sung's guerrilla group became the core of the North Korean regime. In South Korea, the prominence of the 'Manchurians' was manifested in various realms. Those who studied at the three flagship institutes in Manchukuo (Manchukuo Military Academy, Datung Institute, Jianguo University), including Park Chung Hee, would become the leaders of South Korea's developmental state. As low ranking officers in Manchukuo, they gained valuable management experience in the Manchukuo government, the army, the Concordia Association, and in the hospitals. This is a marked contrast to those Koreans who migrated to (or studied in) Japan and were unable to find any jobs other than manual labour during the colonial period. Manchukuo offered a much broader variety of employment to Koreans. For instance, more than 90 per cent of the Korean musicians who had studied in Japan later found jobs in Manchukuo.[28] Musicians from Manchuria, including Kim Sung Tae of the Xinjing Orchestra later became tycoons in the South Korean music world.

These 'Manchurians' initially gained recognition during the Syngman Rhee government by suppressing revolutionary guerrillas. They later joined Park's regime en masse after his military coup, aided in part by the timely and favourable atmosphere provided by the normalisation of relations between South Korea and Japan in 1965, a sort of reunion of Manchurians on both sides, so to speak. In South Korea, the Manchurians were influential not only in the military but also in education and ideology, another pillar of the regime. They promoted *kŏnkuk* (construction of the new state) and *chaegŏn* (reconstruction) ideology, just as the state preachers of the Meiji state and the Self-rule Guidance Committee of Manchukuo did in the initial stages of state formation.[29] 'Manchurians' like Yi Sun Kun and Yi Yin Ki developed *hwarang* ideology (military nationalism) and the Charter for National Education, by combining the corporatism of the Concordia Association of Manchukuo, Confucian loyalty and anti-communism.

Manchukuo and the Cold War on the Korean peninsula

It has long been overlooked that Manchukuo influenced more than the formation of the two Korean states; it also had a profound impact on their competition during the Cold War. During this period, the two regimes nearly grew into garrison states by disciplining their subjects into ideological fighters. Hence, Manchukuo is best understood as a nodal point of the state-formation between old and new states in East Asia, as well as the root of the Cold War confrontation on the Korean peninsula. Above all, the model of their numerous naturalised events, or 'national ceremonies' – such as holding one-minute silent tributes to the war dead in front of monuments, marching, lectures on the 'current emergency situation', movie screenings, making posters, student speech contests, rallies and large athletic events – all too familiar to Koreans for decades, were originally used in Manchukuo, the proto-type for the so-called 'defense state', or for 'total mobilisation' in the Japanese empire.[30] In some realms, the two Koreas were unequal to the enthusiasm of Manchukuo. For instance, the Manchukuo government (as has been recently discovered) created as many as 300 kinds of propaganda posters and 50 kinds of leaflets.[31] Big sports festivals in North Korea, including what is considered the regime's masterpiece, the Arirang Festival in 2002, took their cues from Manchukuo's favourite events.

Confucianism, an official ideology of Manchukuo, was also utilised by the two Koreas to garner the loyalty of citizens to their respective regimes. North Korea, for instance, became a kind of a Confucian corporate state.[32] The official discourse of the DPRK (Democratic People's Republic of Korea) is full of rhetoric of Confucian benevolence and loyalty. The ex-leader, Kim Il Sung was called the *ŏbŏi* (father) of the whole nation. The South Korean regime also diligently mobilised the campaign of Confucian loyalty and obedience to parents in the 1970s.

The very diligent trips made by cadres of the North Korean regime to local industrial spots or farms remind us of the energetic inspections conducted by the Manchukuo bureaucrats. Kim Il Sung himself died during a local inspection in 1994. Officials in Manchukuo were sent on mandatory inspection tours from the capital or provincial capitals throughout the country for up to two weeks every month.[33] Since the founding fathers of North Korea were the very anti-Japanese guerrillas that the Manchukuo officials were trying to monitor, they were likely well-aware of the operations of the Manchukuo regime. While fighting their enemy, the guerrillas came to resemble them. The Soviet element, therefore, was merely one ingredient in the North Korean state-formation.[34]

Although Manchukuo's imprint on North Korea was tangible, the crucial linkage is between Manchukuo and South Korea. The model for the South Korean developmental state, which was praised as the driving force of the so-called 'Miracle on the Han', was also Manchukuo. Manchukuo was the domain of the Kwantung Army, which unblocked by any social forces, was able to freely pursue its grand economic project. The military government there pushed the most extreme planned economy ever attempted in a non-socialist block country.[35]

The legacy of Manchukuo went far beyond the control economy, however. It left a deep impression on the cultural dimension as well. In a way, it shaped the Cold War mentality of confrontation and competition coupled with speedy construction, mobilisation, and strict discipline in the military style in both Koreas, and contributed to the 'relationship of hostile complicity'.[36] Several 'high modern'[37] elements (characterized by strong beliefs in scientific and technological progress) such as American Taylorist production; social engineering and mobilisation in interwar Germany; the idea of a planned economy and the industrial warriors of the Soviet Union flowed to South Korea through Manchukuo. Speed and uniformity were the hallmarks of the South Korean regime. Manchukuo and the two Koreas were literally 'construction states'. Compared to pre-war Japan, the will of the three regimes emphasising uniformity and a straight line shaped their terrain. The three regimes energetically continued to build cities and infra-structure, destroying whatever stood in the way of their projects. The Manchukuo government demolished 700 royal tombs of the Koguryo dynasty in Jian after a ritual service in 1938 in order to continue laying rail lines, for example.[38] South Korean leaders were also resolute in fashioning society and nature in a straight line: one wall of Dŏksu Palace, a Chosŏn Dynasty palace in Seoul, was moved by the mayor of Seoul (a retired general) for the sake of city development in the early 1960s.

Numerous aspects of daily life including streetcars, traditional streets and housing were removed or destroyed nationwide in the spirit of modernity and efficiency in South Korea, just as they were in Manchukuo. The southern part of Seoul and the industrial complex of Ulsan were developed along the lines of Xinjing, the capital of Manchukuo. The agency for developing the Ulsan industrial complex (*t'ŭkpyŏl kŏnsŏlguk*, the Special Bureau for Construction) was named after the one that developed Xinjing. In South Korea in the 1970s, traditional housing in the countryside was entirely removed during the 'New Village Movement'. They were replaced by rectangular houses in the western style with uniform colours and sizes. South Korean leaders also learnt from the Manchukuo rulers the efficacy of summoning citizens to celebrate the foundation of the state, blaming communists for society's ills and cherishing martyrs who died for their countries.[39] The human body also came under the jurisdiction of both regimes. The Manchukuo government spent a great deal of energy on athletics. An athletic meeting was held to celebrate the foundation of the state straight away (later to be called the Manchukuo Olympics). The influential Manchukuo Athletic Association had various branches that built gyms in major cities, and organised all manner of games and activities, including international games (the 'Japan-Manchukuo-China Games' in 1939 and the 'Greater East Asian Games' in 1942, for example). It was an important wing of the government for social education, indoctrinating the people with the official ideology of *jianguo* (construction of the new state), racial harmony and modernity, including sanitation in every province and county. Finally, *jianguo* gymnastics were developed in the name of promoting physical education and ethnic harmony. The Ministry of Education set May 2 as *jianguo* gymnastics day to commemorate Emperor Puyi's visit to Japan,[40] where participants in major national ceremonies would perform gymnastics. From 1937 on, three days were set as *jianguo* gymnastics days.

Leaders of South Korea also successfully linked sports with its competition not only with North Korea but also in the capitalist world system. They slightly changed *jianguo* of Manchuko to *chaegŏn* (reconstruction). *Chaegŏn* gymnastics was propagated through radio broadcasting every morning with a military-style song (a modern version of the song is still played at contemporary South Korean military camps). Politics and sports in the two Koreas were indivisible, and the two regimes fought fiercely in the world of sports. North Korea shocked South Korea in 1972 when a North Korean won a gold medal in the Olympic games, the first Korean from either side of the peninsula ever to do so. This achievement was followed by an enormous investment in sports by the South Korean counterpart.

Winning medals in the Asian and Olympic games became analogous to climbing up the ladder of the world system. In particular, boxing (both amateur and professional) was closely linked to official Korean nationalism. The pose of a skinny boxer crouching forward with clenched fists was the very symbol of the Korean nation advancing forward and overcoming adversities. When Kim Ki Soo fought to become the first South Korean professional world boxing champion in 1966, the fight was set for June 25, the date of the outbreak of the Korean War. President Park Chung Hee watched the match at the stadium and put the champion's belt on Kim himself.[41] When Hong Su Hwan became the second Korean professional world boxing champion in 1974, Pohang Steel Company (Posco) put a full-page advertisement of its huge blast furnace with melting pig iron to celebrate his victory.[42] The association between South Korean boxing and its industrial warriors was perfect.

Conclusion

Nozomi and *Hikari*, the bullet trains in contemporary Japan, were named after the ones that flew from Pusan to Fengtian and Xinjing in Manchuko in the 1930s. This is just one example of how in Japan, Manchuria seems to be a nostalgic memory. In the two Koreas, by contrast, the memory of Manchuria surpassed nostalgia, and the official memory of resistance suppressed other narratives. Bits and pieces of the Manchurian experience were conveniently recalled by the leaders of the two states, most of whom had spent their early careers in Manchukuo either as fighters or as collaborators, and who later subconsciously mimicked the colonisers. This proved to be an incredibly useful strategy for confronting and competing on the peninsula during the Cold War era.

The memory of Manchuria was very conspicuous in South Korea, in particular. Some Koreans had witnessed two historic events in Manchukuo, namely, the military coup-like war initiated by the Kwantung Army without a directive from its home government (the Manchurian Incident of 1931) and state-led industrialisation. This influenced the making of the developmental state and various social engineering projects by coup plotters in South Korea.

The South Korean economic miracle, then, was largely achieved by the 'Manchurians'. Several 'almost the same but not quite'[43] elements filled the process. Slightly modified ideas, catch phrases, spirit, plans, institutes, methods or the very same words from Manchukuo were revived by them from the 1960s. That said, there are a number of reasons why scholars should view Manchukuo very seriously.

Notes

1. Thomas Gottschang and Diana Lary, *Swallows and Settlers: The Great Migration from North China to Manchuria* (Ann Arbor: Center for Chinese Studies, the University of Michigan, 2000), p. 2, 180.
2. On the official ideology of Manchukuo, see Han (2004), 470–4.
3. Thomas Lahusen, 'Introduction,' *South Atlantic Quarterly* vol. 99, no. 1 (2001), 2.
4. Rana Mitter, *The Manchurian Myth: Nationalism, Resistance, and Collaboration in Modern China* (Berkeley: University of California Press, 2000), p. 16.

5. Gavan McCormack, 'Manchukuo: Constructing the Past,' *East Asian History* vol. 2 (1990), 106.

6. Charles Armstrong, *The North Korean Revolution, 1945–1950* (Ithaca: Cornell University Press, 2003), pp. 27–28.

7. Shin Ju Baek, 'Manjuwa haebanghu ŭi kiyŏk' [Manchuria and its memory after liberation], *Manjuyŏnku* vol. 2 (2005), 123.

8. Dae-Sook Suh, *Kim Il Sung: The North Korean Leader* (New York: Columbia University Press, 1988), p. 47.

9. Han Suk-Jung, *Manjuguk kŏnkuk ŭi chaehaesŏk* [the reinterpretation of the Manchukuo state formation] (Pusan: Dong-A University Press, 2007), pp. 73–80.

10. See Hyunok Park, *Two Dreams in One Bed: Empire, Social Life, and the Origins of the North Korean Revolution in Manchuria* (Durham: Duke University Press, 2005).

11. Yamamuro Shinichi, *Kimera-manshukoku no shozo* [chimera and the portrait of Manchukuo] (Tokyo: Chuko Shinshu, 2004), pp. 46, 58.

12. See Yoon Hwytak, 'Manjukuk idŭngkukmin kusilsang kwa husang' [the second class citizen: the reality and illusion], *Yŏksahakbo* vol. 169, (2001), 143–9.

13. 42 per cent of Koreans were in the primary sector, 3.8 per cent in mining and manufacturing, 4.2 per cent in commerce and transportation, 0.9 percent in government and education, and 48 per cent were unemployed. Among the major ethnic groups in the three largest cities (Fengtian, Xinjing, Harbin), Koreans had the highest number in the primary sector and the unemployed. See the 1940 census of Manchukuo, pp. 281–87.

14. Park Kang, 'Manjusabyŏn ijŏn ilbon kwa chaeman han'in ŭi apyŏn, mayak milmaemunje' [Japan before the Manchurian Incident and the problem of illegal opium and drug dealing by Koreans in Manchuria], *Hanguk minjokundongsa yongu* vol. 35, (2003), 325.

15. Kim Suk-Hyung, *Nanŭn chosŏn kongsandangwŏnio* [I am a Korean Communist Party member] (Seoul: Sun'in, 2001), pp. 95–102.

16. About the rumours widespread in Korean society immediately following liberation that Koreans from Manchuria were opium dealers or pimps, see Kim Man Sun's novel, *Kuigukja* [returnees]. p. 565.

17. Prasenjit Duara, *The Sovereignty and Authenticity: Manchukuo and the East Asian Modern* (NY: Rowman and Littlefield, 2003), p. 1.

18. See Kang Jin-Ah, 'Chungguk kwa soryŏn ŭi sahoejuŭi kongŏphwa wa chŏnhu manju ŭi yusan' [the socialist industrialisation of China and Russia and the postwar legacy of Manchkuo] in Han Suk-Jung and Noh Ki Sik (eds), *Manju, tongasia yŏnghap ŭi kongkan* [Manchuria, the space of the East Asian fusion] (Seoul: Somyŏng, 2008).

19. See Carter Eckert, *Offspring of Empire: The Koch'ang Kims and the Colonial Origins of Korean Capitalism* (Seattle: University of Washington Press, 1992); and Chung An-Ki, 'Manju shijang ŭi chulhyŏn kwa chosŏn'in chabon ŭi daeŭng' [the advent of the Manchurian market and the response of the Korean capital] in Han Suk-Jung and Noh Ki-Sik (eds), *Manju, tongasia yŏnghap ŭi kongkan* [Manchuria, the space of the East Asian fusion] (Seoul: Somyung, 2008).

20. Suk-Jung Han, 'From Pusan to Fengtian: The Boundary between Korea and Manchukuo in the 1930s', *East Asian History* vol. 30, (2005), 64–5.

21. See Han Suk-Jung, 'Manjujihyang kwa chongsok: 1930–40nyŏndae pusan ŭi ilbon koryumin ŭi segye' [the Manchurian orientation and dependency: the world of the Japanese settlers in Pusan in the 1930s, 1940s], *Hanguk minjokundongsa yŏnku*, vol. 48 (2006), 271–8.
22. Thomas Lahusen, *Harbin and Manchuria: Place, Space and Identity* (Durham, NC: Duke University, 2000), p. 2.
23. See Peter Duus, Ramon H. Myers and Mark R. Peattie, *The Japanese Informal Empire in China, 1895–1937* (Princeton, NJ: Princeton University Press, 1989).
24. Koshizawa Akira, *Manshukoku no shuto keikaku* [the planning of the Manchukuo capital] (Tokyo: Nihonkeizai hyoronsha, 1997), p. 136.
25. See Philip Corrigan and Derek Sayer, *The Great Arch: The English State Formation as Cultural Revolution* (NY: Basil Blackwell, 1985).
26. See Yamamuro Shinichi, 'Shokumin teikoku nihon no kosei to manshukoku: tochi yoshiki no seni to tochi jinsai no shuryu' [the composition of the empire Japan and Manchukuo: the change of the ruling mode and the circulation of the ruling agent] in Peter Duus and Kobayashi Hideo (eds), *Teikoku to yu genzo* [The illusion called empire] (Tokyo: Aokishoten, 1998).
27. See Kobayashi Hideo, *Manshu to Jiminto* [Manchuria and the Liberal Democratic Party] (Tokyo: Sinchosha, 2005).
28. Li Kang-Sook, Kim Chun-Mi and Min Kyong-Chan, *Uri yangak paeknyŏn* [the century of our Western music] (Seoul: Hyonamsa, 2005), pp. 246, 263.
29. For more on the state preachers and the self-rule guidance committee see Ketelaar (1990) and Yamamuro (2004).
30. Suk-Jung Han, 'Those Who Imitated the Colonizers', in Mariko Tamanoi (ed.), *Crossed Histories: Manchuria in the Age of Empire* (Honolulu: University of Hawaii Press, 2005).
31. Kishi Toshihiko, *Manshukoku no visual, media* [the visual and media of Manchukuo] (Tokyo: Yoshikawakobunkan, 2010).
32. Bruce Cumings, 'The Corporate State', in Hagen Koo (ed.), *State and Society in Contemporary Korea* (Ithaca: Cornell University Press, 1993), pp. 202–10.
33. Han, *Manjuguk kŏnkuk ŭi chaehaesŏk*, pp.110–17.
34. Armstrong, *The North Korean Revolution*, pp. 328.
35. Yamamoto Yuzo, *Manshukoku keizaishi kenkyu* [the study of the Manchukuo economic history] (Nagoya: Nagoyadaigaku Shuppankai, 2003).
36. Lim Jie Hyun, *Chuktaejŏk kongbŏmjadŭl* [hostile accomplices] (Seoul: Sonamu, 2005).
37. James Scott, *Seeing Like a State: How Certain Schemes to Improve the Human Condition Have Failed* (New Haven: Yale University Press, 1998), pp. 88–89.
38. *Shengjingshibao*, Xinjing, 20 November 1938.
39. Han, 'Those Who Imitated the Colonizers', pp. 172–79.
40. *Shengjingshibao*, 8 April 1936.
41. *Dong-A Ilbo*, Seoul, 28 June 1968.
42. *Dong-A Ilbo*, 5 July 1974.
43. See Homi Bhabha, *The Location of Culture* (London: Routledge, 1994), p. 89.

Additional Works Referenced

James Ketelaar, *Of Heretics and Martyrs in Meiji Japan: Buddhism and Its Persecution* (Princeton: Princeton University Press, 1990).

Kim Man Sun, 'Kwigukja' [returnee], *Hanguk kŭndaedanpyŏnsosŏldaegye* [the series of the modern Korean novels], vol. 4 (Seoul: Taehaksa, 1988). Minzhengbu of the Manchukuo government. 1940. *Kangde qinian linshi guoshi: zaimanzhouguo erbenren diaochajieguobiao, quanguopian* [the 1940 Manchukuo census: On Japanese, nationwide]. Xinjing, 1990.

Suk-Jung Han, 'The Problem of Sovereignty: Manchukuo, 1932–1937', *Positions: East Asia Cultures Critique* vol. 12, no. 2 (2004), 457–78.

———. 'Manju ŭi kiŏk' [the memory of Manchuria]. Han-il yŏndae 21 ed. Han-il yŏksainsiknonjaeng ŭi metahistory [the meta-history of the debate of Korea-Japan historical consciousness] (Seoul: Puri wa ipari, 2008).

9
Accomplices of Violence: Guilt and Purification through Altruism among the Moscow Human Rights Activists of the 1960s and 1970s

Barbara Walker

The theme of *samozhertvovanie* (a term meaning both self-giving and self-sacrifice) in the Moscow human rights movement of the 1960s and 1970s invokes considerable passion as activists, opponents and observers have long debated the motives of participants in that movement. Some dissenters and their supporters have focused on the activists' willingness to give up careers, health, social stability and even their lives for the sake of human rights in the Soviet system, while their critics both inside and outside the movement have viewed at least some dissenters as being motivated instead by self-interest, desiring primarily western currency, western contacts and fame. Debate over motives represented as selfless is by no means a new phenomenon in world history; it has played a role in discussions of altruism for as long as those discussions have been recorded.[1] Many apparently find it difficult to believe in the integrity of claims of selflessness.

Yet with regard to the Moscow human rights movement, this issue has acquired a particular emotional intensity, which tells us that there is an important historical issue to be explored here. And indeed, close examination of the contextual implications of the emotions involved offers us a new perspective on the meaning and significance of that movement. We may come to see it as a struggle not only for human rights but also for control over the self-giving or altruistic impulse and its representation in the face of an intensive Soviet state interest in maintaining its own control over that impulse and representation. For participants, this struggle involved seeking or imagining purified social bonds among themselves and even a purified community in which self-giving and solidarity in self-giving were central values. They were motivated in no small part by the desire to cleanse themselves and their milieu of a painful sense of personal and national corruption incurred by their previous commitment to a state responsible for the deaths of a myriad of its citizens.

Historically, the Soviet state had staked, and in the 1960s and 1970s continued to stake, powerful claims on the volunteerism and the altruistic will of its citizens. From the first Five Year Plan to World War II to Cold War classroom collections of money for North Vietnamese children, the theme of self-giving and self-sacrifice in the interest of the state was a significant element of the state-citizen relationship in the Soviet Union. The state also laid absolute claim to its citizens' loyalty and solidarity in self-giving; they were not to give of themselves for any person or entity not sanctioned by the state. The right of the state to claim that loyalty and self-sacrifice was, for reasons that will be delineated next, of vital significance to the state's own interests; therefore it strongly resisted any attempt to encroach upon its power in that area. The Moscow human rights defenders of the 1960s and 1970s were indeed encroaching upon and were in fact implicitly challenging the state's prerogative to control the altruistic impulse and its representation. They did this initially and primarily by forming a spontaneous charity movement for the support of Soviet political prisoners and their families.

That movement, which lies somewhere near the social, cultural and emotional heart of the Moscow human rights movement, began slowly in 1966, with the donation of small change and second-hand clothing. In 1972, it snowballed into the establishment of an unofficial charity fund for political prisoners by Aleksandr Solzhenitsyn. It even drew the material and other support of some westerners, including diplomats, journalists and scholars, who made significant contributions to the survival and success of the dissent movement. Ultimately, this charity movement gave the human rights phenomenon a considerable mate-rial base. Its existence made it a little bit easier for some of the boldest activists to engage in what can be seen as even greater self-sacrifices by rendering themselves vulnerable to arrest with all its dangers to mental and physical well-being, as well as to family survival. And it was also a threat to Soviet state control over the self-giving and self-sacrificial behaviour of its citizens and over-representations of such behaviour, insofar as political prisoners were not preferred beneficiaries of Soviet charity; indeed they were declared enemies of the state.

The charity movement also contributed to a theme of self-giving or altruistic commitment that was immensely important to dissenter iden-tity and that greatly strengthened the passions surrounding that issue in the dissent movement. In recent interviews with former human rights defenders, the strong positive emotional language used in association with the idea of self-giving reveals the power of this element of the dissident experience. What the positive language does not tell us is whether those words reflect emotional experience at the time of dissent or only in retrospect; and indeed whether those words reflect any sort of emotional experience at all. For the historian, so heavily dependent on words and documents, does not have unencumbered access to emotional states. Yet even if these expressed emotions were to tell us less about why dissenters pursued their activities in the past than about how they interpreted that activity, they would at least reveal the importance of altruism as a hotly contested theme in Russian cultural history, whose particularities in this story are well worth uncovering.[2]

While the call upon individuals to give of themselves for the sake of the nation has been a significant phenomenon in the history of the modern nation state (put perhaps most succinctly by the US president John F. Kennedy: 'Ask not what your country can do for you – ask what you can do for your country'),[3] it took on particular importance in the Soviet Union for several different reasons. Above all, it played an important role in the implementation of Marxist ideology in that country, for reasons that have to do with anomalies in Karl Marx's understanding of human self-interest. Marx described world history as driven by the exploitative economic self-interest of one social group after another, culminating in the rise of the bourgeoisie, which, he predicted, would be defeated by the proletariat. Citizens of the utopian world that would emerge from the working-class victory would no longer be driven by self-interest. Social harmony would have to take over, if Marx's dream were to be fulfilled; citizens would operate according to their desire for the good of the community rather than their own self-interest. Marx was astute in his analysis of the motivations of historically successful social groups, but he offered little by way of motivating power to those who would lead a Marxist state (such as the Bolsheviks) beyond a simple call or demand for self-giving behaviour, not just for the behaviour that contributes to the formation and identity of a nation, such as military or civil service, but even for the economic activity that provides the foundation of any society. The impact of Marxist ideology on the Soviet system – and thus on Soviet culture, in this way – cannot be underestimated.

A system based on volunteerism may have made sense to former citizens of the Russian empire for several historical reasons. One was the deep-rooted tradition of service (especially elite service) to the Russian state that was most effectively developed under Peter the

Great, as the nobility was to serve the tsar in both military and civil institutions and the peasantry was to serve the nobility through their agricultural labour. A second reason may have been the tradition of Russian Orthodox Christian exhortations to self-giving and self-sacrifice as a way of imitating the self-sacrifice of Christ and as a significant step toward salvation for Orthodox believers. The Orthodox Church emphasised its superiority over the western church for its commitment to charity and other forms of self-giving.[4] Furthermore, the themes of service and self-giving played a considerable role in the culture of the social class with which Moscow human rights advocates would later most closely identify, namely the Russian intelligentsia.[5] The notion of selfless service to the nation was of great significance to intelligentsia identity in the pre-revolutionary era; and an important component of that desire to serve – especially among the revolutionary intelligentsia, including the Bolsheviks – was the belief in giving of or even sacrificing themselves for the sake of the *narod* or 'the people'.

Intriguingly, in the pre-revolutionary period a Russian counter-discourse on such 'self-giving' reflected a distinct unease with ostentatious claims of both religious and political self-giving. That discourse may help to illuminate concerns about greedy or self-serving dissidents in the later period. Lev Tolstoi, for example, struggled mightily with the question of philanthropy and its motivations in *Anna Karenina*; note Kitty's transition from a false, self-congratulatory notion of charitable behaviour to a deeper, truer and more effective notion of it as an expression of genuine humble love, and Levin's efforts to evaluate the land-owning class's more self-conscious attempts to better the lot of the peasantry. He comes to reject these philanthropic efforts (of landowners such as Anna's lover Vronskii, for example) as self-aggrandising and thus inherently lacking in virtue. 'If goodness has a cause, it is no longer goodness; if it has consequences, a reward, it is not goodness either'.[6] We find a similar critique of the philanthropic impulse in Anton Chekhov's work, as in the short story 'House with the Mezzanine', through the character of Lyda: full of plans for bettering peasant conditions but unable to recognise or express true love.[7]

The notion of self-giving at the political level also attracted distrust and critique, especially following the revolution of 1905. Perhaps the most trenchant expression of that critique came from Sergei Bulgakov in his essay for the *Signposts* collection:

The very foundations of the intelligentsia's faith require worship of the people, be it in the form of the old populism which originated

with Herzen ... or the latest form, Marxism.... But this faith necessarily gives rise not only to the worship of the people but to the
direct opposite as well: an arrogant view of the people as an object
of salvation, as minor, unenlightened in the intelligentsia's sense
of the word and in need of a nursemaid to develop its 'consciousness'. Arguing from a religious point of view, Bulgakov saw primarily
a false pride and will to power in the trumpeting of self-sacrificial
behavior among the revolution minded of the Russian educated
elite.[8]

Despite such critiques and the complicated ideological, historical and
cultural origins of *(samo)zhertvovanie*, images of selflessness, self-giving,
and self-sacrifice soon became staples in the exhortations the Soviet
state made to its citizens, especially in the early years of Stalinism as
it propagated official legends of workers who over-fulfilled industrial
and agricultural plans, for example. World War II led to a powerful
reconstitution of the theme of self-sacrifice, as the state emphasised
narratives of soldiers and partisans who died at the hands of the Nazis
rather than give away or otherwise betray their communist comrades, as
well as the daily sacrifices needed from the entire Soviet population to
keep the war effort going.[9] The theme of altruism was closely entwined
with that of solidarity. Under Iosif Stalin, the state focus on binding the
self-giving loyalty of Soviet citizens exclusively to the state and creating
a vast class of the disloyal in the form of 'saboteurs' and 'traitors' became
a central theme of state rule. The call to altruistic behaviour continued
throughout the Soviet period, as reflected, for example, in the 'Moral
Code of the Builders of Communism' of the 1961 Party Program, which
required 'conscientious labor for the good of society', 'concern on the
part of everyone for the preservation and growth of public wealth', and
'collectivism and comradely mutual assistance'.[10]

   But, in the long run, appealing to selflessness was a difficult way to
motivate people to act in the interest of the state rather than in their
own interest. The national passions for modernisation as a means of
strengthening the country and for waging war when under attack had
only transitory power; over long periods of time, it was less easy to
motivate people to work for the sake of society. Self-interest proved too
important a means of motivation to be avoided. One consequence of
that weakness in the Soviet system was the emergence of an underlying
hierarchical economic system in the form of elite consumer opportunities (special shops, cafeterias and so on for the elites), as well as black
market and other interest-based network relations, all exposing the

Soviet system's altruistic claims and demands as hypocritical, or at least ineffective.

But it was the historical cruelty of the Soviet state as a mass dictatorship that most effectively undercut its claims of altruistic intentions and its demands upon the altruism of its citizens. As former Moscow human rights activist Viacheslav Bakhmin put it most simply and eloquently:

> Now, about the reasons for dissent ... For me the most serious reason was that I understood that for many years they had deceived me. For me this was a very painful process, because after all I was a Komsomol, a Pioneer, and I believed everything because the idea itself was very beautiful, it taught kindness *[dobru]*, it taught [one] to help people, that very humane idea. And behind the facade of that stands an entirely cruel and inhumane system ... which over the decades ... killed an incredible number of people.[11]

That sense of personal corruption due to the brutality and hypocrisy of the Soviet state was a powerful motivation for such activists as Bakhmin to cleanse themselves, their community and indeed the very notion of altruism itself of its pollution.

The social and emotional foundations of the Soviet dissident charity movement that would implicitly challenge the state's right to command the altruistic behaviour of its citizens lay in a social formation that has supported Russian intelligentsia activity for a couple of centuries: the circle or *kruzhok*. The tradition of the intelligentsia circle goes back to the early nineteenth century at least and involves the formation of social networks located in the domestic and private sphere of the educated elite that laid the social foundations for professional, artistic, revolutionary or other activity in the public sphere. Such intelligentsia networks or circles reached their peak of pervasiveness and influence among the pre-revolutionary intelligentsia, and, in the early Soviet period they actually helped to integrate the Soviet intelligentsia into the state.[12] These networks were badly damaged in the Stalin era by both bureaucratic measures and police intervention, as Stalin sought to gain control of all alternative localities of power in Soviet society.

But the culture of independent networks was revitalised with great energy in the Moscow liberal intelligentsia *kompaniias* of the 1950s, as Ludmilla Alexeyeva describes in her book *The Thaw Generation*, which depicts a youthful post-Stalinist world of energetic parties, drinking and discourse in Moscow.[13] Nurtured by the strong emphasis on educa-tion and upward mobility in the post-war era, with its technological advances and ambitions and the growth of educational institutes and institutions, the Moscow *kompaniias* also presented the opportunity for a rise in sociability and intimacy. Following the cold and frightening years of Stalinism, as well as the desperate years of World War II, the *kompaniias* offered a new warmth that laid the social foundations for early dissent. The transition from the general phenomenon of the sociable *kompaniias* to what may be called a dissent movement among a few of those circles began around 1966, following the political trial of Soviet authors Andrei Siniavskii and Iulii Daniel for publishing abroad works critical of the Soviet Union. Closely associated with this transition was the formation of that spontaneous charity movement for the aid of political prisoners.

This phenomenon developed as follows: the Daniel-Siniavskii trial resulted in prison camp sentences for both men. In the camps, both men began to write home to Moscow about their experiences there. In one of his first prison camp letters in 1966, Daniel wrote: 'What amazing people [here]! naive idiots, war criminals [from World War II], raw youths, old guys, people who broke the law intentionally, people who had no idea [that the law they broke] even existed ... I am going to write about all of this'.[14] And so he did, in hundreds of letters home that ended up being read not only by his wife and family but also by his whole network of friends and associates. Through these letters, the *kompaniias* learned of a world largely hidden from them; like most Soviet citizens they had not really understood that the Soviet prison camps continued to gather up significant numbers of political victims so long after Stalin's death. The prison camp memoir published in 1967 in samizdat by one of Daniel's fellow prisoners, Tolia Marchenko, *My Testimony,* soon filled in the gaps.[15] Through the letters and Marchenko's book, the *kompaniias* became aware of a whole realm of political dissent in the Soviet Union that was as yet inchoate and inarticulate.[16]

Learning about this inspired many members of the *kompaniias* to come to the aid of these unjustly suffering individuals, as they saw it. 'People knocked on Daniel's door to offer money, warm clothes, and food', writes Alexeyeva.

At first Larissa [Bogoraz] and Marissa [Siniavskaia] tried to decline, saying that the attorneys had been paid, that Yulik and Andrei had plenty of warm clothes, and that there was no shortage of food on the table. 'In that case, give it to someone who needs it', was the usual reply. Larissa's refrigerator was filling up with smoked sausage, salted fish, and Ukrainian garlic. A pile of flannel shirts, sweaters, fur hats, gloves, mufflers and felt boots grew in a corner of the room.[17]

Soon this provisioning of those in the camps developed into a more systematic affair:

> At first, our parcels went only to Daniel and Siniavskii, but as we learned more names and as gifts and money kept pouring in, we started channeling food and correspondence to every prisoner Yulik and Andrei mentioned in their letters.... In our circle, aid to prisoners was called 'the Red Cross'. 'Red Cross' volunteer work consisted of running around to stores to buy books and magazines, and running around stores to buy powered milk, powdered eggs, dehydrated soups, hard sausage, coffee, canned food, and garlic. After all was purchased and packaged, we stood in line at Moscow's main post office to mail it all to the camps.

There was also a romantic element to this labour: 'Several Moscow women volunteered to write to inmates, ... In a number of cases correspondence led to romance and matrimony'.[18] This was not necessarily simple romance; having a legal spouse could greatly aid prisoners for a number of forms of support could be obtained solely through such a relative.[19] Arina Ginzburg, Aleksandr Ginzburg's wife, began a similar domestically based collection system.[20] In addition, significant fund-raising activities focused on purchasing homes and household goods for those forced into exile.

These seem like small things; and yet as more and more people contributed to charity for prisoners, collecting their kopeks and rubles and their old clothes to pass along, they 'fought Stalinism with felt boots and garlic', as Alexeyeva put it.[21] Furthermore, in doing so they revealed the outlines of a broader community – mostly that of the Moscow liberal intelligentsia – whose members, while they might not possess the courage to take some of the bolder steps of the more prominent dissenters, nevertheless offered what support they could. We see also the outlines of a gender theme here, as women seem to have contributed with particular effectiveness to the charity activity, while men were more likely to engage in the activities that would take them to prison.[22] Yet women (such as Larissa Bogoraz and Nataliia Gorbanevskaia) were also arrested, and men engaged energetically in charitable activities.

Another way of expressing support for political prisoners through self-giving involved going to the homes of those who had been taken away and helping out the families that remained behind by doing the simple but essential chores of domestic life. As Bakhmin explained: 'Simply put, the most helpful thing I could do was to aid the families of those dissidents for whom life was difficult. ... I went shopping, brought visitors, fulfilled requests ... I acted as a courier. I just arrived and asked "does something need to be done?"' Shopping was a crucial matter, given the difficulties of that activity in the weak Soviet economy with its endemic scarcities and long lines. So was childcare, especially for those family members who found themselves embroiled in the never-ending legal and bureaucratic struggle to support political prisoners. Bakhmin also travelled to visit Piotr Iakir – imprisoned in a psychiatric hospital – and with his wife, Tat'iana, helped to clean Iakir's wife's apartment and care for their son with Down's syndrome.[23] Another man who participated in this kind of domestic aid was Viktor Dziadko, who performed similar services for Arina Ginzburg. He and another dissenter, Valerii Abramkin, also travelled to visit those in exile where they helped with such urgent repair issues as heating.[24] Other services included accompanying wives and family members to the distant prison camps where life was very difficult for visitors as well as prisoners and helping them make contact with the prisoners to assure themselves of their health and deliver packages that could not be trusted to the mail. According to Bakhmin, it was in part through such quiet acts of physical and material aid that new supporters were drawn into the networks and began themselves to think about how else they wanted to contribute to the cause.[25]

As they became more assertive, some *kompaniia* members acted in ever more public (and well-known) ways to support political prisoners or political prisoners in the making. They began to circulate letters and petitions. They attended the trials of those who had been arrested, thereby expressing public support in defiance of the security agents who surrounded the trials, or, if there was time, they even went directly to the homes of those who were being searched or arrested. Since it was important to have as many witnesses as possible to such state actions as searches and arrests (the state organs were known to falsify evidence), a practice emerged of calling up as many people as possible to be present in the apartment while a search or arrest was taking place. Another more public form of support was legal aid from a few Soviet lawyers who were willing to defend dissidents in court. Lawyers Sofia Kallistratova and Dina Kaminskaia were soon renowned in the dissident world for their powerful and intelligent commitment to the dissident cause, and their willingness to take the risks that public legal defence of the dissidents involved.[26] Such increasingly public actions, even if not always strictly illegal, most certainly attracted the negative attention of the state and thus involved a willingness to give up peace of mind with regard to one's relations with the state.

The charitable networks that were forming in the dissident community gave strength to those who undertook the even riskier activities that were almost certain to lay them open to the dangers of arrest, such as production and distribution of the *Chronicle of Current Events,* an underground publication providing information about political prisoners (which, in the early years of its existence, involved its own 'charity' operation for the collection of information as well as of paper, typing and distribution), or participation in the public protest against the invasion of Czechoslovakia in 1968.[27] Those who challenged the state knew that if they went to prison for it, people were organised to help them and their loved ones with money, material necessities, domestic aid, legal support and so on. The importance of such a network cannot be overestimated, as the families of those arrested were often placed under severe stress due to lost jobs and lost opportunities to study. Foreknowledge of that material support was one reason why certain people felt emboldened to take great risks in the Moscow human rights movement.[28]

A critical moment in the history of the charity movement of the Cold War era was its institutionalisation: in 1972, Solzhenitsyn's unofficial charity foundation was established. Solzhenitsyn decided to contribute all western (hard currency) royalties for his book *The Gulag Archipelago* to Soviet political prisoners and their families by creating the Fund for the Aid of Political Prisoners. The Aid Fund *(Fond pomoshchi),* as it came to be called, was a highly complex and diffuse organisation based in Moscow about which an important history has yet to be written. It worked at numerous levels and involved a series of tiny cells of people, unknown to one another, who collected information on the existence and whereabouts of political prisoners across the Soviet Union (in this it also supported publication and distribution of the *Chronicle of Current Events)* and distributed funds and other material support to them and their families.[29] Other charitable organisations, such as a Christian Orthodox organisation that collected clothing and other items, passed those donations on to the Aid Fund for redistribution.[30] Through the Working Commission, the Aid Fund also contributed funds for the support of political prisoners who were sent to psychiatric imprisonment.[31] And it paid for the travel expenses of those who travelled to distant trials to support the political dissenters.[32]

Participation in the Aid Fund inspired notable dedication, and some individuals remember to this day the details of their purchases of clothing for prisoners' children whose sizes they did not know, their creation of lightweight dry wooden boxes in which to mail supplies to prisoners and so on. Creating these packages for prisoners took a great deal of creativity given the restrictions on size, weight and content, as well as on who could send packages to which prisoners. A particularly nice example of such creativity was the discovery that if you could get a westerner to buy white chocolate at a *Beriozka* (hard-currency shop) you could pass off this important but forbidden nutritional product (sugar and high-quality fat) as the permitted *sala*, or pork fat.[33] Like other more grassroots-oriented charitable organisations, the Aid Fund did a great deal to provide material support to the dissent movement, and indeed has continued to do so since the 1990s, as it has been revived to support impoverished former dissenters.

The spirit of charitable and other self-giving activities appears to have reached beyond Russian/Soviet culture to engage some of the foreigners living in the Soviet Union at that time: western journalists, diplomats and scholars. According to my Russian informants as well as a few U.S. journalists posted to Russia and numerous scholars with whom I have spoken over the years, certain westerners also engaged in this activity of self-giving, from bringing food, clothing and medicine, through donating or mailing books and clothing that unemployed and impoverished dissidents could sell on the black market, or carrying documents and manuscripts across the border that was so impermeable for Soviet citizens, to giving urgently needed western publicity to endangered prisoners. They donated both to individuals and to central domestic collection points. Such contributions from foreigners were vital to the dissidents, both for their survival and for getting word of their cause to the outside world, and evoked strong expressions of appreciation from some of the dissidents I interviewed. Yet it was precisely the material goods accumulated through these charitable efforts that led to concern about new sources of corruption particular to the dissent movement: the domestic charitable collections, the western currency brought into the mix by the Solzhenitsyn Aid Fund, and the access to western goods and support. Alexeyeva reports that at one point she discovered that some individuals, prisoners' wives, were double-dipping, so to speak, by asking for donated gifts both from her 'Red Cross' and from Arina Ginzburg's charity operation.[34] Solzhenitsyn's Aid Fund seems to have been plagued by particular tensions, due in part to the sheer volume of charity that was available. Its problems may have been exacerbated by the fund's weak institutional structure and accounting, and its need to do much of its work in secret, while at the same time reaching those who needed aid. Another factor was the domestic foundation for Aid Fund work, as food for prisoners' families mingled with food for the Aid Fund workers' families in the same refrigerator, for example.

Accusations of nepotism, favouritism and simple theft of Aid Fund money were notable; Alexeyeva, for example, eventually stopped working with the fund because,

> in the first place, I caught a glimpse of some people from a very unattractive point of view with regard to money, and in the second place because I saw that I myself was suspected of somehow using a part of that money for my own family because we were living in such difficult circumstances at the time, and [suspected] of favoritism, of helping my friends more than other people. I tried not to do that, but maybe it happened somehow unconsciously, but I tried to help everyone equally, and I know that I took nothing for my family.[35]

The hard currency (Solzhenitsyn's western royalties) upon which the Aid Fund was based generated a particular source of tension. As an e-mail correspondent put it, 'I ... have some gloomy memories of the workings of the Solzhenitsyn fund, and what hard currency did to the mood of the movement'.[36]

Soviet state media attacks on the dissent movement focused intensively on the purity of dissident motivations, or rather the putative lack thereof. The media were particularly concerned to point out the seeming advantages that dissenters accrued through their associations with westerners. For example, they frequently cited the arrest of dissenters on the grounds not only of 'parasitism' (not having a job, a common condition after one had lost one's job and employability due to dissident activity) but also of such base activities as selling icons or scurrilous secrets for western money, gum or jeans and for possession of hard currency, which state agents 'found' in human rights activists' apartments, such as Aleksandr Ginzburg's.[37] It is difficult to tell to what extent the state initiated such accusations of self-interest in the debates over dissenter integrity and to what extent it echoed concerns already expressed inside the movement; the potency of the theme is in any event evident, reflecting the powerful social and ideological reverberations of the discourse on altruism.

Westerners were not immune from accusations of operating on the basis of cynical self-interest either. Western journalists, for example, came under attack for not doing enough for human rights in the Soviet Union. Some dissidents, such as Andrei Amalrik, accused them of failing to cover the dissent movement adequately due to careerism. He was particularly scathing about what he saw as the cowardice of western journalists with regard to meeting with dissidents in their homes. He also believed that western journalists should demonstrate greater solidarity with one another in defending their right to report on whatever they wished (presumably through greater coverage of dissent activity) despite the Soviet state's tendency to simply eject those who reported on topics the state disliked, such as human rights. With some acidity, Amalrik noted that the only solidarity exhibited among western journalists was over their right to order and receive western domestic goods in Moscow.[38]

Solzhenitsyn had his own complex critique of westerners, one that reveals the extent to which the theme of self-giving played a role in dissenter identity, as well as a certain degree of pride in that identity:

> It is not an inherent quality of people in the West that they should be calculating to the point of pettiness or that the more amiable they appear on the surface, the more hard-hearted they are in reality. It is all a question of which 'force-field' they are drawn to. In Russia, despite Soviet oppression, there has long been a field tugging us in the direction of generosity and self-sacrifice, and it is this force that is communicated to certain Westerners and takes hold of them— perhaps not for all time but at least while they are among us.

That he believes that this 'force-field' is concentrated in the (presumably Russian) human rights movement is made clear when he writes that some westerners were 'willing to leave their mercenary habits behind and risk their necks' upon encountering participants in the movement.[39]

Solzhenitsyn's tone of moral self-satisfaction as well as of Russian nationalism in such comments as these may help to illuminate some of the discomfort that dissident claims of *(samo)zhertvovanie* have inspired.

So there was (and still is) plenty of tension surrounding the question of altruism among contributors to the human rights movement. Furthermore, there may have been a temporal limit to the self-giving fervour some of the participants described as characterising the early stages of dissent; some western participants portrayed a growing sense of entitlement with regard to western support among some dissidents by the mid- to late 1970s and early 1980s that they found disturbing.

Yet despite these negative overtones, the power of the language of positive emotion in connection with a sense of self-giving through the human rights activity of the 1960s and 1970s in recent interviews is impossible to dismiss. Many participants in the dissident community of networks have expressed signal emotional satisfaction or even joy in the belief that through their supportive activities they were giving of themselves in the context of community. 'Those were the happiest days of my life', Arina Ginzburg said in a 2003 interview, describing her work in gathering charitable donations for political prisoners and their families and at the Aid Fund.[40] A search through interview transcripts and notes for the particular associations that trigger that kind of satisfaction reveals the persistence of the theme of community solidarity and mutual support. As Arsenii Roginskii, historian and head of the organisation Memorial, put it with appreciation: 'Those were times of true solidarity'.[41] Aleksandr Podrabinek, who did much to bring the plight of political prisoners in mental institutions to the attention of the world, gives a sense of how westerners could be drawn into that experience of solidarity: 'It was an astonishing atmosphere that western people fell into. People with responsive hearts, they were drawn into it, they became a part of that atmosphere, part of that dissident culture, they were even participants, to a greater or lesser degree'. Podrabinek also described a sense of purity in dissident association: 'those mutual goals, that general atmosphere, it's very difficult to convey that in words ... not mercantile, very pure'.[42] Perhaps the most eloquent expression of that sense of pleasurable solidarity and purity comes from Viktor Dziadko. When asked why he had subjected himself to the great difficulties of dissent and arrest, he exclaimed: 'For the sake of love!' 'Love for whom or what?' I asked him. 'For my friends', he replied.[43] Tolstoi and Chekhov would have understood and approved entirely.

These are potent words: happiness, solidarity, purity, love. Exactly what they tell us about the movement or even about memory of the movement is not easy to disentangle. They may reflect no more than nostalgia. Perhaps the passage of time has obscured the difficulties of the past; perhaps those memories of dissent are tied up with memories of youth as much as anything else; or perhaps the fact that the former human rights activists have received little national support in Vladimir Putin's Russia contributes to such possible nostalgia. Or there may even be a cultural script that leads interviewees to believe that they should have felt or should feel, and express, positive emotion with regard to solidarity or altruistic behaviour.

But whether real, imagined or constructed, one vibrant theme that comes through these words is the emotional importance of the human bonds being described. The ideas of 'solidarity', of 'responsive hearts', of 'love for my friends' all reveal the experience of human connection as a vital part of this experience and its memory. Furthermore, these expressions suggest a highly personal sense of that connection. While the term *solidarity* may sound as much political as personal, such phrases as 'love for my friends' and 'responsive hearts' indicate the highly personal quality of that sense of solidarity: the importance of face-to-face relationships with all their potential emotional engagement. Whether in nostalgic memory or real experience, the explanations provided for this engagement reflect the passion of self-giving or self-sacrifice in the context of warm human association.

But what such words and phrases do not particularly reveal is why members of this community or imagined community might have extended that personal sense of self-giving solidarity to those with whom they had no personal ties – to unknown political prisoners, for example – and how those connections might have contributed to the sense of emotional satisfaction or joy Arina Ginzburg expressed when she called her time as a dissident 'the happiest days of her life'. One way to approach this conundrum is to explore the Russian historical tradition of concern about and charity for prisoners more generally. That tradition goes back as far as the medieval period in Russia, when those who were imprisoned were entirely dependent on outside support for food, clothing and other daily necessities; providing that support was considered a collective responsibility, as Horace W. Dewey and Ann M. Kleimola tell us.[44] The situation was little better by the age of Catherine the Great; the state paid only a minimal amount toward the prisoners' daily needs, and poor prisoners might well be reduced to begging for alms in order to provide for themselves.[45] One response to the sheer misery of impoverished prisoners was personal charity of the sort described by the noblewoman Anna Labzina in her early nineteenth-century memoir.[46] This charitable concern for prisoners continued through the nineteenth century and, as Adele Lindenmeyr has pointed out, it inspired a number of charitable groups toward the end of that century and the beginning of the twentieth century.[47] Prisoners as a social group were, perhaps because of their patently desperate conditions, viewed less as justly punished sinners but rather as unfortunate creatures deserving of aid.[48] That view of prisoners is vividly articulated in pre-revolutionary art and literature as well; a renowned example in literature is Chekhov's detailed description of the appalling lot of those imprisoned on Sakhalin. And a classic female figure in literature who responds with generosity to a miserable sinner and prisoner is Fedor Dostoevskii's Son'ia, at the end of *Crime and Punishment*.[49] In the visual arts, the famous painting by Il'ia Repin of convicts pulling a boat along the Volga River also reflects a culture of attention to and sympathy for the plight of prisoners. And, of course, historically the Decembrists' wives, who followed their exiled husbands to Siberia following the 1825 uprising against the autocracy, both demonstrated their loyalty and created an impact through their memoirs.

The tradition of giving aid to prisoners was embedded in a broader tradition in Christian Orthodoxy of charity for the sake of religious salvation. This was founded in a religious ideology that prescribed the appropriate use of wealth as distribution to the poor.[50] Lindenmeyr describes the *podvigy* or 'feats' of charity and self-giving accomplished by holy figures, often women, in the medieval and imperial era, which included not only providing material support but also physically caring for and sheltering the poor. This type of charity to prisoners required uncritical love and compassion for the object of care, but it could produce a joy in the humility of this activity, and the notion of obtaining salvation through charitable work to prisoners may give emotional colour to some of the narratives of self-giving that we find in the imperial period.[51] Anna Labzina describes the pleasure she obtained through such charity in the following terms:

> At the time of my departure they were with me every day for the entire two weeks, especially the convicts they soaked my hands with tears ... they were very close to my heart every day God had presented me with an opportunity to do good for those around me ... Oh, how contented my heart was then![52]

In this 'contentment' we may catch an early echo of the enthusiasm (whether real or scripted) for charity toward prisoners that was to be so notable among human rights activists of the 1960s and 1970s. This is not to argue that human rights activists were directly guided by Orthodox Christianity, of course (though a number of former human rights activists have turned to Orthodoxy in the post-Soviet era); many were Jewish, and many considered their movement entirely secular. Nor is it to argue that the human rights activists of the 1960s and 1970s drew directly on a pre-revolutionary cultural phenomenon in pursuing their charitable activities. Yet given its prominence, this phenomenon offers intriguing insight into the cultural and historical meaning of those activities, as well as the emotional satisfaction expressed in association with them.

Certainly, the cultural legitimacy of concern for prisoners, political prisoners in particular, extended into the Soviet period, due in no small part to their great numbers and the great numbers of those who had been closely associated with them prior to their incarceration. Also important was the fact that charity toward political prisoners was one form of altruism that had been neither arrogated nor contaminated by the state. Samizdat brought numerous materials to the *kompaniia* and human rights scene detailing the appalling circumstances and conditions of Soviet imprisonment, particularly for political prisoners, many of them by authors of great moral authority and literary eloquence. Anna Akhmatova's description in her poem *Requiem* of waiting with other women in front of a prison to try to bring aid to their imprisoned loved ones; Nadezhda Mandel'shtam's tale of her husband's descent into imprisonment and death; Eugenia Ginzburg's prison camp memoir *Journey into the Whirlwind;* and of course Solzhenitsyn's *One Day in the Life of Ivan Denisovich,* which achieved public distribution under Nikita Khrushchev in 1962, and his *Gulag Archipelago* (published in Paris) that represented an intensively researched history of the prison camp system and experience (and whose western royalties Solzhenitsyn devoted to the Aid Fund): all of these contributed to the cultural legitimisation of political prisoners as particularly deserving of self-giving or self-sacrificial endeavour.[53]

Thus far we have explored two possible reasons for the emotional satisfaction that is evident in many recent interviews with Moscow human rights defenders of the 1960s and 1970s: the powerful gratification provided by human contact and acts of generosity within a face-to-face community, and the echoes of a tradition of 'contented' self-giving and self-sacrifice for the sake of prisoners in Russian Orthodox religious culture. Another approach to this question is to explore more closely the meaning of the reference to 'purity' in the human rights movement. Of course the first question that arises in response to such a term as *purity* is: 'very pure' (as Podrabinek put it) in comparison to what?[54] What is the 'contaminant' in question? Podrabinek gives us an important clue in his contrast of the word pure (*chistyi*) to the word commercial (*merkantilnyi*): such 'purity' indicates an absence of the contaminant of self-interest and again reflects the power of the idea of altruism in this discourse.

But I am arguing that a particular kind of self-interest led to a particular sense of contamination experienced in the context of the Soviet system and that this must be understood in order to grasp the full problematic of the idea of 'purity' in the human rights movement. This was the self-interest in personal survival and success that led those compelled by it into intimate moral association with a state and a system imbued with the glaring contradiction between social ideal and social reality as Bakhmin expressed it above: 'the idea itself was very beautiful, it taught kindness *[dobru]*, it taught [one] to help people, that very humane idea. And behind the facade of that stands an entirely cruel and inhumane system ... which over the decades ... killed an incredible number of people'.[55]

This painful contrast between ideal and reality had a particularly powerful impact on the highly (state-) educated individuals with professional aspirations from whose ranks many human rights activists sprang. Their success or survival in the context of state-controlled educational and professional channels required intensive engagement with and also affirmation of the state. Bakhmin was by no means the only one to experience a feeling of profound dissonance as a result of this engagement: such renowned dissenting authors as Solzhenitsyn ('Live Not by Lies'), Boris Shragin *(Challenge of the Spirit)*, and Vaclav Havel of the Soviet bloc country of Czechoslovakia ('Power of the Powerless') all express a similar sense of dislocation and alienation as well as anguished feelings of personal contamination, stress and guilt.[56]

In 'Power of the Powerless', Havel elucidates these contradictions in the most illuminating detail:

> This system is so thoroughly permeated by hypocrisy and lies: government by bureaucracy is called popular government; the working class is enslaved in the name of the working class; the complete degradation of the individual is presented as his ultimate liberation; depriving people of information is called making it available ... the repression of culture is called its development; the expansion of imperial influence is presented as support for the oppressed, etc. ... Individuals need not believe all of these mystifications, but they must behave as though they did, or they must at least tolerate them in silence, or get along well with those who work with them. They need not accept the lie. It is enough for them to have accepted their life with it and in it. For by this fact, individuals confirm the system, fulfill the system, make the system, *are* the system.[57]

Solzhenitsyn affirms this sense of personal responsibility as well: 'It is not they who are guilty – it is ourselves, only we:' his sense of the corruption of the social and political system of the Soviet Union is expressed in his typically vivid use of the word *gangrenous* to describe it.[58] But perhaps most eloquent is Shragin, who brings us back to the systemic contradiction that most concerned Bakhmin – the state brutality that exposed all its claims of altruism as false and that for him was most contaminating of all:

> One becomes the accomplice of violence; it corrupts us and corrodes our will. ... And gradually, without noticing it, one turns into the sort of person one would have previously shunned. This kind of spiritual disintegration, the loss of one's own self and the dishonor of serving iniquity is more frightening to a conscious human being than bodily suffering or physical annihilation.[59]

This is not, of course, to assert that participation in the Soviet state or system was in itself inherently corrupt or hypocritical; such social scientists as Alexei Yurchak have sought to delineate the enormously complex aggregation of belief, ritual and pragmatism that contributed to living in the Soviet Union.[60] Nor is it to argue that this participation was any more contaminating than participating in any other human community that requires personal compromise – that is to say, in any other human community. But it is worth elaborating on the particular experiences that led to the feelings of contamination that some who lived in the Soviet system have expressed, and the deep sense of personal stress that could result.

Alexeyeva described experiencing such stress when she was obliged to stand as a teacher before a group of working-class students following Khrushchev's Secret Speech on 'the crimes of Stalin' in 1956 and keep silent about her personal feelings about Stalin: 'I wanted to tell them that I shared their indignation ... but I had a role to play. So, every morning, I walked into the seminar and faced their anger in silence. I felt like I was being flogged in a public square'. Deciding that she could no longer continue in this job or accept an offered promotion in the form of a professorship of Marxism-Leninism, Alexeyeva told her husband: 'If something happens to you and I have to feed the children, I will take up prostitution. It's cleaner'.[61]

Petro Grigorenko, a highly successful member of the Soviet military establishment (a general), described a similar sense of stress triggered by the public discourse following Khrushchev's denunciation of Stalin:

> After the 20th party Congress and all the hypocritical conversations about the cult of Stalin, a new cult was being created and I was

uneasy. I found it difficult to tolerate the hypocrisy of the rulers.... At this point the thought that had long been haunting me returned with new strength: 'You must speak out' ... Time passed and my thoughts changed again. 'What do I care about some collective farmers or workers who are trotting [around] in prisons and concentration camps.' And then: 'What a rat you are, Pyotr Grigoryevich'.[62]

Perhaps the most evocative Soviet description of the mental distress that could result from full self-interested engagement in the Soviet system is to be found in Vasily Grossman's *Life and Fate*. In this novel written during the 1950s about the Stalinist Soviet Union during World War II, Grossman describes the struggles of the nuclear physicist Viktor Shtrum to survive professionally while still being able to live with himself. Pushed to sign a public document making assertions that he knows to be untrue and supporting state acts of violent injustice, Shtrum's anguished thoughts demonstrate the profundity of his sense of personal corruption: 'He had sacrificed his inner freedom.... . There was no peace anywhere. Everything he did, even his smiles and gestures, no longer seemed a part of him; they were alien, hostile.... . Why had he committed this terrible sin?' His agony is relieved only when it occurs to him that he may be able to make up for his 'sin' in the following fashion: 'Then he realized that it wasn't too late.... Every hour, every day, he must struggle to be a man, struggle for his right to be pure and kind'.[63]

In each of these cases, note the predominance of the theme of contamination. For Alexeyeva, 'prostitution is cleaner' than accepting the professional rewards of supporting the Soviet system; Grigorenko is overcome by the sense of being a (dirty) 'rat'. And Shtrum, too, feels himself to be contaminated by his 'sin' to the point that he can face neither himself nor his community. But, as Shtrum's realisation that 'it wasn't too late' reveals, pollution can be relieved: through 'purity' and 'kindness'. Shtrum's sense of relief as described by Grossman (who himself signed such a public document in the 1950s, supporting Stalin's conspiracy theory of a Doctors' Plot) offers us another way of looking at the language of emotional satisfaction and pleasure cited earlier, especially in relation to the notion of 'purity' in the Moscow human rights movement. We may see that language as expressing a sense of release or potential release from the personal feelings of contamination engendered by forced engagement with what some experienced as a hypocritical and corrupt Soviet state and society. It is the celebration of cleansing and of spiritual purification, something that bears a very close resemblance to spiritual atonement, through acts of kindness, or altruism. It sheds light on the charitable activity of participants in and supporters of the human rights movement as a form of self-purification that has been explored by anthropologists and social psychologists as a human spiritual phenomenon more broadly.[64]

But personal purification was not the only thing that was at stake: in the specific context of Soviet history, also at stake was the problem of community purification in a society whose ideological foundations and historical development had led to a glaring contrast between social ideal and social reality. Proposed and propagandised as a source of social bonding and solidarity, self-giving solidarity with the Soviet state and society had been revealed to be, for some at least, a potential source of pollution and alienation instead. One source of the emotional potency of the social bonds among the Moscow human rights activists and the political prisoners, whether real or imagined, appears to have been their offer of a community solidarity in altruism that was an alternative to the perceived hypocritical claims of and demands upon its citizens' altruism by the Soviet state. And the condemnation of any sign of a weakening of purity in *(samo)zhertvovanie* among participants in the movement, as well as by a state that sought to destroy the movement, reflected the centrality of that theme of purity to its very meaning, The importance of these social bonds and this community was not just the human rights activism that they produced but also their very existence (or imagined existence) as alternatives to and implicit critiques of the mass dictatorship of Soviet state rule.

Notes

An earlier version of this chapter first appeared under the title "Pollution and Purification in the Moscow Human Rights Networks of the 1960s and 1970s" in *Slavic Review* (vol. 68, no. 2, Summer 2009), published by the Association for Slavic, East European, and Eurasian Studies, and is reprinted in the book with the permission of the publisher.

1. Robert H. Bremner, *Giving* (New Brunswick, NJ: Transaction Publishers, 1996), p. xii.
2. See Anke Stephan, *Von der Küche auf den Roten Platzz: Lebenswege soowjetischer Dissentinnen* (Zurich: Pano Verlag, 2005), pp. 33–71, for a sophisticated and wide-ranging review of the issues of memory, narrative, and genre in dissident memoirs and oral histories.
3. Inaugural address by John F. Kennedy on 20 January 1961 at http://www.famousquotes.me.uk/speeches/John_F_Kennedy/5.htm [Last accessed 26 February 2009].
4. Adele Lindcnmeyr, *Poverty Is Not a Vice: Charity, Society, and the State in Imperial Russia* (Princeton: Princeton University Press, 1996), p. 7.

5. As one memoirist wrote: 'The old intelligentsia no longer existed, but we wanted to believe that we would be able to recapture its intellectual and spiritual exaltation.' Note however, that I am not arguing that Soviet human fights activists of the 1960s and 1970s were drawing unmediatedly on pre-revolutionary intelligentsia culture, but rather that that culture may have contributed to early and continuing Soviet state and popular acceptance of the centrality of a notion of altruism to the functioning of Soviet society and economy. Ludmilla Alexeyeva and Paul Goldberg, *The Thaw Generation: Coming of Age in the Post-Stalin Era*, 2nd ed. (Pittsburgh: Pittsburgh University Press, 1993), p. 97.

6. Leo Tolstoy, *Anna Karenina*, trans. David Magarshack, intro. Priscilla Meyer (New York: Signet Classics, 2002), p. 915.

7. Anton Chekhov, *Five Great Short Stories* (New York: Dover, 1990), pp. 30–44.

8. Marshall S. Shatz and Judith E. Zimmerman (eds. and trans.), *Signposts: A Collection of Articles on the Russian Intelligentsia* (Irvine, CA: Charles Schlacks, Jr., publisher, 1986), pp. 35, 42–43.

9. To understand the impact that images of partisan self-sacrifice could have on future dissenters, see Alexeyeva and Goldberg, *The Thaw Generation*, pp. 19–20. Alexeyeva recounts the tale of Tanya, the partisan who reputedly cried out just before she was hanged by the Germans: 'It is a great privilege to die for your people!'

10. Philip Boobbycr, *Conscience, Dissent and Reform in Soviet Russia* (London: Routledge, 2003), 64.

11. Viacheslav Bakhmin, interview, Moscow, 20 July 2005.

12. Barbara Walker, *Maximilian Voloshin and the Russian Literary Circle: Culture and Survival in Revolutionary Times* (Bloomington, IN: Indiana University Press, 2005), pp. 1–23.

13. Alexeyeva and Goldberg, *The Thaw Generation*.

14. Iulii Daniel', *'Ia vse sbivaius' na literaturu—': Pisma iz zakliucheniia, stikhi*, ed. Aleksandr Daniel' (Moscow: Memorial, 2000), p. 30 (letter of 14 March 1966).

15. Anatolii Marchenko, *My Testimony*, trans. Michael Scammell (London: Pall Mall Press, 1969).

16. Ludmilla Alexeyeva, *Soviet Dissent: Contemporary Movements for National, Religious, and Human Rights*, trans. Carol Pearce and John Glad (Middletown, CT: Weslyan University Press, 1985), p. 287.

17. Alexeyeva and Goldberg, *The Thaw Generation*, p. 138.

18. *Ibid.*, p. 140.

19. Hence the importance *of Istoriia odnoi golodovki*, a tale in documents about Aleksandr Ginzburg's efforts to gain legal recognition for his partnership with Arina Ginzburg while he was imprisoned. *Istoriia odnoi golodovki*, (eds) Iulii Daniel, Aleksandr Ginzburg and Leonid Borodin (Frankfurt am Main: Posev, 1971).

20. Arina Ginzburg, interview, Paris, 1 May 2003. See also Alexeyeva and Goldberg, *The Thaw Generation*, p. 248.

21. Alexeyeva and Goldberg, *The Thaw Generation*, p. 138.

22. See Stephan, *Von der Küchwe auf den Roten Platz;* for a thorough and thoughtful discussion of gender in the Soviet human rights movement.

23. Viacheslav Bakhmin, interview, Moscow, 20 July 2005.

24. Viktor Dziadko, interview, Moscow, 25 June 2005.
25. Viacheslav Bakhmin, interview, Moscow, 20 July 2005.
26. Dina Kaminskaya, *Final Judgment: My Life as a Soviet Defense Attorney*, trans. Michael Glenny (New York: Simon Shuster, 1982); E. Pechuro (ed.), *Zastuimusa: Advokat S. V. Kallistratova, 1907–1989* (Moscow: Zveniia, 1997).
27. For information on the *Chronicle of Current Events*, see Aleksandr Lavut, interview, Moscow, 18 July 2005.
28. Viacheslav Bakhmin, interview, Moscow, 20 July 2005.
29. On the importance of this network for the *Chronicle of Current Events*, see Aleksandr Lavut, interview, Moscow, 21 July 2005.
30. Valerii Barshchev, interview, Moscow, 1 July 2006.
31. Viacheslav Bakhmin, interview, Moscow, 20 July 2005; Aleksandr Podrabinek, interview, Moscow, 21 July 2005.
32. Aleksandr Lavut, interview, Moscow, 21 July 2005.
33. Tat'iana Mikhailovna Bakhmina, interview, Moscow, 4 July 2005.
34. Alexeyeva and Goldberg, *The Thaw Generation*, p. 248.
35. Ludmilla Alexeyeva, interview, Moscow, 26 June 2006.
36. One of my informants who describes him/herself as peripherally involved in the dissident movement and in the workings of the Aid Fund, e-mail, 28 March 2006.
37. See, for example, 'The Dissidents vs. Moscow', *Time*, 21 February 1977; Memorial Archive, f. 161 (Fond pomoshchi), AC no. 5403, excerpts from the 'confession' of Valerii Repin on Soviet television in Leningrad in March 1983. For more details on this confession, see 'Around the World: A Soviet Dissident Implicates U.S. Agents', *New York Times*, 4 March 1983.
38. Andrei Amalrik, *Notes of a Revolutionary*, trans. Guy Daniels (New York: Knopf, 1982), p. 3640; Amalrik, 'News from Moscow', *New York Review of Books* vol. 16, no. 5 (25 March 1971).
39. Alexander Solzhenitsyn, *Invisible Allies*, trans. Alexis Klimov and Michael Nicholson (Washington, DC: Counterpoint, 1995), p. 265.
40. Arina Ginzburg, interview, Paris, 1 May 2003.
41. Arsenii Roginskii, interview, Moscow, 14 July 2006.
42. Aleksandr Podrabinek, interview, Moscow, 21 July 2005.
43. Viktor Dziadko, interview, Moscow, 25 June 2005.
44. Horace W. Dewey and Ann M. Kleimola, 'Suretyship and Collective Responsibility in Pre-Perrine Russia', *Jahrbücher für Geschichte Osteuropas* vol. 18, no. 1 (March 1970), pp. 337–54.
45. Isabel de Madariaga, 'Penal Policy in the Age of Catherine II', *Politics and Culture in Eighteenth-Century Russia, Collected Essays by Isabel de Madariaga* (London: Longman, 1998), p. 117.
46. Anna Labzina, *Days of a Russian Noblewoman: The Memories of Anna Labzina, 1758–1821*, ed. and trans. Gary Marker and Rachel May (DeKalb, IL: Northern Illinois University, 2001), pp. 9, 92–95.
47. Lindenmeyr, *Poverty Is Not a Vice*, pp. 15–16, 22, 110–11, 113, 221–22.
48. *Ibid.*, p. 19.
49. Lindenmeyr gives an extensive list of literary works depicting 'Russians' unusually tolerant attitudes toward criminals' as well as their donations to prisoners in such works as Dostoevski's *House of the Dead* and Tolstoi's *Resurrection;* she also cites George Kennan's Siberia and the Exile System

(London: Osgood, McIlvaine & Co., 1891). Lindenmeyr, *Poverty Is Not a Vice*, p. 19.

50. Lindenmeyr, *Poverty Is Not a Vice*, pp. 7–11.
51. *Ibid.*, pp. 13–16.
52. Labzina, *Days of a Russian Noblewoman*, pp. 93–94.
53. Anna Akhmatova, *Requiem and Poem without a Hero*, trans. D. M. Thomas (Athens, OH: Ohio University Press, 1976); Nadezhda Mandelstam, *Hope against Hope*, trans. Max Hayward (New York: Trade Cloth, 1970); Eugenia Ginzburg, *Journey into the Whirlwind*, trans. Paul Stevenson and Max Hayward (New York: Harcourt Brace & Co., 1967); Alexander Solzhenitsyn, *One Day in the Life of Ivan Denisovich*, trans. Ralph Parker (New York: Dutton, 1963); Alexander Solzhenitsyn, *The Gulag Archipelago, 1918–1956: An Experiment in Literary Investigation*, trans. Thomas P. Whitney and Harry Willetts (New York: Harper and Row, 1974–1978).
54. Aleksandr Podrabinek, interview, Moscow, 21 July 2005.
55. Viacheslav Bakhmin, interview, Moscow, 20 July 2005.
56. Alexander Solzhenitsyn, 'Live Not by Lies', *Washington Post*, 18 February 1974 at www.columbia.edu/cu/augustine/arch/solzhenitsyn/livenotbylies. html [Last accessed 26 February 2009]; Boris Shragin, *Challenge of the Spirit*, trans. P. S. Falla (New York: Alfred A. Knopf, 1978); Vaclav Havel, 'Power of the Powerless', in idem, *Open Letters: Selected Writings, 1965–1990*, ed. Paul Wilson (New York: Vintage Books, 1992), pp. 135–36.
57. Havel, 'Power of the Powerless', pp. 135–36. Emphasis in the original.
58. Solzhenitsyn, 'Live Not by Lies'.
59. Shragin, *Challenge of the Spirit*, p. 12.
60. See, for example, Alexei Yurchak, 'Soviet Hegemony of Form: Everything Was Forever, Until It Was No More', *Comparative Studies in Society and History* vol. 45, no. 3 (July 2003), 480–510, and Yurchak, *Everything Was Forever; Until It Was No More* (Princeton, NJ: Princeton University Press, 2005).
61. Alexeyeva and Goldberg, *The Thaw Generation*, p. 78.
62. Petro G. Grigorenko, *Memoirs* (New York: Norton, 1982), p. 233.
63. Vasily Grossman, *Life and Fate: A Novel*, trans. Robert Chandler (New York: Harper and Row, 1985), pp. 839–41.
64. See, for example, Jonathan Haidt, 'The New Synthesis in Moral Psychology', *Science* vol. 316, no. 5827 (18 May 2007), 998–1002; Paul Rozin and Carol Nemeroff, 'The Laws of Sympathetic Magic: A Psychological Study of Similarity and Contagion', in James W. Stigler, Richard A. Schweder and Gilbert Herdt (eds), *Cultural Psychology: Essays on Comparative Human Development* (Cambridge, UK: Cambridge University Press, 1990); Chen-be Zhong and Katie Liljenquist, 'Washing Away Your Sins: Threatened Morality and Physical Cleansing', *Science* vol. 313, no. 5792 (8 September 2006), 1451–2. Legal theorist William Ian Miller makes an important argument about 'disgust' in the form of moral revulsion against what he calls the institutionalized vices of human society, such as hypocrisy, betrayal, and cruelty, in *The Anatomy of Disgust* (Cambridge, MA: Harvard University Press, 1997), pp. 179–205.

10
Consuming Fragments of Mao Zedong: The Chairman's Final Two Decades at the Helm

Michael Schoenhals

Nikita Khrushchev was not to Mao's taste. The CCP Chairman showed no craving for *gulyáskommunizmus*. He hungered for something different. In the remarkable art film *The Ming Tombs Reservoir Fantasy* from 1958 (in which Mao appears briefly in person), we are served a sampling of what it may have been.[1] Set in 1978, ten years after the liberation of Taiwan and with New China well into the 'higher phase of communist society [when] ... all the springs of co-operative wealth flow more abundantly', the film has young revolutionaries gathering in the shade of a tree from the branches of which grow bananas, apples, pears, loquats, lychee ... and living among farmers who each rear an average of 365 pigs a day (!) to meet some of the dietary needs of a population that has found a cure for cancer (massive quantities of Turfan grapes) and whose members live to the ripe old age of well past a hundred.[2] It is a unique record of the Utopia of Mao's Great Leap Forward, a sweet Chinese dream of plenty.

Poverty, Mao had argued a few months prior to the shooting of *The Ming Tombs Reservoir Fantasy*, gave rise to a powerful desire for change (*bian*).[3] Perhaps the blandest of words expressing the act or instance of becoming different, 'change' was in Mao's conceptual universe intimately related to epistemology – knowledge, as understood by him, both stimulating and feeding on change. In 1958, after two years of digesting the implications of its direction in the Soviet Union since the CPSU's 20th Congress and its progress in China since the forced abortion of the 'Socialist Upsurge' of 1956 (a.k.a the First Leap Forward), Mao set about to pursue change barely distinguishable from chaos. Chaos came with 'the immense advantages of chaos', he was to assert in 1964, and it was on this very point that Mao's evolutionary thinking was in fact cutting-edge. As Stuart Kauffman's and Christopher Langton's research has since suggested, being 'on the edge of chaos ... provides the greatest

evolvability'.[4] It was away from an oppressive past by way of an imperfect present that Mao sought *at any cost* to evolve China into a communist society. For fellow revolutionaries of his own generation satisfied
with anything less than living on the border of disorder, he had only
contempt. Pride in progress was fine, but contentment was revisionist!
On the first day of the year 1976, his last at the helm of the CCP, China's
radio stations broadcast a poem in which Mao's communist roc interrupted a revisionist sparrow salivating over the prospect of piping hot
potatoes and beef in the land of plenty, telling her: 'Quit farting! Look,
the world is being turned topsy turvy!'[5]

In what follows, Mao's reflections on the subjects of change and
knowledge bulk up a chronocollage of the final two decades of his
life – from the Great Leap Forward and the nightmare famine that followed, to the 'Four Cleanups' and successive 'revolutions within the
Chinese revolution'.[6] Taking my cue from Richard J. Parmentier's *The
Sacred Remains* and being aware of how ideology undoubtedly seasons *all*
sources, I make no attempt at straining out false consciousness in order
to lay bare a 'raw truth' behind the dissimulation of Mao's extant *oeuvre*,
but seek instead to uncover in the metaphors of the man the principles
of his ideological flavouring, colouring, and texturising.[7] The visceral
effectiveness of Mao's ideas always rested on the appeal of the metaphors
he chose to work with. To recognise this is not altogether different from
what students of creative writing learn to do early on: 'Sensory details,
telling details, the "divine" detail, this is where the truth lies... Fact:
We had dinner at 6 P.M. Detail: We had dinner of roast chicken, boiled
red potatoes, corn on the cob, and tomatoes. It was a little early for the
corn ...'[8] The reader be forewarned: this is not a paper in the literary or
cultural vein, albeit that in its chosen methodology it attempts a transfer
from one meaning to another through a personal operation based on
impressions that the readers must experience for themselves.[9]

Where *do* correct ideas come from?

> *Without the participation of intellectuals,*
> *victory in the revolution is impossible.*
>
> Mao Zedong, 1 December 1939

Much has been written about the broader political and historical context
in which Mao's ideas ended up, in one form or another, on paper. Rather
fewer attempts have been made to capture the intimate circumstances
under which he produced what eventually became Mao Zedong Thought.

In recent years, however, the memoirs of former bodyguards and personal staffers have begun to throw fascinating new light on how some of Mao's most fertile ideas emerged after a prolonged process during which Mao, it turns out, was remarkably vulnerable.

Li Yinqiao, a former bodyguard of Mao's, recently fleshed out considerably the context that students of Mao Zedong Thought had to contend with in the past. The time: autumn of 1947. The place: north China countryside. Mao, Li recalled, had been sitting at his desk, poring over maps, occasionally consulting the *Cihai* encyclopaedia and a dictionary, now and then grabbing his pen making notes, jotting something down. 'Suddenly,' Li recalled,

> the CCP Chairman frowned and moments later grabbed some paper and headed for the door. I hurried along behind him. In the doorway he informed me: 'I need to relieve myself. Bring along a shovel and help me dig a hole.' I quickly grabbed a shovel and flashlight and, staying right behind Mao Zedong, headed out into the wild yonder on the outskirts of the village.[10]

Having dug a hole for Mao, Li stood by, keeping a watchful eye on the surroundings. Done, Mao turned to him on the way back and asked: 'Tell me, when do you think is the best time to reflect upon a problem (*sikao wenti*)?' Li suggested that perhaps it was when lying in bed. 'Wrong!' said Mao, moving closer to Li in the dark: 'I'll tell you, it's when you shit. The best time to contemplate things (*xiang shiqing*) is while you're taking a shit.'[11] Needless to say, ethnographic information of this sort forces historians to consider alternative readings of part of the CCP canon, most notably Mao's 1963 essay entitled 'Where Do Correct Ideas Come From?' in which he had asked: 'Where do correct ideas come from? Do they drop from the skies? No. Are they innate in the mind? No. They come from social practice, and from it alone ... '.[12]

Rather than dismiss the information leaked by Li Yinqiao as just so much rubbish, we need to let it feed our imagination – our thinking about Mao, about his politics and about the nature of his relationship to the men and women around him. Marshal Lin Biao was prior to his demise in 1971 described as Mao's 'most outstanding pupil', though about *what* he learnt from his teacher that earned him the epithet we know precious little. In the case of Premier Zhou Enlai – described in 1968 as 'Chairman Mao's close comrade-in-arms and outstanding pupil' – we know rather more, thanks to the disclosures of *his* personal staff.[13] That the ingredients of Zhou's politics always differed from Mao's is well-known; but in his epistemological practice the Premier was by the mid-1950s no less Maoist than the Chairman. A personal secretary of his between 1949 and 1957 has since revealed that Zhou's toilet was referred to by herself and her colleagues as the First Office (*di yi bangongshi*) and it was here that, every morning, the Premier would reflect long and hard on problems and contemplate matters of state, as well as sign off on government decrees and occasionally even hold closed-door high-level meetings. In an interview with a Peking University historian published under the title 'Are the Common People of Beijing able to Get Vegetables Like These?' a man who served as one of Zhou's bodyguards from 1945 to 1968 described a visit to the busy First Office by a senior colleague of Zhou's. Not only did Zhou not object to the visitor who burst in unannounced but even had him pull up a chair to talk policy. 'My business is finished', the visitor is said to have remarked as he left. His visit 'left a very deep impression on me', Zhou's former bodyguard remembered.[14]

Great leap

> *The zeal for revolution and for construction*
> *that the people are showing in 1958 is higher*
> *than at any time in the past.*
>
> Mao Zedong, 16 January 1958

In his lecture notes *On Dialectical Materialism* Mao had observed in 1937 how 'If you want knowledge, you must take part in the practice of changing reality. If you want to know the taste of a pear, you must change the pear by eating it yourself.'[15] Twenty years later, at a November 1957 Meeting of the Representatives of the Communist and Workers' Parties of Twelve Socialist Countries in Moscow, Mao picked up the same theme, commenting thus on the hitherto fruitless attempts of socialism's enemies to change socialist reality:

> If it were not for the Soviet Union, we would probably all be swallowed up by the other side. Of course, by this I do not mean to say that without the Soviet Union the socialist countries would all be swallowed up and digested by imperialism and all their peoples would perish.[16]

Mao's crucial point here was one of strategy: knowledge could only be acquired gradually and change not be effected all at once. 'Strategically,' Mao elaborated, still in Moscow that same week, in front of delegates representing some 64 communist and workers' parties.

we take the eating of a light meal lightly, we are sure we can manage it. But when it comes to the actual eating, it must be done mouthful by mouthful: you cannot swallow an entire banquet at one gulp. This is called the piecemeal solution and is known in military writings as destroying the enemy forces one by one.[17]

Upon his return to China, Mao appears to have found that 'the piecemeal solution' had begun to taste tired. Why, we may never know – but rather than seek to revive it, he chose to throw it onto the proverbial compost heap of history. Changing reality from its imperfect present into an altogether new communist form had, after the Moscow visit, acquired a rare urgency. Of course, compared to not all that long ago, parts of China had by 1958 *already* been changed beyond recognition. In Mao's own words, 'We've consumed the large end (*datou chidiaole*), the bureaucrat-capitalist class. Should the small end, the national bourgeoisie, attempt to resist, it would be powerless to do so.'[18] But it was as if Mao saw his old recipe for success as ripe for radical change. In a *People's Daily* editorial, Mao held out the prospect of an irresistible new desert in the form of 'bountiful economic fruit' that 'entirely in accordance with the laws' would be awaiting those who were prepared to join him in attempting more 'faster, better, and more economically'.[19]

Knowledge of how to proceed was far from easy to come by: 'All knowledge is acquired in the course of difficulties and setbacks', Mao would lament in front of his political secretaries.[20] Where epistemology intersected with development strategy, scaling down while simultaneously increasing numbers seemed initially to resolve the conflict Mao had identified in Moscow. Taking the notion of small as beautiful to its extreme, Mao in May 1958 expressed admiration for an unlikely agent of change:

> There are certain microbes called germs who, though small in size, are in some sense more powerful than men. They have no superstition and are full of energy. They strive for greater, faster, better, and more economical results and for the upper reaches. They respect no-one and fear neither heaven nor earth.[21]

The enemies of progress and of communism were, meanwhile, viewed by Mao as subject to an evolution that made them increasingly vulnerable to germs, to decomposition, to rot. In 1961, Mao would compare them to 'ghosts'; in 1958, he still envisaged them as tigers, albeit made of cellulose, of meat, of coagulated soy milk.[22] Elaborating, Mao put the following on paper during a Central Committee plenum near the end of 1958: they were 'real tigers who devoured people, devoured people by the millions and tens of millions'; but if they had not already, they would in the end – all of them without fail – change into 'paper tigers, dead tigers, bean-curd tigers. These are historical facts. Haven't people seen or heard about these facts?'[23]

Famine

> *This man-made disaster is not one our*
> *enemies have created, but one we have*
> *created ourselves.*
>
> Mao Zedong, 30 December 1960

By the end of the summer of 1959 it seemed increasingly unlikely that China would get a good taste of communism in the near future: the tree in *The Ming Tombs Reservoir Fantasy* was growing none of Mao's 'bountiful economic fruit'! With alarming frequency, the Ministry of Public Security's Top Secret *Public Security Work Bulletin* and *Public Security Intelligence* told, instead, of ever more severe domestic food scarcities. If this was the onset of communism, a lot of ordinary Chinese privately admitted, they craved none of it. One report quoted a senior 'democratic personage' in Beijing as saying 'in the villages, the suffering is terrible: while they [the CCP] speak day in and day out of ever bigger harvests, what the people have to eat becomes less and less with each passing day ... '.[24] Mao's urging to fellow CCP Politburo members at the end of a particularly confrontational July 1959 meeting, about what was going wrong and who was to blame, had a sharp and caustic poignancy: 'Comrades', he said in an agitated state at the end of what Roderick MacFarquhar has characterised as a 'brilliant debating performance', 'you should analyse your own responsibility and your stomach will feel much more comfortable if you move your bowels and break wind'.[25] Mao's words did little to turn the situation around, however. Nobody would, in the weeks and months that followed, 'feel much more comfortable'. At a meeting of senior party leaders at the end of 1960, Mao commented on the 'communist wind' by saying that 'unless there is a degree of suffering, a degree of pain, [people] will never learn a lesson'.[26]

Between 1959 and 1961, large parts of China were in the grip of a famine that ended up taking an estimated 20 to 30 million lives.[27] 'Ample food and clothing will not drop from the skies!' Mao was quoted as saying in the *Fujian Daily* in the summer of 1961, as if to admit that he had by then run out of 'correct ideas' that might at this stage improve the lives of the tired, poor, and starving.[28] And so with none of it dropping from the skies, ordinary Chinese went looking for food elsewhere. The class enemy, no less opportunistic than the energetic germs that Mao had paid tribute to in 1958, did not hesitate to go *up* the food chain: In Hubei, according to a report in *Public Security Work Bulletin*, a family of thieves and robbers running a hostel in the isolated mountains of Badong county had killed and consumed no less than six passing travellers in the winter of 1959.[29] And in April 1960, the Xinhua News Agency's Top Secret *Internal Reference* had carried news of how:

> statistics from eleven counties and municipalities in Gansu, the Ningxia Muslim Autonomous Region, and Guizhou, tell of seventeen cases of 'cannibalism' [*chi renrou* – lit. 'eating human flesh'] since the beginning of the year. Of these cases, eleven occurred in Gansu, and three each in Ningxia and Guizhou. The seventeen cases involved the slaughter and murder of fifteen individuals (of which three were young children) and the excavation and consumption (*juechi*) of sixteen corpses. The altogether twenty-two offenders involved in these cases included eleven rich-peasant, landlord, counter-revolutionary, or bad elements; two members of reactionary sects; two middle peasants; three poor peasants; one petty trader; and three housewives.[30]

As the report's wording indicates, these were not the kind of practices that the communist ideal of an all-consuming revolution endorsed; which is not to say that grassroots officialdom never ever indulged in something similar. In Guangdong's Lianping county, police officers had on one occasion in the early 1950s 'without asking for permission executed two people and without considering the impact this might have permitted the masses to cut them up and take pieces of flesh with them home.'[31] During the Cultural Revolution (when, coincidentally, the slogan 'There is class struggle at the pointed end of the chopsticks!' was described in *Red Flag* as a 'very simple and plain, very vivid' example of the 'language of the masses'[32]), the brain and tongue and heart and testicles of counter-revolutionaries were on a handful of rare occasions eaten in the wake of executions in remote parts of Qiaojia county in Yunnan and Wuxuan county in Guangxi.[33]

Ordinary Chinese were in 1960 and 1961 forced to go down the food chain, to eat flowers, leaves, roots, bark, seeds and bulbs. Nowhere to be seen were Mao's pears and the sweet taste of knowledge they provided; mushrooming, instead, were 'substitute foods' from which too big a bite could prove as lethal as political ignorance. Mao – who himself went on a vegetarian diet in October 1960 – had always maintained that 'to attempt to cover the objectively existing poisonous weeds with mud and dirt and in this way prevent them from appearing' was 'idiotic' and showed 'no understanding of the tactics of class struggle'. Confident in the common sense of ordinary people, he had announced at the beginning of the Great Leap Forward that 'the party is convinced the masses have the capacity to distinguish the poisonous weeds and to conquer the poisonous weeds.'[34] But was his confidence realistic? This is an example of what *Public Security Work Bulletin* had to report in November 1960:

> When the urban residents of Ji'nan in Shandong and Wuhan in Hubei visit the [rural] suburbs in search of substitute foods (*daishipin*), they grab whatever they can get their hands on. More than 2,000 people come each day to the fields surrounding the two production brigades of Wuhan's Dai Mountain [People's] Commune to scavenge for vegetables... As of recently, large numbers of workers and urban residents from the cities of Ji'nan and Qingdao in Shangdong province visit the surrounding rural areas daily in search of edible wild plants. They take whatever they can find.[35]

Widespread food poisoning occurred where Mao's confidence proved misplaced. 'Since October', a ministerial report on 5 November 1960 explained, there had been '5404 known cases of food poisoning from eating the Siberian Cocklebur Fruit' in the cities of Taiyuan and Changzhi in Shanxi province alone. In Tangshan, Qinhuangdao, Changli, and Yutian in Hebei province, the fruit (actually a herb, poisonous when digested in large quantities, used in traditional Chinese medicine to dispel wind and damp) had 'in early October poisoned an estimated 7900 persons and claimed the lives of 34'.[36]

Yet some of the worst suffering in actuality, if not in memory, had limited natural causes. As an investigation conducted by a Ministry of Public Security task force in 1962 discovered in the province of Qinghai:

> Because the scope of attack has been excessive and large numbers of people have been offended these past years, close to 300,000 died in the province as a whole, and the masses show signs of displeasure. Add to this that in quite a few regions, the food grain available to the peasants is only half a *jin* while in some places social order is no good, and there is even the possibility of unrest.[37]

What sort of criminally misguided Great Leap Forward was it that managed to terminally 'offend' 0.3 million Qinghai residents? What kind of punitive 'communism' was it that fed people but half a *jin* of grain per person per month?

It takes a leap of the imagination to find the key. The publication of the 'brutal, obscene and disgusting' (these are its author William Burroughs' own characterisation of it) novel *Naked Lunch* in the United States in 1962 prompted, in due course, a Massachusetts court to ask if the title 'relates to capital punishment'? Testifying on behalf of *Naked Lunch*, Allen Ginsberg responded 'No, no. It relates to nakedness of seeing, to being able to see clearly without any confusing disguises, to see through the disguise.' A full naked 'lunch', Ginsberg asserted, would in this case correspond to 'a complete banquet of all this naked awareness'. Ginsberg said he understood *Naked Lunch* to point at 'the number one World Health Problem, which, he [Burroughs] feels, is this tendency on the part of – the tendency in a mechanised civilisation for very few people to get control of enormous amounts of power'.[38] In China, punishment, nakedness, health and the concentration of power were meanwhile intersecting in ways that showed Burroughs to have been remarkably perceptive:

> On 1 October [1960], Liao Jun, general [party] branch secretary in Zhuanghou brigade, Gushi township, Suichang county, Zhejiang province, announced at a meeting of cadres at and above the rank of team leader and at a mass meeting of members of the Guanling production team to celebrate National Day that 'petty thieves have no sense of shame. Merely to hang them up and beat them doesn't do the trick. You also have to remove their clothes, their trousers, strip them naked.' In accordance with his instructions, altogether eleven members of the masses (five males, six females) in the brigade subsequently ended up having their clothes removed and being paraded naked through the streets. Six of them were members of the Guanling production team. On 2 October, the middle peasant Zheng Lifa (aged 28) had been caught stealing nine corn ears and was taken to the brigade where the [party] branch secretary Zheng Yanhuo told four militia members at a mass meeting to remove all of Zheng Lifa's clothes and put him on public display for over an hour... On 5 October, the poor peasants from the same team Ye Aichai (female, aged 47), Xu Genlan (female, aged 55), and Zhou Moying (female, aged 60) each took two, three *jin* of corn ears and when Zheng Yanhuo found out he immediately sent the militia to remove their clothes and parade them naked through the streets. On their knees, Ye and the others pleaded for mercy while members of the masses, one after the other, asked Zheng to show forgiveness. But he insisted on them removing all of

their clothes and furthermore ordered Zhou Moying to bang a gong while walking naked up front, militia escort following close behind, for one *li* and a half. Afterwards, Ye Aichai was so devastated with shame she wanted to kill herself, but her husband managed to talk her out of it. On 9 October, the woman Chen Jinjuan (aged 18) was spotted by the head of the brigade as she took three corn ears growing by the roadside on her way home from the production brigade where she had bought some cooking oil. He immediately insisted on fining her eight Yuan, money which she was unable to produce. When she pleaded for mercy, crying, he refused to give way and demanded she take off her clothes and leave them as collateral instead. She was only able to return home after her family had turned up with another set of clothes for her to wear.[39]

Coming clean

> *Some leading comrades ... have puffed up the*
> *arrogance of the bourgeoisie and deflated the*
> *morale of the proletariat. How poisonous!*
> *Viewed in connection with the Right deviation*
> *in 1962 and the wrong tendency of 1964 which*
> *was 'Left' in form but Right in essence, shouldn't*
> *this make one wide awake?*
>
> Mao Zedong, 5 August 1966

Nakedness is next to cleanliness and 'Clearly, cadres had to be clean if they were to carry conviction', Rod MacFarquhar has concluded from his analysis of famine realities in *The Origins of the Cultural Revolution*.[40] Since the 'banquet of all this naked awareness' of 1959–1961 indicated that large numbers of powerful CCP cadres were in fact *not* 'clean', a drastic remedy needed to be devised. Though Mao and his colleagues would eventually split over just how to proceed, there was initial agreement on what the remedy was to entail. Mao announced that the gist would be 'cadres, relying on the poor and lower middle peasants, washing their hands and taking baths ...'[41] Peng Zhen explained in an extended discourse on the subject that

leading comrades will be taking a preliminary bath. It's been well over ten years since they last did this... It's better to take an early bath than a late bath, and even a belated bath is better than no bath at all... For years, Chairman Mao has been proposing that we wash our faces every day...[42]

Though Mao spoke of them needing to wash their hands, he did not mean that cadres were to disclaim responsibility for their actions. As one contemporary source had it, '[we] must stress and point out in particular that the aim of the bath is to overcome any and all thinking and behaviour *not conducive to socialism*'.[43] They were meant to act as role models for ordinary Chinese who might themselves also have been in one way or other tainted. CCP Vice-Chairman Liu Shaoqi suggested that 'once the cadres have taken a bath and really given themselves a thorough cleansing, the masses will naturally follow and take a bath too. It need not take too long, a few days should do it.'[44] The reality of the 'Four Cleanups' – as the remedial cleansing became known – was related in texts like a report from Di county in central Shanxi entitled 'Some Impressions Gained from Organising Rural Grass-Roots Cadres to Wash Their Hands and Take Baths' which spoke of how

> according to their positions and duties, the nature of their problems, their attitudes being good or bad, etc. research was conducted into the scope of cadres needing a bath and the methods of bathing. As a norm, brigade cadres would wash themselves in the brigade, team cadres would wash themselves in the team, while party and league cadres would wash inside the organisation...[45]

The starved peasant women from Zhejiang mentioned earlier had been forced to walk naked down the village street because they had stolen two, three *jin* of corn ears each; in Di county, three out of four commune cadres 'needed to take baths' when it turned out that the total 'value of what they had eaten and taken that exceeded their share was 249,128 Yuan'.[46] Hereupon, 'in the course of bathing, they confessed to having stolen 2300 *jin* of grain and expressed their resolve to show through action their repentance.'[47]

Purging the entire system: The Cultural Revolution

> *Before the movement, a lot of people kept saying*
> *they were ill and needed expensive drugs and rest,*
> *maybe seven or eight months a year. When the*
> *Cultural Revolution began, their illnesses disappeared.*
> Mao Zedong, 5 October 1968

The very orderliness that Mao saw emerge in the 'Four Cleanups' made him concerned. Signs of a rethink of the initial remedy began to appear as time passed. A crucially important programmatic document circulated in January 1965 as CCP Central Document *Zhongfa* [1965] 26 hinted in vague terms at what Mao was contemplating and at where he might be going next. It signalled a decreased concern with external cleanliness overall in that it stated clearly that work team members 'don't necessarily have to be all that "clean"'.[48] 'The class content of purity is different in different societies. There are so-called pure officials in capitalist societies as well', Mao told Chen Boda three days after Chen had presented him with an early draft of the document, 'and they are all big tycoons'.[49]

What Mao had in mind or was reflecting upon was not disclosed beforehand. As Roderick MacFarquhar and I have noted elsewhere, Mao played his cards very close to his chest, pursuing a 'deliberate opaqueness' that kept even some members of his inner circle in the dark.[50] Hence there remained, well into the autumn of 1966, when the Four Cleanups drew to a close nationwide, something ambiguous about much that was being said: even statements made by Mao's 'most outstanding pupil' could be interpreted simultaneously as presaging more of the same *and* as foreshadowing something completely different. Compare the following:

> I don't mean to say that all [powerholders] must take their trousers off in front of the masses ... [But] when standing in front of the masses, should we adopt a posture that involves making a thorough self-criticism and an equally thorough self-denunciation – comparable to pouring water off a steep roof – by taking our trousers off? Or should we adopt the posture of organising some of the masses to protect us? If we adopt a posture of thoroughly denouncing ourselves, dispense with our nauseating airs, and take our trousers off, then we shall succeed in mobilising the broad masses to denounce us and turn the spear of attack against us ... [51]

Unless they managed to intuit something very different from Mao's behaviour, members of Lin's audience could plausibly and rationally interpret his words as simply describing the run-up to 'taking a bath' and cadres 'giving themselves a thorough cleansing'. And there were numerous precedents that suggested just that.

The possibility that to 'take our trousers off' might be a prelude to something very different did not dawn on many until the end. Which is not to say that from a position of hindsight one cannot already discern where things were moving, for example, in the CCP's counter-revisionist discourse on *gulyáskommunizmus*. In the Soviet Union, in the words of Liu Shaoqi,

> Large contingents of bourgeois intellectuals have come to the fore that are seen as having grown up on socialism. While in their mother's womb and while on mother's milk, that which they consumed was socialism's milk. So, we ask, do they still count as bourgeois intellectuals? They may not count as such, but in actuality they are![52]

Truly consequential impurities, in other words, would for the duration be on the inside. 'Like the Monkey King' in *Journey to the West*, Mao would eventually be quoted as saying, they provoked 'counter-revolutionary activities' in the belly after having penetrated it by way of clever use of 'military tactics'. In some cases, 'conceit, self-complacency, lack of vigilance and absorption in the day-to-day job to the neglect of politics on our part as revolutionaries' might even allow them to 'penetrate our liver'.[53] Unless this slow process of *internal* absorption was interrupted and reversed well before it had run its full course, the effect would (as the Soviet case showed) ultimately be full blown revisionism.

None had a better command of Mao's metaphors than the men who at one time or other had served him as ghost-writers and/or alter ego 'theorists'. They could produce a discourse that was for all practical purposes as much Mao as Mao's own. It is hence as the emulation and near-perfect simulation of the CCP Chairman's thinking that we must read and understand the following assertion by Hu Qiaomu (style-editor of Mao's *Selected Works*) dating from the time of the 'Four Cleanups' and describing a very different process to which 'take our trousers off' was *also* a perfectly appropriate prelude. In 1970, Mao's brief and cryptic order, 'Expel waste matter' would be duly included in the PLA's massive 2200-page *Index to Quotations From Chairman Mao* (the entry, sourced to *Red Flag*, read *in full*: 'Expel waste matter, ...');[54] in what follows, Hu Qiaomu elaborates on the why and wherefore of what Mao *really* expected the cadres to do with their trousers down:

> Here is a kind of social phenomenon consisting of faeces produced by socialist society in a manner similar to man's having to eat and defecate every day. If man does not defecate, there will be a reshuffle (*gaizu*) in his internal organs. Once he has eaten, man needs to defecate, which is of course a bother, since it involves a waste of time

as well as of paper. On the other hand, it is not a bad thing either, since unless we defecate, how do we rid ourselves of the waste matter? Societies are like that, [like people] they also have to defecate, which is not a bad thing. Once this truth has been made clear to people, it will no longer appear strange to them. Of course, differences in essence as well as process distinguish defecation by socialist societies from defecation by capitalist or feudal societies.[55]

The Cultural Revolution, the name that Mao would give his grand experiment, would subject the CCP and officialdom to a purge of unprecedented ferocity.

A revolution is not a dinner party

> *Maybe in a few more years,*
> *we'll have yet another revolution.*
> Mao Zedong, n.d. [1973]

'A revolution is not a dinner party', the *Quotations from Chairman Mao* had the CCP Chairman musing. By the autumn of 1968, the organ of the CCP Central Committee *Red Flag* was quoting him in an editorial as saying (in words officially described as 'embodying extremely profound dialectics') that 'if we don't expel waste matter, don't absorb fresh blood, the party will have no vitality.'[56] The editorial, drafted by Yao Wenyuan, contained an entire paragraph dissecting the waste matter Mao had in mind and listing its components – politically suspect 'elements' of one kind or another.[57]

The first Cultural Revolution was to leave many CCP members more than satisfied: Mao's successors were unable to stomach even the mere thought of a second one or even worse, successive revolutions 'every seven to eight years' as Mao now and then threatened. One of the last occasions on which he elaborated on the dialectic of change and epistemology was, as far as we know today, the CCP's 9th National Congress in April 1969, an informal pre-dinner conversation on 11 April, with the congress secretariat and regional delegation leaders. No complete official transcript of what was said on that day has since been declassified by the CCP, yet historians have at present no less than five different *unofficial* transcripts of it, all of them equally authoritative in the sense of being rough stenographic records taken down either by someone who was present or someone who heard a tape recording of Mao and his 'comrades in arms' speaking.

Prior to taking a short break, Mao had explained why it was imperative 'for our comrades to be thoroughly familiar with our party's historical experiences, in order to avoid repeating past mistakes.'[58] After the break, he had begun to speak again but quickly found himself interrupted by Kang Sheng. Transcript #1 notes that it was Kang's interjection that prompted Mao to elaborate as follows:

> A person has to eat and he has to shit. After all, he cannot only eat and not shit. There has to be a process of digestion between eating and shitting. Dialectics expresses itself by way of a process. Infants, right after they're born, will both eat and shit. If we only remember to eat, and not remember to shit, how's that going to work? After all, one cannot wait until the moment one has to shit to dig a pit. At any given period, there's always a principal contradiction.[59]

Vintage Mao Zedong Thought, one might at first be inclined to believe. Transcript #2, however, complicates the ascription of direct (1969) authorship to Mao of this passage by suggesting that the speaker was Kang, interrupting Mao and apparently summarising what Mao had said in Yan'an decades earlier about the importance of correctly digesting experience. Transcripts #3 and #4 are almost identical in their syntactic imperfections, both possibly suggesting Kang *was* at least partially responsible for what was being recorded.

On the basis of the likely intent of the person(s) providing a variant text of Mao's, Timothy Cheek some two decades ago defined the stubbornly persistent conceptual category of the 'genius edition'.[60] It basically assumes that the provider (typically one of the best minds of a generation starving to recreate the syntax and measure of the Chairman's prose[61]) regarded Mao as a 'lone genius not subject to revision by any collective leadership' and looked upon editorial tinkering with the Chairman's Word the same way Jack Kerouac had looked upon *ex post facto* alterations of his own: 'Once God moves the hand, you go back and revise it's a *sin!*'[62] If we apply Cheek's categories to the five different records of what Mao is meant to have said at the 9th National Congress, it would at first appear as if they all fall squarely within the 'genius' category. Nothing appears to have been done to them to enhance the *form* for the sake of making the content more intelligible. At the same time, however, the fifth record actually manages to fuse the 'genius' with a rather impudent category – the *'homogenised'* 'collective wisdom' that Cheek for some reason hesitates to call by its rightful name the *Antimao*.[63] Transcript #5 makes a powerful case for treating Mao's knowledge as collective, reproducing as it does a kind of conversation, in the middle of which Mao very pointedly even downplays his own role:

> (*Revered Kang [Sheng]:* The Chairman said already a long time ago that after all, you can't work and sleep or eat and relieve yourself simultaneously. He said in Yan'an that at any one time, there is always one that is the major one) I didn't say that in Yan'an. (*Revered Kang:* The Chairman said it numerous times while discussing dialectics, that there has to be a process, that we relieve ourselves when we've eaten, that like infants sucking the breast, they eat and shit at the same time.) (*Everybody laughs*) It's only when we have to shit while our troops are on the march that we dig a pit, some of us even digging one ourselves. (*The Premier:* We make mistakes, not remembering to dig a pit) (*Xu Shiyou:* Once in the barracks, we would no longer be digging.) The barracks have segregated our military from the workers and peasants and that is not a good thing, though of course not having any of it would not be good, the common people would resent that as well.[64]

Who *are* historians to say that it was *not* exchanges like this one that the CCP Central Committee had in mind when, with Mao dead and gone, it insisted that 'numerous outstanding party leaders made important contributions to the formation and development of Mao Zedong Thought'?

* * * * *

And so we return to the men and women on Mao's personal staff and security detail. Young Miss She from the PLA worked for two and a half months for Mao in Wuhan in 1964; the record has it that the other women in her detail were flush with envy when she received her assignment. Her officially sanctioned account of what it entailed (duly censored for political correctness, published by a prestigious arm of the official CCP history establishment three decades later) has it that she 'provided Chairman Mao with boiled water, tidied his bed, cleaned his room, washed his bathtub, and flushed his toilet for him.' Of their conversations, a poignant snippet survives. Miss She: 'To be able to serve the Chairman makes me really happy!' Mao: 'Really? You serve me and I serve the people.'[65] No official resolution on party history drives it home with greater punch, no academic scholarship at Harvard or Peking University can really afford to be that blunt in describing the deal between Mao and *800,000,000 – The Real China*. Because, does that one intimate soundbite not say, I serve you a revolution and you clean up the mess when I'm done?

Notes

This chapter was first published in *A Critical Introduction to Mao*, ed. by Timothy Cheek (New York: Cambridge University Press, 2010), pp. 110–128.

1. Shisanling shuiku changxiangqu, based on a play by Tian Han, directed by Jin Shan, and produced by the Beijing Film Studio.
2. Karl Marx, Critique of the Gotha Programme, http://www.marxists.org/archive/marx/works/1875/gotha/ch01.htm
3. Jianguo yilai Mao Zedong wengao, vol. 7, p. 178.
4. Edward O. Wilson, *Consilience: The Unity of Knowledge* (New York: Alfred A. Knopf, 1998), pp. 88–90. See also http://www.edge.org/3rd_culture/kauffman03/kauffman_index.html and http://www.santafe.edu/research/publications/workingpapers/93-06-040.pdf [Accessed on 9 February 2008].
5. I was there. I heard the broadcast; Jianguo yilai Mao Zedong wengao, vol. 11, p. 466.
6. Cf. the title of John K. Fairbank and Roderick MacFarquhar (eds), *The Cambridge History of China*, Volume 15, The People's Republic, Part 2: Revolutions within the Chinese Revolution 1966–1982 (Cambridge: Cambridge University Press, 1991).
7. Richard J. Parmentier, *The Sacred Remains: Myth, History, and Polity in Belau* (Chicago: University of Chicago Press, 1987).
8. See http://www.judyreeveswriter.com/truth_in_details.htm [Accessed on 2 January 2008].
9. Slightly abbreviated definition of metaphor lifted from Bernard Dupriez, *A Dictionary of Literary Devices* (Toronto: University of Toronto Press, 1991), p. 276.
10. Sun Mingshan (ed.), *Lishi shunjian III* (A Moment in History III) (Beijing: Qunzhong chubanshe, 2004), p. 191.
11. *Ibid.*, p. 192.
12. Jianguo yilai Mao Zedong wengao, vol. 10, pp. 299–300.
13. Chongqing gongren bianjibu (ed.), *Yi Mao zhuxi weishou de wuchanjieji silingbu wansui* (Long Live the Proletarian Headquarters Headed by Chairman Mao) (Chongqing, 1968), pp. 304–05.
14. Cheng Hua (ed.), *Zhou Enlai he tade mishumen* (Zhou Enlai and His Secretaries) (Beijing: Zhongguo guangbo dianshi chubanshe, 1992), p. 178, 381.
15. Stuart Schram (ed.), *Mao's Road to Power: Revolutionary Writings 1912–1949*, vol. 6 (Armonk, NY: M. E. Sharpe, 2004), p. 606.
16. Michael Schoenhals, 'Mao Zedong: Speeches at the 1957 "Moscow Conference"', *The Journal of Communist Studies* vol. 2, no. 2 (June 1986), 113.
17. *Ibid.*, p. 120.
18. Du Sulian Zhengzhi jingjixue jiaokeshu shehuizhuyi bufen de tanhua jilugao (Record of Some Conversations on the Section Devoted to Socialism in the Soviet Textbook on Political Economy) (Beijing, 1975), p. 226.
19. Michael Schoenhals, *Saltationist Socialism: Mao Zedong and the Great Leap Forward 1958* (Stockholm: Föreningen för orientaliska studier, 1987), pp. 40–43.
20. Du Sulian Zhengzhi jingjixue jiaokeshu shehuizhuyi bufen de tanhua jilugao, p. 359.

21. *Mao Zedong sixiang wansui (1958–1959)* (Long Live Mao Zedong Thought (1958–1959)) (N.p., 1967), p. 55.
22. Jianguo yilai Mao Zedong wengao, vol. 9, p. 426.
23. *Ibid.*, vol. 7, pp. 610–13.
24. Gongan qingbao, no. 4, 23 January 1960, p. 2; no. 29, 26 March 1960.
25. Roderick MacFarquhar, *The Origins of the Cultural Revolution 2: The Great Leap Forward 1958–1960* (New York: Columbia University Press, 1983), pp. 218–21.
26. http://tieba.baidu.com/f?kz=82661598 [Accessed on 17 February 2008].
27. Li Chengrui and Shang Changfeng, 'Sannian kunnan shiqi fei zhengchang siwang renkoushu yanjiu shuping' (Survey of Research into the Number of Abnormal Deaths During the Three Bad Years), unpublished conference paper, Yan'an, 2007, p. 14.
28. Fujian ribao, 29 July 1961. Reprinted in and here quoted from Mao zhuxi yulu suoyin (Index to Quotations from Chairman Mao) (N.p., 1970), p. 272.
29. Gongan gongzuo jianbao, no. 21, 11 March 1960, p. 10.
30. Neibu cankao, no. 3032, 14 April 1960, p. 25.
31. Yiting [pseud.], 'Wushi niandai Guangdong zhenfan' (The Suppression of Counter-revolution in Guangdong in the 1950s), Tianya wangwen (Net Articles from Remote Corners of the World). This 3-part study was posted on the Hainan website Tianya on 8 October 2007 (when the author downloaded it in full) but has since been removed by the PRC Cyber Police.
32. Wenzhang xuandu (pinglunwen bufen) (Selected Readings (Critiques Section)) (N.p., 1970), p. 4.
33. Roderick MacFarquhar and Michael Schoenhals, *Mao's Last Revolution* (Cambridge: Harvard University Press, 2006), p. 259.
34. Jianguo yilai Mao Zedong wengao, vol. 7, pp. 93–94.
35. Gongan gongzuo jianbao, no. 80, 18 November 1960, p. 5.
36. Gongan gongzuo jianbao, no. 73, 5 November 1960, pp. 4–5.
37. Gongan gongzuo jianbao, no. 14, 29 April 1962, p. 10. The original recipient of my copy (#234) of this now declassified Top Secret report has written in pencil next to the casualty figure '14.4% of the entire population'.
38. William S. Burroughs, *Naked Lunch* (New York: Grove Press, 1966), pp. xxi–xv.
39. Gongan gongzuo jianbao, no. 81, 23 November 1960, p. 5.
40. Roderick MacFarquhar, *The Origins of the Cultural Revolution 3: The Coming of the Cataclysm 1961–1966* (New York: Columbia University Press, 1997), p. 341.
41. Mao Zedong sixiang wansui (1960–1967) (Long Live Mao Zedong Thought (1960–1967)) (N.p., 1967), p. 51.
42. Zhonggong zhongyang zuzhibu bangongting (ed.), *Zuzhi gongzuo wenjian xuanbian 1963 nian* (Selected Documents on Organization Work from the Year 1963) (Beijing, 1980), p. 103.
43. Shanxi sheng Wenshui xian Macun Shangxian dadui shehuizhuyi jiaoyu yundong juti jingyan huibian (Collected Concrete Experiences from the Socialist Education Movement in Macun and Shangdian Brigades in Wenshui County, Shanxi Province) (Beijing: Zhonggong zhongyang Huabeiju xuanchuanbu, 1964), p. 16.
44. Pipan ziliao: Zhongguo Heluoxiaofu Liu Shaoqi fangeming xiuzhengzhuyi yanlun ji (Criticism Material: Collected Counter-Revolutionary Revisionist Utterances by China's Khrushchev Liu Shaoqi), 3 vols. (Beijing: Renmin chubanshe ziliaoshi, 1968), vol. 3, p. 598.

45. Guanyu zhaokai gongshe sanganhui zuzhi ganbu xishou xizao de jige cailiao (Some Material on Convening Meetings of Three Levels of Commune Cadres for the Purpose of Bringing Cadres to Wash Their Hands and Take Baths) (Taiyuan: Zhonggong Shanxi shengwei nongcun siqing bangongshi, 1965), p. 26.
46. *Ibid.*, p. 23.
47. *Ibid.*, p. 24.
48. *Shejiao wenjian* (Socialist Education Documents) (Lanzhou: Zhonggong Gansu shengwei nongcun shejiao bangongshi, 1965), p. 65.
49. Mao Zedong sixiang wansui (1960–1967), p. 124.
50. MacFarquhar and Schoenhals, *Mao's Last Revolution*, pp. 47–48.
51. Lin Biao wenxuan (Selected Works of Lin Biao), 2 vols. (Xi'an: Xi'an yejin jianzhu xueyuan geming weiyuanhui xuanchuanbu, 1967), vol. 2, p. 391.
52. Zhonggong Shanghai shiwei bangongting geming zaofandui (ed.), *Liu Shaoqi zai gedi sanbu de xiuzhengzhuyi yanlun huibian* (Shanghai, 1967), p. 226.
53. Mao Zedong sixiang wansui (1949.9–1957.12) (Long Live Mao Zedong Thought (1949.9–1957.12)) (N.p., 1967), pp. 51–55.
54. Mao zhuxi yulu suoyin, p. 2004. Ellipsis points as in original.
55. Tantan baozhi gongzuo (On Newspaper Work) (Beijing: Xinwen yanjiusuo, 1978), p. 55.
56. Hongqi, no. 4, 14 October 1968.
57. *Ibid.*; Jianguo yilai Mao Zedong wengao, vol. 12, p. 580.
58. Pang Xianzhi and Jin Chongji, *Mao Zedong zhuan 1949–1976* (Biography of Mao Zedong 1949–1976), 2 vols. (Beijing: Zhongyang wenxian chubanshe, 2003), pp. 1550–51.
59. 'Mao zhuxi jianghua: 4 yue 11 ri xiawu 4 dian 30 fen dao 6 dian' (Chairman Mao Talks: from 4. 30 to 6 P.M. on 11 April), in 'Jiuda' ziliao huibian (Collected Materials on the 'Ninth Congress') (Ji'nan: Ji'nan tieluju Ji'nan chelianggu 5.7 zhongxue, 1969), p. 5.
60. Timothy Cheek, 'The 'Genius' Mao: A Treasure Trove of 23 Newly Available Volumes of Post-49 Mao Zedong Texts', *The Australian Journal of Chinese Affairs*, no. 19/20 (January–July 1988), 318–19. Personally, I think Cheek got it wrong, but as Stuart Kauffman put it: 'Definitions are neither true nor false; they're useful or useless' (see http://www.edge.org/3rd_culture/kauffman03/kauffman_index.html) and Cheek's definition is nothing if not useful.
61. Cf. the lines from Howl not reproduced in Umberto Eco, 'Intertextual Irony and Levels of Reading', in *Umberto Eco on Literature*, Martin McLaughlin, trans. (Orlando: Harcourt, 2002), pp. 212–35.
62. Quoted in Charles E. Jarvis, *Visions of Kerouac*. 2nd edition (Lowell: Ithaca Press, 1974), p. 7.
63. Cheek, 'The 'Genius' Mao', p. 327.
64. '4 yue 11 ri xiawu 5 shi zhi 6 shi ban de jianghua' (Talk from 5 to 6.30 P.M. on 11 April), in Mao Zhuxi zai Zhongguo gongchandang di jiu ci quanguo daibiao dahui shang de zhongyao zhishi (Chairman Mao's Important Instructions at the Ninth National Congress of the CCP) (N.p., 1969), p. 7.
65. Zhonggong Hubei shengwei dangshi ziliao zhengbian weiyuanhui (ed.), *Mao Zedong zai Hubei* (Mao Zedong in Hubei) (Beijing: Zhonggong dangshi chubanshe, 1993), p. 318.

11
The Lived Space of Recollection: How Holocaust Memorials Are Conceived Differently Today

Jörg H. Gleiter

Since the mid-1980s Germany has witnessed a change in the conception of memorials against the crimes of National Socialism. In contrast to previous concepts the new memorials renounce any kind of pathos irrespective of whether generated by a technique of mimetic imagery or geometric abstraction. While earlier memorials were recognised as works of art through their exposed position in public space, the new memorials pursue an opposing strategy of dissimulation in everyday life, at times even culminating in their complete disappearance, as in the case of Jochen Gerz's 'Memorial against Fascism, War and Violence' in Hamburg-Harburg. Over the period of seven years and under the watchful eyes of the population, the memorial was slowly lowered into the ground until it was no longer visible, leaving as a reminder nothing more than a simple commemorative plate. Through techniques of dissimulation in everyday life the new memorials dispense with their recognition as art, which was thought to be essential for empathetic expression, but was always an obstacle for critical reflection. Forty years after the end of the war, as witnesses gradually died off, the conception of the Holocaust memorial started to change. As the recollection of the Nazi regime and its atrocities moved on from 'communicative memory' – as Jan Assmann terms the recollection of authentic experience[1] – to cultural, mediatic memory, the new memorials began to liberate admonitory commemoration from artistic-aesthetic formalism and to carry it back to where National Socialist terror started: the context of everyday life. They dispense with artistic representation and rather rely on a technique of diachronic correspondences in everyday life. They succeed in doing so by shifting the focus from mass murder to its preconditions in 'lived space'.

Dissimulation in everyday life

Three memorials and three processes can be cited as examples of the dissimulation of memorials in the context of everyday life. The first is the 'Memorial against Fascism, War and Violence – and for Peace and Human Rights' by Ester Shalev-Gerz and Jochen Gerz in Hamburg-Harburg. This initially consisted of a 12-metre high square stele covered in lead, erected in the centre of Hamburg-Harburg. An explanatory panel requested citizens to stop for a moment in their everyday routines and take an active part in the memorial: 'We invite the citizens of Harburg and visitors to the town to add their names here to ours. In doing so we commit ourselves to remain vigilant.' Whenever the lower part of the stele was covered with inscriptions – of whatever kind – the stele would be gradually lowered into the ground to make space for further

Figure 11.1   Memorial against Fascism, War and Violence – and For Peace and Human Rights by Ester Shalev-Gerz and Jochen Gerz, Hamburg-Harburg 1988–1993

inscriptions. The project lasted for several years, from 1986 to 1993, when the last part of the stele was covered with inscriptions and could finally be lowered into the ground. The memorial worked like a mirror, less however for the problematic past than for the current political consciousness of the citizens. If not enough signatures against fascism, war and violence and for peace and human rights were gathered, the stele could not have been lowered into the ground and would instead have turned into a memorial to the political ignorance and the lack of civic commitment of the citizens of Hamburg-Harburg. Today only the upper surface remains visible as a reminder of the action, while from the square below it is possible to view the sunken stele through a narrow window.

Another procedure of dissimulation and spatial-diachronic correspondence in everyday life is performed by the "Monument: Places of Remembrance" erected by Frieder Schnock and Renata Stih in 1993 in the Bavarian quarter of Berlin. Some 16000 upper-middle class Jews

Figure 11.2 Monument: Places of Remembrance by Frieder Schnock and Renata Stih, Berlin 1993

lived in the Bavarian quarter in 1933, also known at that time as 'Jewish Switzerland', until it was declared 'Jew-free' after the last raids in 1943. Today, 80 panels are distributed around the district as inconspicuously as traffic signs, fastened to lamp posts. Only on closer inspection can their messages be read: on one side they show a coloured pictogram, while on the other is one of the many decrees that limited and gradually suffocated the life of the Jewish population in the area. For example, a multicoloured pictogram of a thermometer can be seen on a board, which reads on the back side: 'Jewish physicians may no longer practise. 25.7.1938'. On the back of a pictogram of a blackboard is written: 'Jewish children may no longer attend state schools. 15.11.1938'. Another panel states: 'Jews will no longer receive eggs. 22.6.1942'. Depending on the topic, the signs are affixed locally in front of doctor's offices, schools, shops and the like. Once we recognise them, they wrench us out of our everyday routine, as we cannot help but extrapolate the creeping

Figure 11.3 Monument: Places of Remembrance by Frieder Schnock and Renata Stih, Berlin 1993

Figure 11.4 Monument: Places of Remembrance by Frieder Schnock and Renata
Stih, Berlin 1993

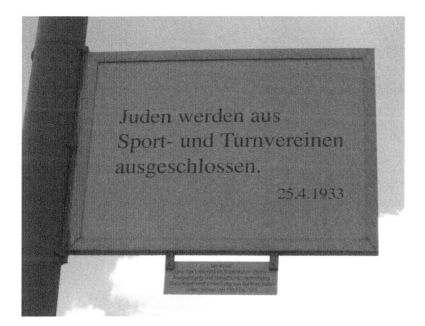

Figure 11.5 Monument: Places of Remembrance by Frieder Schnock and Renata
Stih, Berlin 1993

Figure 11.6   Monument: Places of Remembrance by Frieder Schnock and Renata Stih, Berlin 1993

restrictions on the everyday lives of the Jewish population onto our own lives.

Another memorial almost inconspicuously integrated into everyday life is Gunter Demnig's *Stumbling Blocks* (*Stolpersteine*). It consists of concrete cobblestones with bronze surfaces. These are engraved with an inscription, beginning with the words: 'Here lived...', then followed by the name, year of birth and – where known – the year and place of death. With the help of local volunteers, archives and also relatives of victims, Demnig places the stumbling blocks in front of the houses from which people were deported, murdered or driven to commit suicide. 'I imagine my stumbling blocks as a large, decentralised memorial',[2] writes Demnig. Since 1997 over 20000 stumbling blocks have been placed in German, Austrian, French and Polish cities, among others. They manage without any kind of artistic impetus, at first gleaming brightly and visible from afar, then accumulating a patina that makes them increasingly fade into the grey pavements.

Figure 11.7 Monument: Places of Remembrance by Frieder Schnock and Renata Stih, Berlin 1993

Empathy

As can be gathered from the outline, calling the new memorials counter-monuments or abstract monuments, as is often the case, does not do them justice. They are abstract in their formal and, if we wish, in their intellectual appearance, but not in their impact. It is true that the new memorials refuse any appealing, mimetic pictorial character, but this in no way impinges on their ability to produce affective reference, as hardly anyone will be able to avoid the trepidation produced by the 'Monument: Places of Remembrance' or when stumbling over the Stumbling Blocks. The effect is not the result of any empathy arising from a metaphorically pictorial, artistic object, but rather, from the extrapolation of the histori-cal facts onto our own life circumstances, as they actually exist at this moment and in this place in the realities of the lives of current observers. We stand *in* the monument, rather than before it as with conventional

Figure 11.8   Stumbling Blocks by Gunter Demnig, Berlin

memorials. The memorial is *around* us, but less as a material, artistic artefact as in its spatial-atmospheric qualities, than as a horizon of an imagined, potential threat.

This becomes comprehensible when comparing these memorials with Alfred Hrdlicka's 'Memorial against War and Fascism' or the 'Memorial for Jewish Deportees' in Levetzowstrasse in the Moabit district of Berlin. Hrdlicka's memorial was completed in 1991 it stands on the Albertinaplatz in Vienna and consists of a group of sculptures of roughly hewn granite. Distorted, tormented bodies are visible in a sort of half-relief, representing the various groups that were persecuted under fascism, including the sculpture of a Jew cleaning the street on his knees, a reference to a historical occurrence. The artist describes it as an 'accessible' memorial on account of the openness of its positioning on the Albertinaplatz. The same could also be said of the *Memorial for Jewish Deportees*, created in 1988 by Peter Herbich, Theseus Bappert and Jürgen Wenzel, which consists of different elements, including a high steel wall listing the 63 transports that took people from the Levetzowstrasse synagogue to various concentration camps, with a table showing the reliefs of the 36 Berlin synagogues. The central element is a railway wagon captured

Figure 11.9   Memorial for the Jewish Deportees by Peter Herbich, Theseus Bappert and Jürgen Wenzel, Berlin 1988

in solid steel. On it stand several large marble blocks carrying the top of the wagon, separate from the chassis. These are not, however, simple stone blocks; the outlines of human figures can be seen in them, making them into human bodies metaphorically carrying a massive load that is simultaneously crushing them. In front of the railway wagon, on a ramp, stands another group of people made of marble, tied to one another by a steel cable that cuts deeply into the stone.

Both memorials are marked by an artistic strategy of figurative representation. Their anthropomorphic language attempts to represent pictorially the humiliation, violence and physical and psychological pain of persecution. In conceptual terms, they thus subscribe to an aesthetic of empathy. In his 1872 volume *On the Optical Sense of Form*, Robert Vischer described empathy as 'the unconscious ability to project its own bodily form – and with this also the soul – into the form of the object'.[3] This is because, in the words of Heinrich Wölfflin, 'our own

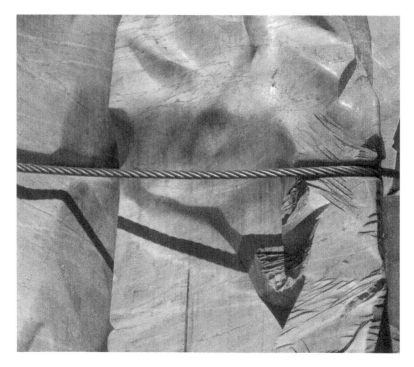

Figure 11.10   Memorial for the Jewish Deportees by Peter Herbich, Theseus Bappert and Jürgen Wenzel, Berlin 1988

bodily organisation is the form through which we apprehend everything physical',[4] such as well-being, illness or even pain. Empathy was for Vischer a condition for the sensory perception of the environment by humans: he did not differentiate between artistic and natural forms. That we incorporate our own physical form into objective forms applied just as much to the organic, material world of trees, rock formations and landscapes as to human creations.

Vischer excluded only purely technical artefacts, but the 'imbuing of forms with souls' or the 'unifying, and contractive feeling [Zusammenfühlung]'[5] of an I and a not-I means more than simply a physical feeling for the aesthetic of empathy. It aims at the transformation of external, sensuous impulses into 'an internal and a directly spiritual sublimation'.[6] It is thus not limited to physical sensation but possesses with its 'mental sublimation' an epistemological focus, so to speak. Herein lies its meaning for memorials. We are to project ourselves into Hrdlicka's Jews and experience not just the physical torment but also the humiliating degradation; as we project ourselves into the stone figures in the Moabit memorial, the steel cable cuts not only into their flesh but also into ours, thus provoking our critical consciousness. Although the memorials are not natural artefacts, but rather artificial, and therefore artistic ones, it should not be ignored that the act of empathy cannot be separated from the formal-aesthetic, iconographic and artistic status of the memorial. This remains a condition for the act of empathy, meaning that empathy is always linked to an aesthetic judgment that ultimately determines the success of the empathic projection into the artistic object, irrespective of how conscious or unconscious the aesthetic judgment itself is. In conventional memorials the work of art, the memorial as work of art, always stands between the Holocaust and our empathic participation.

Fading of memory

The new memorials refuse to represent the Holocaust and thus the aesthetic of empathy, particularly in the elevation as postmodern sublime, as Jean-François Lyotard described the inconceivable potential for destruction of modern civilisation, formulating this in aesthetic terms as the 'representation of the unrepresentable'. This term has hitherto been used to attempt to conceptualise the non-pictorial nature of the new memorials within postmodern aesthetics oriented toward the sign-character of things. Doubts rightly arose as to whether 'this historical event would elude all artistic representation as no pictorial representation could capture it',[7] and whether the graphic representation of the Holocaust inevitably leads to the artistic dilemma of either trivialising its machinery of destruction in familiar pictorial forms or missing the point of its banality of evil in elitist image concepts. It was thus acknowledged that restrictions were imposed by the reduction of the means of artistic expression solely to their sign-character, to the techniques of representation and rhetoric, of metaphors and images. Nevertheless the paradigm of representation was retained and with it the semiotic understanding of art as sign and representation, if only in the negative formulation of the 'representation of the unrepresentable'. It was not considered that the new memorials were pursuing a different aim – that they were not concerned with an artistic coding and an emblematic reference to something absent and past, but rather with a spatial strategy of diachronic correspondences between those affected at the time and today's viewer in his or her sensual-physical totality.

The question now is why the change in the concept of memorials occurred in the middle of the 1980s, forty years after the end of the war.

Why not before, or why not later? The answer becomes clear in the work of Jan Assmann: it lies in the specific structure of human memory. In his book *Cultural Memory*, Assmann writes, 'The vivid memory of today can be passed on tomorrow only with the help of some medium'.[8] Assmann shows that 40 years after a historical event, a transformation process begins from the so-called communicative memory to the cultural memory, that is from the 'living memory' of contemporary witnesses – the communicative memory – to the medialised memory – the cultural memory. After approximately 80 years, and as the last contemporary witnesses die off, the communicative, experience-based memory is replaced by the cultural, institutionalised memory. This is precisely what the new memorials are opposing. They must be understood as a critical reaction to the increasing medialisation of the memory of the Holocaust and its accompanying gradual disappearance from the consciousness. Their dissimulation in everyday life is an attempt to restore the Holocaust and its commemorative remembrance to the living, lived space, thereby keeping it in the general consciousness.

Communicative memory can, on account of the participatory perspective of contemporary witnesses, be described as a 'history of everyday life' or as a 'bottom-up history' that is 'biographically' connoted by those involved. Its nature is based on social interaction. On the other hand, cultural memory is no longer rooted in everyday life but is communicated via media: we can also describe it as a 'top-down history'. As Assmann shows, in oral cultures cultural memory was passed on through great epic works, songs or rites, while in text-based cultures this is the function of books and images, and now of sound recordings or films. Thus cultural memory no longer forms an immediate part of everyday life, as it requires an elite (sociologists of knowledge) that administers the cultural memory in this medialised way. In former times this was the role of shamans, priests or balladeers, while today it is writers, scientists and historians. As Assmann states, 'the cultural [memory] is not automatically disseminated, but requires careful introduction into the code of its medialised communication'.[9]

This 'halfway point of the 80-year limit'[10] represents such a critical threshold in the switch from communicative to cultural memory in the public consciousness that, in his book *Strategies of Remembrance*, Christoph Heinrich could write of a practically exploding interest in monuments and memorials since the middle of the 1980s. A major cause for this was the historical speech made on 8 May 1985 by the then West German President Richard von Weizsäcker. In it he warned of the 'fading'[11] from memory of the unparalleled genocide of the Jews. The speech was marked by a deep distrust of the motivations of human behaviour and culminated in the demand for a reflexive culture of memory. Without an insight into our darker side, Weizsäcker said, we humans are always endangered. We can only learn from negative history what human beings are actually capable of doing; an enlightened humanism can only be a humanism that is reflected by history, he stated soberly. Weizsäcker thus saw the dwindling memory of the Holocaust from public consciousness as an experience of cultural loss that posed a massive threat to societal self-perception.

Correspondences

The re-conceptualisation of memorials is a reaction against this type of cultural loss. It wishes to counteract the fading of living memory. The passing of the last contemporary witnesses cannot, of course, be reversed. The new memorials, however, represent an attempt, against the anthropological condition and genetics of memory, to maintain the memory of the Holocaust in the wider consciousness, even beyond the anthropological threshold of cultural memory. The primary requirement is the overcoming of the formal-aesthetic, artistic conceptions of memorials and a physical and spatial phenomenological widening of their previously largely graphical conception into everyday life; into the lived space of everyday life. This is evident in the memorial in the Bavarian quarter and its dissimulation in the numerous traffic signs and notices in the public space. It is not eye-catching – indeed, it is not even made for the eye. Only through each individual encounter and the repeated perception of individual elements does the memorial gradually develop. It becomes a memorial through the correspondences between our own lived realities of today and the realities of the Jewish population of that time in the same quarter, whose lives were not anthropologically different from those of today. The only difference is that, in the Third Reich, the degrading decrees were published in the Jewish press and the non-Jewish population was not aware of them. The panels thus become a memorial when, through extrapolation of the reprisals of the time onto our current lives, something of the existential threat leaps across, when the mental condition of the viewer is shaken and the vulnerability of everyday life is experienced as happening to ourselves. This was to an extent noticed when in 1993 some local residents reacted in anger to the recently installed panels. They had misunderstood them as a repetition of the discrimination against the Jews. Thereupon a small sign was attached under each panel explaining that these are part of the memorial *Monument: Places of Remembrance*.

As has now become clear, the new memorials practice another kind of reference to the Holocaust. It is not that of contemporary witnesses, but rather one of intervening in the physical-sensory mental condition of viewers, one of diachronic correspondences. This does not, however, contradict Assmann's theory of cultural memory as there is also a physical-phenomenological component in that theory, even if not explicitly stated. Communicative memory, then, does not draw its authenticity solely from the knowledge of the occurrences of that time. On the contrary, the knowledge of the contemporary witnesses is essentially something of the experiencing subject, experienced in the unity of the life-worldly reality, i.e. in the actual entirety of the respective experience. Communicative memory is also based on the experience of the present-related space in its entire 'essence, value and life reality'.[12] This is precisely what distinguishes it as authentic knowledge. Like Count von Dürckheim, the author of this observation, the present-related space is always both an objective and a personal space, insofar as the objective space as, 'an object space currently being experienced [always] gains a current-personal meaning, but also in its objective meanings is itself based in the totality of the personal life reality'.[13]

The new memorials appear in objective spaces where 'personal significances' and 'personal qualities' also constantly resonate, and without which absolutely no experience of the space is possible, but where, conversely, the individual experience and personal space themselves are also more or less socio-culturally and semantically pre-structured. The new memorials make this inherent in different forms. The decrees written on simple panels, the stumbling blocks or the sunken stele in Hamburg-Harburg can never be registered purely as information. It is the diachronic correspondence and identity of the lived, physical space through which they tinge our everyday life experience and existentially shake us in our corporeality.

The lived space of memory

The memorials can now, according to their function and impact, be differentiated with respect to three categories of lived space, depending on how the personal and pathic of cultural layers of experience are overlaid. Count Karlfried von Dürckheim's book, *Investigations into Lived Space*, propounds this view. Even if, as Hermann Schmitz pointed out, he failed in this endeavour, Dürckheim was the first to attempt a classification of the human spatial experience. Three kinds of space can in fact be identified and systematised in this trailblazing book, as Jürgen

Hasse and Robert Kozljanic demonstrated: the lived-atmospheric space, the experienced-aesthetic space and the remembered-historical space. There is no doubt that *Monument: Places of Remembrance* by Frieder Schnock and Renata Stih draws its effectiveness from the first category, i.e. from the presence of the lived-atmospheric space. Compared with the other memorials, the connection to the actual lived reality of the viewer is very close, irrespective of residence in the Bavarian quarter. The memorial is from the very first moment part of the life-worldly reality of the viewer. It does not require any great historical background knowledge, nor any intellectual act. The memorial gains its pathic dimension when, through the extrapolation of the degrading decrees to the viewer's own life reality, the atmosphere of the space experiences a momentary change and a threat (albeit imaginary) penetrates into his or her everyday life. That is, not just any everyday life but the everyday life of the individual viewer. The spatial identity and correspondence turn the lived-atmospheric space into a medium of commemorative remembrance and thus into the memorial.

Gunter Demnig's *Stumbling Blocks* on the other hand overlay the diachronic, spatial correspondence experience with a historical experience category. Although the Stumbling Blocks are let into the pavement in front of the former houses of the persecuted, here (in contrast to the memorial in the Bavarian quarter) the place of the deed to which the Stumbling Blocks refer – such as transportation, concentration camps or Gestapo jails – is separate from the immediate life reality of the viewer. Thus the stones bear inscriptions such as 'here lived ...', 'deported to ...' or 'murdered on ...'. Demnig demands a higher power of imagination, separate from the current atmospheric space experience. His memorial thus belongs to the space category that Hasse and Kozljanic describe as the experienced-aesthetic. Here, the spatial correspondence that directly touches the lived everyday life –the house of those deported and murdered – recedes behind the aesthetic imagination. The fact that the people came in and went out here and walked on this pavement is overlaid by categories of imagination and perception that are abstracted from personal experience.

The 'Memorial against Fascism, War and Violence – and for Peace and Human Rights' corresponds in its turn to Dürckheim's category of remembered-historical space. This is because here, the memorial is distinguished less by its atmospheric, physical or physiognomic aspects than by the socio-cultural, cognitive dimension of the space. The same memorial could quite possibly be located in another corner of the square or in another place altogether. The erecting of the stele in a pedestrian precinct in Harburg is of course advantageous, in particular on account of the height that allows people to view the sunken stele through a small window. This is not, however, a necessary condition; the memorial's character would hardly be diminished without it. Much more important are the socio-cultural meanings and significances, meaning that the metaphorical pictorial content plays a substantially more important (if also ambivalent) role. Thus the shape of the stele reminds us on the one hand of the chimneys that remained after the barracks had been burnt down at Auschwitz, while on the other, it possesses a direct local reference by alluding to Ernst Barlach's stele to the memory of the dead of the two world wars opposite the Hamburg Alster Arcades.

As the 40-year mark has now passed, the three memorials employ three different spatial strategies to react to the change and shift from the communicative to the cultural memory. Against the background of the progressive loss of contemporary witnesses, and thus the loss of a personal communication of history, they all attempt to bring the commemorative remembrance of the Holocaust back to where it all began: into the context of everyday life and lived space. They aim at the experience of diachronic correspondences in lived space, in as it were the shift from the orientation towards mass murder to its preconditions in everyday life. As architecture and urban spaces (and this includes omissions and gaps in the townscape) always hold traces of the past, diachronic correspondence means that the lived space of today is aligned with the lived space of that time in the imagined experience, and with the threatened consequences for our personal lives, so that the current, lived space can be seen and experienced in its potentiality as a space of the deed.

Notes

1. Jan Assmann, *Das kulturelle Gedächtnis* (München: Beck Verlag, 2000).
2. Annelies Fikentscher, 'Ein Strich durch das kollektive Vergessen', Neue Rheinische Zeitung (2 January 2008), <http://www.nrhz.de/flyer/beitrag. php?id=11922&css=print> (22 January 2012).
3. Robert Vischer, 'On the Optical Sense of Form: A Contribution to Aesthetics', in Harry Francis Mallgrave and Eleftherios Ikonomou (eds), *Empathy, Form, and Space: Problems in German Aesthetics, 1973–1893* (Santa Monica: The Getty Center for the History of Art and the Humanities, 1994), p. 92.
4. Heinrich Wölfflin, 'Prolegomena to a Psychology of Architecture', in Mallgrave and Ikonomou (eds), *Empathy, Form, and Space*, p. 157.
5. Robert Vischer, 'On the Optical Sense of Form: A Contribution to Aesthetics', p. 90.
6. *Ibid.*, p. 57.

7. Guido Boulboullé, 'Mahnmale gegen die nationalsozialistischen Verbrechen', <http://www2.dickinson.edu/glossen/heft1/guido.html> (22 January 2012).
8. Jan Assmann, *Das kulturelle Gedächtnis* (München: Beck Verlag, 2000), p. 51.
9. *Ibid.*, 54 f.
10. *Ibid.*, p. 51.
11. Richard von Weizsäcker, 'Zum 40. Jahrestag der Beendigung des Krieges in Europa und der nationalsozialistischen Gewaltherrschaft. Ansprache des Bundespräsidenten Richard von Weizsäcker am 8. Mai 1985 in der Gedenkstunde im Plenarsaal des Deutschen Bundestages', <http://www.hdg.de/lemo/html/dokumente/NeueHerausforderungen_redeVollstaendigRichardVonWeizsaecker8Mai1985/index.html> (22 January 2012).
12. Graf Karlfried von Dürckheim, 'Untersuchungen zum gelebten Raum: Erlebniswirklichkeit und ihr Verständnis. Systematische Untersuchungen II', in Volker Albrecht et al. (eds.), *Natur. Raum. Gesellschaft* vol. 4 (Frankfurt/M.: Selbstverlag 2005), p. 16.
13. *Ibid.*, p. 54.

Index

Lightning Source UK Ltd.
Milton Keynes UK
UKOW06n0622260216

269166UK00018B/252/P